BEYOND BLAME

BEYOND
BLAME

■ ■ ■ ■ ■

Freeing Yourself from the Most
Toxic Form of Emotional Bullsh*t

■ ■ ■ ■ ■

Carl Alasko, Ph.D.

JEREMY P. TARCHER/PENGUIN

a member of Penguin Group (USA) Inc.

New York

JEREMY P. TARCHER/PENGUIN
Published by the Penguin Group
Penguin Group (USA) Inc., 375 Hudson Street, New York, New York 10014, USA • Penguin
Group (Canada), 90 Eglinton Avenue East, Suite 700, Toronto, Ontario M4P 2Y3, Canada
(a division of Pearson Penguin Canada Inc.) • Penguin Books Ltd, 80 Strand, London WC2R 0RL, England •
Penguin Ireland, 25 St Stephen's Green, Dublin 2, Ireland (a division of Penguin Books Ltd) • Penguin Group
(Australia), 250 Camberwell Road, Camberwell, Victoria 3124, Australia (a division of Pearson Australia Group
Pty Ltd) • Penguin Books India Pvt Ltd, 11 Community Centre, Panchsheel Park, New Delhi–110 017,
India • Penguin Group (NZ), 67 Apollo Drive, Rosedale, North Shore 0632, New Zealand (a division
of Pearson New Zealand Ltd) • Penguin Books (South Africa) (Pty) Ltd, 24 Sturdee Avenue,
Rosebank, Johannesburg 2196, South Africa

Penguin Books Ltd, Registered Offices: 80 Strand, London WC2R 0RL, England

Most Tarcher/Penguin books are available at special quantity discounts for bulk purchase for sales promotions,
premiums, fund-raising, and educational needs. Special books or book excerpts also can be created to fit specific needs.
For details, write Penguin Group (USA) Inc. Special Markets, 375 Hudson Street, New York, NY 10014.

Library of Congress Cataloging-in-Publication Data
Alasko, Carl.
Beyond blame : freeing yourself from the most toxic form of emotional bullsh*t / Carl Alasko.
p.   cm.
ISBN 978-1-58542-876-2
1. Faultfinding.   2. Blame.   3. Criticism, Personal.   4. Emotions.   5. Interpersonal relations.   I. Title.
BJ1535.F3A43   2011   2011013249
158.2—dc22

Printed in the United States of America
1   3   5   7   9   10   8   6   4   2

Book design by Katy Riegel

CONTENTS

■ ■ ■ ■ ■

Introduction: Why I Wrote This Book   *vii*

PART ONE

Digging into the Roots of Blame:
Where Blame Comes from and How It Works

1. Blame Is Our Most Destructive and Confusing Behavior   3
2. Why Blame Is So Misunderstood: The Mistaken
   Beliefs of Blame   13
3. Blame Is Deeply Rooted in Our Biology—and Our Society   26
4. Blame Is More Than Just a Single Incident   37
5. Blame Comes from Many Directions at Once   46
6. Blame Is a Three-Part Syndrome Initiated
   by a Blame Attack   67
7. Part Two of the Blame Syndrome: The Emotional Impact   78
8. The Third Part of the Blame Syndrome:
   The Reactive Response and the Blame Spiral   90

PART TWO

Blame Busting: Learning to Use Positive
Accountability Instead of Blame

9. What Do I Use Instead of Blame?   105
10. Dilemmas of Dating: Using Positive Accountability
    in New Relationships   135
11. Marriage: The Proving Ground of Accountability   159
12. Parenting and Positive Accountability   192
13. Using Positive Accountability in the Workplace   213

PART THREE

Advanced Work with the Law
of Personal Limitations

Introduction to Part Three   231
14. Dealing with Personal Limitations:
    Always Start with Your Own   233
15. Exploring the Foundations of the Law
    of Personal Limitations   250
16. Testing the Law of Personal Limitations on Yourself   271
17. Pulling It All Together: Living Beyond Blame   284

The Take-Home Message: Living Beyond Blame   317

INTRODUCTION

■ ■ ■ ■ ■

Why I Wrote This Book

TWENTY-FIVE YEARS as a clinician, and many more as a husband, parent and friend, have taught me a great deal about what works best when people try to communicate a need or share a feeling. And I've certainly learned what does *not* work: blame tops the list.

Blame always makes things worse. It makes anyone on the receiving end of criticism or accusation feel much more resentful and angry. It also causes anxiety and pain, and pushes people away from finding solutions to their problems.

Blame is always destructive.

In my previous book, *Emotional Bullshit*, I focused on three of our most common interpersonal dynamics: *denial*, *delusion* and *blame*. I called them the Toxic Trio, because they work together to *deny* reality, create an alternate *delusional* condition and then allow us to *blame* someone else when things fall apart. Of these three dynamics, blame is the most confusing—and also the most damaging. For these reasons, blame requires its own book.

Do we really need a book entirely on blame? Yes. Because blame has seeped so deeply into how we think and how we communicate that we use it unconsciously, without realizing its destructiveness. We use it constantly because we grew up with it, and it's everywhere—it permeates our thoughts, ideas, beliefs and attitudes. But mostly we use it because we are unaware of how blame damages our relationships.

Most of us assume that blame fulfills an essential role in relationships. If we can't criticize or accuse people, how can we get them to correct mistakes, to change bad behaviors? But the problem is that whenever people are blamed, it always feels *bad*. When you're told that you're responsible for someone else's behavior or feelings, it feels *wrong*. When you're criticized for making a mistake, or accused of being wrong, inevitably you feel resentment. And if you're the one who's using blame, you still end up feeling bad because your connection to the other person has been damaged.

This book will change all that. You will learn that you won't *ever* need to employ blame's destructive arsenal.

This may sound revolutionary—if not impossible. It is revolutionary. Yet it's entirely possible and practical.

This book is based on the following components of blame:

- Blame means finding fault by criticizing, accusing and shifting responsibility.
- People are hardwired to use blame when they feel frustrated, want something and/or want to vent a feeling.
- Using blame always makes things worse.
- Blame can be entirely replaced with Positive Accountability.

As these points are meticulously discussed throughout the book, you'll learn that blame is a highly destructive behavior that serves no useful purpose in your relationships, and especially when you use blame against yourself in the form of self-blame.

Part One of the book will explore the numerous ways blame is used within our relationships, including the Blame Cycle, Blame Attacks and the deadly Blame Spiral.

In Part Two of the book, I'll provide a step-by-step method for replacing blame with what I call Positive Accountability.

Part Three presents the Law of Personal Limitations, a truly radical method for eliminating blame, and internally reorganizing your attitude toward the mistakes, errors and offensive behaviors of those around you—including your own!

■ LIVING BEYOND BLAME IS BOTH REALISTIC AND WORKABLE

My decades of experience with patients have taught me that even a basic understanding of how to replace blame with Positive Accountability can have life-changing effects.

Couples on the brink of divorce can learn to stop the Blame Attacks that have kept them engaged in a seemingly endless Blame Spiral. They can rebuild their relationships and return to the happiness and joy that originally brought them together.

Individuals caught in a downward spiral of depression, guilt and self-blame can find a practical way to understand their humanity and stop using blame against themselves, creating a sense of contentment and self-acceptance.

Anyone who's stuck in their career or feels abused by coworkers can learn skills that harness the positive energy of accountability, thus advancing their career and building professional confidence.

Parents can learn to guide children toward responsibility and accomplishment without blame. These approaches generate amazing changes in parents' relationships with children of all ages, including through the challenging period of adolescence.

Even your first attempt in substituting Positive Accountability for blame will provide a dramatic improvement, reducing your anxiety and resentment. When you can live your life entirely without blame, you will have reached the level of happiness and fulfillment you absolutely deserve.

Your first experience of living Beyond Blame will instantly make your life better. That's my promise to you.

PART ONE

■ ■ ■ ■ ■

Digging into
the Roots of Blame

■ ■ ■ ■ ■

Where Blame Comes from
and How It Works

CHAPTER ONE

■ ■ ■ ■ ■

Blame Is Our Most Destructive and Confusing Behavior

I'M SITTING WITH Mitch and Jessica in my consulting room. They're in their early thirties, trim and athletic. Jessica complains about her problems communicating with Mitch.

Jessica says, rather softly, "Mitch, I'm not blaming you. I'm just trying to share my feelings. I really wish you weren't so defensive."

Mitch is looking at his shoes. He grimaces. "Defensive? If I say anything to you at all, if I even ask a simple question, I get nailed for being defensive. I'm sick of it!"

I intervene. "Jessica, do you think you could tell Mitch about how he hurt your feelings without criticizing him? Without using blame?"

She thinks for a moment. "Sure. How about I use one of those 'I' statements you therapists seem to like so much. Mitch, *I* don't understand why it's so difficult for you to call me when you know you're going to be late. *I* think work is more important to you than me." Mitch cringes. I think to myself, can Jessica really believe that she's not criticizing her husband by telling him that he doesn't love her because he puts work first.

Now Mitch is upset. "Have you forgotten that my *work* pays the mortgage? I think you're obsessively controlling and impossible to please. That's what I think!"

Jessica wipes away tears and turns away, obviously feeling hopeless.

Mitch and Jessica are caught in what I call a Blame Trap. Each of them is so entangled with blame that every time either one tries to solve even a minor problem, the one can't help but find fault with the other and they both use criticism or accusation in a destructive attempt to fulfill their needs.

Marcie Arrives at Work and Is Heading for the Staff Meeting when a colleague, Jim, tells her it has been canceled. Irritated and upset, she asks, "And why wasn't I kept in the loop?"

Jim reacts angrily. "Hey, it's not my job to keep you posted." Marcie tries to backpedal, saying she didn't mean to imply it was. Jim is miffed and walks away. For the rest of the day Marcie worries about having offended Jim—how stupid of her! By the time Marcie leaves work, she's convinced her coworkers are against her. Jim is still upset. He wishes Marcie would shape up.

Daniela Divorced Her Husband Four Years Ago After His Second Affair. She complains about him to everyone, and is especially angry because he doesn't help out with their teenage daughter. The daughter rarely studies and is always on the phone, so Daniela is angry at her too. She often barks at her daughter, "Why can't you help out? Do I have to do everything? You're so selfish!"

Her daughter rolls her eyes, mumbles "bitch" under her breath and goes to her room. A few days later Daniela discovers prescription drugs in her daughter's things. Daniela is crushed and feels like a failure: as a wife, as a mother and as a person.

■ WHAT DO THESE STORIES HAVE IN COMMON?

The basic theme that runs through the lives of Mitch and Jessica, Marcie and Jim, and Daniela is that their relationships are permeated with our most *common, destructive* and *least understood* behavior: **blame.** Almost everything they say is a setup, a Blame Trap. It may seem obvious to us that the people in these stories don't have a clue as to how blame is directly responsible for their unhappiness and lack of relational fulfillment—but sadly, it isn't so clear to them.

Blame has become such an integral part of their thinking and behavior that they can't seem to break free of its grasp. And they're not alone. Many of us are scarcely aware of how often we use blame, and even less aware of its negative effects on our lives. Blame has ravaged our most precious relationships for far too long—for centuries—and its rampage continues.

We desperately need to examine blame's destructiveness. We need another way of approaching and solving problems. We simply can't afford to allow blame to dominate our relationships just because we don't know how to stop it.

The first step in learning how to move Beyond Blame begins with exploring how it functions.

■ A DESCRIPTION OF BLAME'S TWO PRIMARY FUNCTIONS

The main reason blame is so confusing is that it's comprised of several reactions and behaviors. Let's start with the two primary functions:

1. Blame finds fault with another person (or group) through criticism and accusation, punishment and humiliation.
2. Blame transfers responsibility onto someone else—by using criticism and accusation.

The first function of blame involves our most *destructive emotional behaviors*:

- criticism
- accusation
- punishment
- humiliation

Can there be anything even remotely positive or constructive about these behaviors? Definitely not.

The second function of blame *shifts responsibility* for our own behaviors onto individuals or a group, distorting reality and creating confusion and reactivity. When responsibility is denied, solving any problem becomes all but impossible. This function plays an enormously destructive role in every relationship, from our casual friendships to the most intimate and permanent: marriage and parenting.

When an *individual* is blamed—accused of making a mistake—that person is accused of *being* wrong, of *being* defective. His or her value is diminished, and is pushed further away in the relationship.

When a group is blamed—accused of being responsible for something bad—the group is also seen as *being* defective, and is marginalized and isolated physically (as in a ghetto), or acted against violently. Sometimes **blame is used to generate destruction and terror,** such as in Rwanda in 1994, when hundreds of thousands of Tutsis were massacred; or during World War II, when the Nazis blamed the Jews and other non-Aryans for their problems, resulting in the Holocaust.

Countless other times in history, blame has been used to justify isolation of a people or violent atrocities against them.

No wonder blame is such a difficult subject to tackle, and so dangerous. Blame seems to be everywhere and active in all our affairs. And its effects are always destructive.

◼ THE FOUR FUNCTIONS OF BLAME: Why Do We Use Blame Even Though It's Destructive?

As we begin an examination of our most destructive interpersonal behavior, we need to examine WHY we use blame so frequently even though it hurts our relationships. The following four functions of blame explain how blame appears to fill several necessary purposes. We use blame:

1. when we want to change another person's behaviors through criticism, accusation, punishment or humiliation;
2. when we need to vent a feeling such as anxiety, anger, resentment, pain or fear;
3. when we attempt to escape personal responsibility by shifting it onto someone else; or
4. when we try to protect ourselves from being seen as wrong or bad.

At a minimum, blame serves these four purposes.

In actual practice, we use blame even more often. Some examples of blame are subtle and passive, as in passive-aggressive behavior, exemplified in being chronically late, constantly forgetting things, lapsing into moodiness, isolating into silence, overworking and so on.

Other forms of blame disguise themselves within our "good intentions." And there's an extremely toxic form of blame that **buries itself deeply inside us like a cancer: self-blame.** We shall explore all of these forms of blame in the following chapters.

The situation between Jessica and Mitch, which we saw at the beginning of the chapter, illustrates how the four functions of blame became mixed up in their lives and the unhappy results. Both Jessica and Mitch are using all four functions in one form or another. Both are trying to correct each other's behaviors, want to vent irritation or anxiety, want to escape responsibility and are furiously protecting themselves from accusation.

How did Jessica begin? *"Mitch, I'm not blaming you. I'm just trying to share my feelings. I just wish you weren't so defensive."* Jessica is using Functions One and Two: she's trying to (1) correct Mitch's behavior and so accuses him of defensiveness.

She is also (2) venting her feelings of anxiety and resentment because he doesn't call if he's working late. Underneath these behaviors is her *fear* that he doesn't love her enough.

Mitch replies angrily because he thinks he's just been attacked. *"Defensive? If I say anything to you at all, if I even ask a simple question, I get nailed for being defensive. I'm sick of it!"*

Mitch is trying to (4) protect himself from being wrong by accusing her of being impossible to please. He's also (2) venting his own anger at being called defensive, as well as (3) shifting responsibility back onto Jessica by saying he can't even ask a question without being nailed.

Jessica then tries an "I" statement. *"I don't understand why it's so difficult for you to call me when you know you're going to be late. I think work is more important to you than me."* Now she's accusing Mitch of not loving her by declaring that work is more important. She's still trying to (1) correct his behavior, escalating the criticism: there must be something wrong with him, he's defective, if he can't even make a phone call.

Mitch is now angry. He fires back a barrage of more blame, more criticism, accusation and punishment, and vents his anger (1, 2). *"Have you forgotten that my work pays the mortgage? I think you're obsessively controlling and impossible to please."*

Isn't this exhausting? Imagine actually being part of these toxic communications!

Both parties are caught in what I call a Blame Trap. Their heartfelt desire for happiness is being destroyed by their inability to communicate without criticism, accusation, punishment and humiliation.

■ BLAME IS DESTRUCTIVE BECAUSE IT CREATES MULTIPLE REACTIONS— ALL NEGATIVE

Let's track what happens when blame is used during an ordinary, everyday interaction, at home, between two people. John and Mary have been together only a few years, but already their communication style is permeated with blame.

1. John can't find something in the refrigerator, and becomes frustrated. "Darn it, Mary, why can't I even find the mustard! This refrigerator's a mess." He vents his feelings by finding fault with Mary: she's disorganized.

2. Mary feels unjustly attacked. She experiences the negative emotions of anger, anxiety and pain. "It wouldn't be a mess if you put things back where they belong. You're the slob around here, not me!" She discharges her emotions by escalating, throwing out another accusation.

What actually happened between these two people? Their physical reactions are triggered.

3. Anger and anxiety activate Mary's fight/flight syndrome, releasing adrenaline into her body; her pulse accelerates and her blood pressure rises.

4. Mary believes that she's being wrongly accused. This belief accelerates her physical reactions, and she fights back with a verbal attack employing yet more blame.

5. Now John also feels under attack. His body floods with adrenaline and his rational thinking is affected. He doesn't

> understand why he's being attacked, but because he's physically agitated, all he can do is respond with more criticism and accusation.

Now it's going to be a lot more difficult for John and Mary to solve the problem of the refrigerator because they're both angry. Now the focus is *retribution*, not resolution.

Of course, the impulse to strike back when you're under attack is entirely "natural." However, this reciprocal use of blame is a highly destructive impulse leading to the most common dynamic in relationships: the Blame Cycle.

▪ THE RECIPROCAL USE OF BLAME CREATES THE "BLAME CYCLE"

In just a few seconds, John and Mary have become caught up in a Blame Cycle—a back-and-forth argument between two people (or groups) in which each party uses criticism and accusation against the other.

The constructive resolution of a problem becomes impossible.

In close committed relationships, being blamed feels so bad that you feel compelled to defend. How? By attacking the other person. And it happens instantly. Within seconds a highly destructive and dangerous Blame Cycle begins.

Each person asks a silent question: "Why are you treating me this way? Why are you criticizing and accusing me? How dare you hurt me this way!" That's when the heavy artillery of punishment and humiliation is used. Each person blasts away at the other. "I'll teach you to hurt me! I can hurt *you* even worse!"

Doesn't that sound terribly immature? Well, it is. When the

Blame Cycle takes over, it feels as if small children have taken over the argument. Working toward a solution becomes impossible. Love and trust are eroded. Animosity grows.

The quick explosion between John and Mary illustrates one of the main reasons why blame is so destructive. Namely, that blame has worked its way into our lives in so many ways that we use it without thinking about the inevitable consequences. In almost every instance, people involved don't really understand that they're using blame, and rarely do they understand how it's damaging their relationships.

Which is exactly why blame is so misunderstood.

CHAPTER TWO

■ ■ ■ ■ ■

Why Blame Is
So Misunderstood

The Mistaken Beliefs of Blame

THE MAIN REASON there's so much confusion about blame is that we've accumulated a series of Mistaken Beliefs about how blame works and what it does.

We assume that blame assigns responsibility and solves problems. Therefore blame is necessary. *Wrong!* This is a *Mistaken Belief*.

We also assume that criticizing another person's behavior, ideas or even their feelings is the way to get them to change. *Wrong! Mistaken Belief*.

We believe that defending ourselves by counterattacking the other person will stop the accusation and criticism. *Wrong! Mistaken Belief*.

In fact, blame actually diverts us from solutions by creating animosity and divisiveness, which erode trust and push everyone involved further away from happiness. As the previous examples of the Blame Cycle illustrate, what really happens is a back-and-forth of more criticism and more accusation.

In the worst cases, blame can kill. People can be pushed so far away from solving a vital problem that violence can erupt or critical situations go ignored. Someone can die.

Here's what happened to my patient Maureen. Her brother accused Maureen of being excessively controlling of their elderly mother's care. They fought back and forth, fully engaged in the Blame Cycle. Somewhere in the middle of the accusations, Maureen assumed her brother was on duty to deal with her mother's medications. Somehow, their mother didn't get her medicines on time and she died. Each sibling now blames the other for killing their mother. Not only did they lose their mother, they lost their relationship with each other!

A similar critical situation happened between Rachel and Doug. They blamed each other for a credit card bill and became so angry over it that they refused to deal with another pressing issue, their homeowner's insurance. Some months after the insurance expired, a fire broke out in their kitchen and it was a total loss. Of course they blamed each other for not renewing the insurance. Then they had to deal with the physical destruction, as well as the destruction to their relationship.

Here are some other Mistaken Beliefs about blame that show why it's so misunderstood:

■ WE DON'T SEE BLAME AS INHERENTLY NEGATIVE

When we criticize, accuse and punish, we're just doing what we've always done and what everyone around us is doing. Since blame is so common, it must be okay. Mistaken Belief.

- Fifteen-year-old Jenny walks into the kitchen and her father says, *"You're going to school dressed like that?"* Jenny gives her dad a quick glare and stalks out. He is criticizing his daughter's choice in clothing, and also accusing her of not having the sense to dress properly. In the extreme, he's accusing her of dressing like a slut. But he believes that he's just doing his job as a parent by criticizing her (Mistaken Belief). But Jenny goes to school angry and feeling humiliated. Now she's even more anxious about her life because she feels criticized and devalued, and grows more distant from her father. Her self-esteem suffers. Of course we all want our children to wear appropriate clothing, but glares, sarcasm and accusation are part of blame.

■ WE BELIEVE BLAME IS NECESSARY TO CHANGE SOMEONE'S BEHAVIOR

When we use blame, we believe that our intention is well-meaning. That is, we don't (usually) *intend* to hurt the other person. But, you might think, if you don't criticize and accuse someone, how are you going to get him to change? When someone is doing something wrong, or has offended you, that person must be forced to face the consequences. In fact, these are Mistaken Beliefs.

- Christie watches her boyfriend ogling another woman, and says, "You know, Jake, if you think she's so gorgeous, why don't you get up and ask her for a date? I'm leaving!" And she walks out. Her Mistaken Belief is that she has a right to blast him with her anger and stalk out. Yes, Jake's staring is rude, but getting angry and leaving abruptly now puts the focus on her angry reaction, and not on his behavior. Solving the issue becomes more difficult.

■ "Why can't you even park the car properly? Is that so hard?" Adam says accusingly to his wife. He believes (Mistaken Belief) that he will motivate her to park more carefully if he accuses her of being inept. In fact, she's so angry at his criticism and accusation that she hands him the keys and says, "You park it!" The last thing she wants to do now is please him.

To repeat: Criticism and accusation shift the focus onto the explosion that follows, and away from the behavior that needs to be addressed.

■ WE BELIEVE BLAME IS AN EFFECTIVE WAY TO EXPRESS AN EMOTION

When we're upset over just about anything, criticizing and accusing another person feels like a good way to discharge anxiety, resentment or anger.

■ "See what you made me do!" the mother says angrily to the child. The mother made a mistake and is upset, so she unloads her irritation onto the child.

■ "You know, Marge, I have to work for my living." Your friend wants to go to a pricey restaurant for lunch and you know you can't really afford it. Because you are single, and Marge's husband has a high salary, you say something accusatory to discharge your anxiety.

These examples show how blame has become such an intrinsic part of how we communicate that we use it without thinking, and minimize its destructiveness. We don't realize how often it shows up in our speech and thinking, or how often we thoughtlessly criticize and accuse. As children we begin absorbing criticism when we're scolded for making ordinary mistakes, such as spilling something or making a mess, and the habit of using blame takes hold in our personalities.

- "Can't you do anything for yourself? I'm not your mother!" You're angry because your partner leaves a wet towel on the bathroom floor—again. Your comment is demeaning and creates resentment, which can build up over time. No one likes to hear belittling comments.
- "I just said that the salad was a bit bland. You don't have to get so upset!" You think that you're just giving your partner some necessary feedback (Mistaken Belief). But your criticism is blaming her for not performing to your standards. When she's hurt, you accuse her of being too sensitive. Then, to compound the hurtfulness, you'll often pile on the blame by saying, "She tells me to share my feelings, and when I do, she goes into a crisis! I can't win!"

WE USE BLAME BECAUSE WE DON'T KNOW WHAT ELSE TO DO

When we try to solve a problem or express a feeling, we typically use criticism and accusation because . . . what else is there? When we're feeling anxiety or anger our impulse is to make the other person feel the same way. If we don't criticize, accuse and punish, do we just let people get away with things? We tell ourselves that alternatives to blame are too complicated to use in everyday life, or they're useless. Worse yet, that they're enabling.

- "Jim needs to hear that he screwed up! You don't expect me to just overlook this mistake, do you?" You're angry at Jim's mistake, and you're going to give him both barrels. You believe that's the best way to teach him (Mistaken Belief). Unfortunately, the severe reprimand will be so humiliating that Jim won't think about how the error occurred; he'll focus on the humiliation. And he'll feel less willing to put things right.
- "My son knew he had to make a B+ average. Since he only made a B, he's losing the car for the entire summer." You believe that if your son doesn't suffer draconian consequences, he won't respect your word, and learn his lesson to study harder.

We've briefly looked at blame's destructiveness, and now we need to explore why it shows up in so many situations.

■ HOW BLAME DESTROYS OUR RELATIONSHIPS WITH OTHERS

Why do we use blame so often? Because in the heat of the moment, blaming not only seems *necessary*, but seems like the correct thing to do.

When we're feeling offended, frustrated, upset or irritated—and especially when we feel anxious or worried—we believe (*mistakenly*) that the most logical thing to do is find fault with someone or something else. So *we criticize, accuse or punish and humiliate* the other person.

What we're actually doing, though, is *discharging emotion*, mostly anxiety. We are literally wrapping our feelings around a rock, symbolically shouting, "Here, take this!" and throwing it. We certainly feel justified. After all, what else can we do when someone has made us feel uncomfortable, anxious or afraid?

Or we use blame (also known as defensiveness) when we believe we are being accused . . . of anything. Admitting error feels risky and threatening: who knows where it will end if we admit to making a mistake? So we instantly and reactively shift the responsibility onto someone else. Either way, we're discharging, shifting and deflecting our negative emotions onto another target.

- "When my husband forgot my birthday, I didn't talk to him for days. And when he tried to apologize, I ignored him." Punishing him for being forgetful makes you feel vindicated, and also teaches him a lesson. (Mistaken Belief)
- "You're never in the mood for sex! So don't be surprised if I end up . . ." Rather than discuss your sexual frustration and work toward a solution, you discharge your anger at your partner through punishment, humiliation, threat. You have a right to be nasty! (Mistaken Belief)
- "I was so upset when Gerri missed her deadline that I didn't include her in the meeting. She got the message." Instead of directly confronting Gerri about the deadline issue, you dump your anger passive-aggressively by humiliating her. That'll teach her! (Mistaken Belief)
- "After all your nagging, I need a couple of drinks to help me chill out." There's a reason why your wife nags, but rather than addressing it, you numb yourself with alcohol

and punish her by withdrawing into silence. She'll learn that there's a price to pay for nagging you. (Mistaken Belief)

- "Hey, I wasn't the idiot that got us into this mess." Shifting the responsibility certainly won't resolve the problem. But calling the other person a derogatory name feels justified and discharges anxiety about the problem. (Mistaken Belief)
- "Grow up! You're not a baby anymore!" Speaking this way to a child merely increases his anger and resentment toward the parent. But Dad seems to believe that humiliating his son will motivate him to be more responsible. (Mistaken Belief)

Every one of these incidents demonstrates how we use blame to discharge our negative emotions and shift responsibility. All because we feel uncomfortable, threatened or at risk.

Blame is a completely wrongheaded attempt at solving the problem. It only makes matters worse. Because every statement is brimming with criticism, accusation and punishment, *powerful negative emotions are triggered*, both in ourselves and in any others involved. The Blame Cycle continues, and it often escalates uncontrollably.

There's yet another form of blame that works like an emotional cancer inside our minds and bodies: self-blame. This is our *most unexplored* and *most toxic* form of blame.

■ HOW BLAME DESTROYS OUR RELATIONSHIPS WITH OURSELVES

We not only use blame as a weapon against others, but also attack ourselves. Blame's toxicity grows inside us like a cancer, creating misery and despair.

Self-blame occurs when we turn criticism, accusation and especially *punishment* and *humiliation* inward; when we criticize our own behaviors and accuse ourselves of being incompetent for making a mistake—and *don't let up.*

Self-blame is often fueled by a deep-seated belief that we're inherently flawed, that there's something fundamentally wrong with our personality, or even our humanity.

Of all the Mistaken Beliefs that can take root inside your soul, the one that you're "inherently flawed" is the most damaging and dangerous. It makes you despair of ever finding solutions to your problems. Over time you come to feel like you don't deserve happiness. You criticize your every move. Nothing you do seems to turn out. Even when it does, you don't believe or trust it.

The reason this is a Mistaken Belief is that *everyone is fundamentally flawed.* There are no exceptions to this rule because we're all human.

Everyone has inherent human limitations. People just have different methods of working with their limitations that may be more (or less) successful. We'll explore this complex issue in Part Three, when we discuss the Law of Personal Limitations.

For now, let's look at some brief examples of self-blame. In each case, the person believes that whatever mistake he or she has made is too great to be forgiven, so the self-criticism and self-accusation continue relentlessly. Moving on becomes impossible.

- "I completely ruined my kids' childhoods by leaving my husband. Sure, he was having affairs, but I should have found a way to live with it." You can't accept the fact that you did a pretty good job with them and struggled against formidable odds.

- "I really screwed up my life by taking this job. I can't do anything right." In fact you deliberately chose a more secure job and can't accept the inherent trade-offs built into any job.
- "I suppose I wasn't destined to be happy. I try my best, but there's got to be something wrong with me." You refuse to appreciate the security and comfort you've attained and always believe that everyone else is happier.

These are just a few of the thousands of negative comments we use to blame ourselves for life's missed chances and random acts of folly and tragedy. We punish ourselves for an ordinary mistake, a well-intentioned decision or even bad luck.

Toxic self-blame is far more than reviewing a situation in an effort to understand what happened. It's an endless Blame Cycle of self-punishment—with no relief.

Learning to live Beyond Blame means using specific techniques—techniques we'll explore in this book—to stop using blame on yourself, and to stop self-criticism, accusation and punishment from destroying your self-worth.

■ HOW BLAME OPENS THE DOOR TO DANGEROUS BEHAVIORS

Sometimes our ethics or sense of fairness inhibits the fulfillment of a desire, impulse or craving. But if we conveniently shift responsibility onto someone or something else, we can create an excuse to fulfill our desire . . . anyway.

Using blame in this way can have serious, life-altering consequences:

- "It's your fault I had an affair—you're so difficult and unloving." If I can blame you for pushing me to break my marriage vows, I don't have to admit I'm behaving unethically. I'm no longer responsible to maintain my vows; an affair is justified.
- "I only took the money because they don't pay me enough." Stealing isn't intrinsically wrong or illegal if the boss is unfair. Then it's justified. I don't have to be responsible for my ethics if I'm treated badly. I'm not really being dishonest.
- "Because of your pissy attitude I canceled the whole trip." I can throw a tantrum and cancel the trip because you were grumpy. I don't have to be a responsible adult when you act this way. And it's my right to punish you.
- "I'm really sorry, but . . . it was meant to be. A Greater Power took over." I'm not responsible for my personal decision: fate and destiny were more powerful.
- "We have to do something about those people. They cause all our problems." By demonizing another group, we don't have to be responsible for our ethical behavior toward other people. We no longer have to work together and solve mutual concerns.

Each of these statements bluntly shifts the responsibility onto someone else—or onto a *thing*, such as destiny or another group or a Greater Power. (We'll explore this topic in a following section.)

◼ HOW BLAME HIDES IN SARCASM AND FALSE SYMPATHY

Blaming can also be more subtle. It doesn't need to take full operatic form or wave red flags with big block letters proclaiming

"Blame!" to create unhappiness. Blame can also lurk behind sarcasm or false sympathy. Each of the following can easily be critical and accusatory, according to emphasis and tone of voice. Try to hear their tone as sarcastic and false.

- "I'm so glad you finally found some time to join us."
- "Well, you're looking well rested. Have a nice nap?"
- "Yeah, well, it's been fun."
- "Great job! I didn't know you were so talented."
- "Gee, thanks!"

How would you feel when someone used these versions of sarcasm on you? Wouldn't you feel bad? Concealed in each comment is a sharp splinter of criticism, a poison pill of disdain. They tell you that you don't measure up, don't make the cut. Sarcastic comments are part of the many little cuts and abrasions that wear away at the internal structure of relationships, eroding well-being and our connections to others.

In summary, it's important to keep in mind that blame isn't always loud and angry. It camouflages itself in literally dozens of different guises.

IGNORANCE ABOUT BLAME WON'T PROTECT YOU

The world of relationships functions with rules similar to those of the physical world. Just as ignorance of gravity won't protect you from falling off a cliff, not understanding the destructiveness of blame won't stop you from being harmed by its effects.

Yet finding out more about blame has not been easy. Even

though its negative effects are obvious, little has been written about blame as a specific behavior. Even less has been available about a practical alternative.

Why hasn't our ignorance of blame been vigorously addressed? Why hasn't the world of psychology taken on this destructive problem seriously? It's because blame is so widely diffused in our culture, and is part of so many of our interactions, that its toxic effects are really hard to pin down.

In my research, I've been continually confronted by the confusion and ignorance that surround this toxic behavior—and the *apparent lack of a viable alternative.*

This confusion hides blame's negative effects. The vortex of negative emotions (the Blame Cycle) makes it very difficult to isolate its cause.

To directly confront the qualities of blame is to swim against a deep current. I'm asking you to make a radical shift in your thinking. Even though blame is deeply embedded in our interactions, it doesn't mean that it must continue its reign of destruction indefinitely.

I promise you this: Every amount of effort you put into living Beyond Blame will instantly pay off in greater happiness and success in all your relationships.

CHAPTER THREE

■ ■ ■ ■ ■

Blame Is Deeply Rooted in Our Biology—and Our Society

MARIO GRABS a crayon from Ben's desk. Ben yells at him. The kindergarten teacher intervenes. Mario is worried he's going to be punished so he claims, "Ben took it from me first!" Ben protests, "No I didn't!" and calls Mario a name. Now Mario's angry and throws a pencil at Ben.

Why do children resort to blame at the first sign of conflict? For the same reasons adults do. "I didn't do it! It's your fault! I'm innocent!" is one of our most fundamental responses. Underlying these protests is the message, "I'm not defective!"

As we mature, the impulse to blame others when we've been accused doesn't go away. By the time we become adults, blaming has become such a part of how we communicate that we use it automatically. We also become subtler and sneakier in its use.

There are two major sources of blame's power in our lives, biology and psychology. Let's begin with examining the biology of blame.

Blame is a structural part of our fight/flight syndrome, connected to a primal instinct, the *biological* and *psychological* need to protect ourselves. People are often surprised to learn that we are, in fact, programmed to use blame. We're hardwired both physically and *psychologically.* It's a double whammy. However, our physical reactions are so tightly wired to our emotions that it's often very difficult to know which comes first. Is the release of adrenaline calling for instant anger? Or is the rise of anger, pain or fear what provokes a physical response?

To understand this mechanism, we need to look more carefully at what's happening between the two kindergartners, Mario and Ben.

Mario has taken Ben's crayon, and Ben protests. That's entirely expected. Now Mario finds himself in an internal struggle and he doesn't like it. Mario feels the emotion of *anxiety* because he's been caught. He's being accused, which *feels* very bad. He tries to escape by blaming Ben; he *accuses* Ben of taking a pencil first. Mario is trying to shift responsibility away from himself. If he can appear to be innocent, he will have lowered his anxiety.

And like all humans, Mario is programmed to do whatever it takes to feel less anxious. Why? Because our body does not like anxiety, which is a variation of fear. The negative emotions of anxiety and fear are extremely distressing.

So whenever we feel anxiety, stress or fear, whenever something in our world isn't working well, whenever we're being attacked in any way, this physical hardwiring kicks in and we defend ourselves by striking back. We use blame to attack someone, to vent an emotion or to shift responsibility, usually onto whoever is closest to us.

We'll do whatever it takes to lessen our anxiety.

■ ■ ■ ■ ■

THE CONNECTION BETWEEN
BIOLOGY AND EMOTIONS

Within human behavior, biology and psychology are so closely linked that it's virtually impossible to separate the two. Our response to the emotion of fear is so rapid that fear *feels* like a physical reaction. In fact, fear is an emotion that triggers the fight/flight syndrome that can instantly flood our body with adrenaline. To truly understand blame's negative effects on our body and our relationships, we must understand the biological and psychological connections.

What controls this reflexive response? The amygdala, an almond-sized node that's part of our limbic system, and which drives our primitive *fight/flight syndrome*. This structure has been referred to as the "lizard brain" because it's primitive.

For hundreds of thousands of years we have had to physically defend ourselves from attack. At the first sign of conflict, the amygdala instantly floods our body with adrenaline, preparing us to fight or escape.

In the struggle between Mario and Ben, Mario's anxiety pushed him to respond with a physical reaction: he threw a pencil.

HERE'S THE CATCH: We don't have to be physically assaulted for this syndrome to activate. The attack can also be social or psychological. In addition, the *perception of an attack* is enough to trigger the fight/flight syndrome. The attack (criticism, insult and so on) does not have to actually happen, we simply have to believe that it has, or that it will.

This fact is immensely important. Wars have been fought and thousands of lives lost because of a ruler and a nation's *perception* of insult. "We must avenge our honor!" When this happens, our need to survive *psychologically* (with our honor intact) becomes inseparable from our biological need to survive *physically*. That is, we convince ourselves that death would be preferable to the *perception* of dishonor.

Similarly, as individuals, we must survive within our social group, tribe or clan. The need for social survival can be linked (in our minds) to our need for physical survival. Within our social life, an attack is usually verbal, and an insult or gesture can trigger rage or fear almost as effectively as if someone came at us with a club.

So as members of a society, we place a very high *value* on being seen as right and good. This value isn't frivolous or arbitrary. It's directly connected to our status, our standing in the community. If our standing becomes too low, we risk ostracism.

> **THE POINT: We're hardwired to defend ourselves from blame, to be seen as right and good, to protect our reputations.**

Keep in mind, once again, that blame is actually a combination of several behaviors: criticism, accusation, punishment and humiliation. So our "program" to protect ourselves from being blamed (from being criticized and so on) is deeply wired into our psychology and our behavior. To be blamed is to be *accused* of being bad and wrong. And we'll do almost anything to make sure that we're not seen as bad or wrong (or dishonest or immoral), and thus be relegated to the bottom of the status pyramid.

■ OUR NEED TO BE RIGHT HAS ANCIENT SOCIAL AND RELIGIOUS ROOTS

Why do we so strongly resist being seen as wrong? Why is it so difficult for most of us to make a simple mistake, accept the responsibility and move on? The reason is that we expect punishment to follow. The phrase "being in the wrong" succinctly explains it.

If I'm *in the right*, I can expect approval from the community. If I'm *in the wrong*, I can expect punishment, condemnation and loss of status. Either my mate or my peers will punish me. Therefore the value we place on ethics and morality has a direct, practical and sometimes life-and-death application.

The need to be in the right is strongly supported within every major religion. It plays a major role in the Judeo-Christian heritage. The Old Testament God punished wrongdoers, beginning with Eve, who was kicked out of paradise for going against the rules. According to the Christian religion, bad and sinful people suffer for eternity. In contrast, honesty and goodness are connected with heaven and paradise.

Understanding how criticism and accusation are connected to our personal and social well-being (and even our physical survival) is essential to our understanding how deeply the roots of blame are intertwined with our thinking, beliefs, attitudes and behaviors. Indeed, with every aspect of our lives.

■ WE USE BLAME TO PROTECT OUR STATUS WITHIN OUR RELATIONSHIPS

We depend on our social structure (family, marriage, neighborhood and workplace) for our happiness, and our survival. We must protect ourselves from anything that diminishes our status within all our relationships, especially our committed relationships, such as marriage. Whatever might threaten our status with our mate threatens our security and happiness. The more committed the relationship, the greater the dependency, and the greater the vulnerability. Thus the greater the risk to our safety.

For instance when John asks his wife Mary, "Why are you always losing your car keys?" John isn't asking where the keys are. He's blaming (criticizing) Mary for being forgetful. Mary grimaces at his criticism, but she also becomes angry because her competency, her value as a human being, is being diminished. In essence, John is *telling* Mary that she's too stupid to keep track of her keys. Which means that this interaction is not really about car keys, but about Mary's sense of equality in the relationship.

At a primal level, Mary understands that if she allows John to attack her about the car keys, he'll feel free to criticize other things too. If her status in the relationship drops too low, John might take over all her decisions. Mary risks losing her autonomy. She's not about to let that happen, so she argues back. And waits for a chance to get even.

And sure enough, the very next day, Mary challenges John: "You didn't buy another stupid gadget, did you?" Why does she criticize John? Maybe Mary is worried about money, but she's also blaming John for spending money foolishly. She's pointing out that he too makes mistakes. He bought something stupid, so he must be stupid. If she can devalue him, his attacks will have less sting.

Naturally, John snaps back. What's going on below the surface for him? He believes that his ability to manage money (and make independent decisions) is being attacked. If he allows Mary to chip away at his competency and decision-making, she might take over everything. He's surely not going to allow that to happen. The argument intensifies.

We intuitively know that if our status (or autonomy) is diminished within an intimate relationship, we'll lose our personal power and become subservient. Centuries ago that might have meant a physical challenge, a battle to the death.

> **THE POINT: We instinctively know that we must fight back when we're criticized or insulted, because if the insult isn't dealt with, our status and personal power will diminish.**

Within a group of, say, friends at school, we're afraid that our "competitors" will find allies and the insults will increase. And if we lose too much status, we risk ostracism. This struggle for status can take the form of bullying, which is a vicious form of blame, because it typically involves all four behaviors of blame: criticism, accusation, punishment and especially humiliation. Not only is it terribly painful to the victim, in extreme cases it can lead to suicide. These behaviors can become systematic and chronic. The child who can't fight back or escape is frequently targeted for continued attacks.

We use the term "pecking order" to describe how some people in a group have higher status and are therefore not "pecked on" by others. This term comes from observing chickens in the barnyard. The same dynamic happens in the schoolyard.

Now let's examine more in depth one of the most common uses for blame: displacing our uncomfortable or difficult feelings onto other people.

■ WE USE BLAME TO SHIFT ANXIETY ONTO SOMEONE ELSE

Blaming is probably the most common tactic for shifting uncomfortable or painful feelings onto others. The instant we feel frustration or anxiety we search for someone who's responsible for our upset and blame that person: "See what you made me do!" "You push me over the edge!" "Why are these people so slow? They hire just anyone for this job."

Or we dump our anxiety and frustration onto an available target: "Marsha is such an idiot!" "Oh sure, you expect me to believe you." "That #@%& drives like a moron!" "It's these kind of people who are ruining our country!" Each of these statements finds fault with someone else as a way to alleviate our own anxiety.

During a therapy session, Barbara complained about Michael always blaming her for anything that went wrong. She gave an example about something left to go bad in the refrigerator.

"But that's not blame!" Michael protested. "I just made an observation!" (He justifies his comment.)

"Observation?" replied Barbara. "You sneered about keeping things in the fridge wasn't rocket science. It's so simple!"

I asked Barbara, "Did you think you were being criticized? Accused of being dumb?"

"I sure did!" Barbara responded. "And I got upset. So I shot back, 'Why can't you do something like make an omelet? It's so simple!'"

Michael continued to defend himself by attacking. "It's stupid getting into a fight over a silly comment. Barbara's way too sensitive." (He's criticizing her for being too demanding and sensitive.)

Now Barbara was even more upset. "Oh, so it's my fault that I get upset when you call me stupid?"

"I didn't call you stupid."

They were locked into a Blame Cycle. If I wasn't present to stop the argument, it would have continued to escalate into an ever more destructive fight.

This exchange demonstrates why it can be so difficult to understand the connection between feeling anxiety and finding fault with someone else. We lapse into using blame as a way to vent our anxiety or frustration. We have become so habituated at finding fault that we do it without thinking. And then, as Michael did, we deny it, or accuse the other person of being too sensitive . . . which launches another round of criticism.

The proof that it's an episode of blame is how it feels on the receiving end. In Barbara's case, she definitely felt criticized and accused, even somewhat humiliated. And, amazingly, so did Michael.

Here's a personal story about discharging anxiety.

A while ago my wife was getting in the car to leave and I said I'd call her later to talk about our schedule. She looked at her cell phone and said, "Darn, the battery's almost dead."

Instantly I shot back, "Well, how did that happen?" That's blame. It's a criticism. When I asked, "How did that happen?" I was not seeking information, I was criticizing her for being forgetful. Because I felt a surge of anxiety about not being able to call her, I instantly discharged my anxiety onto her. It's your fault for causing my anxiety. You *deserve* to be criticized!

My wife frowned slightly, shook her head and drove off. Later

I apologized, and that ended it. We did not get locked into a Blame Cycle.

Does that little interaction seem familiar? But don't all of us find fault through criticism and accusation as soon as we feel some tension or anxiety?

THE POINT: Even minor incidents of blame carry consequences. And the resulting negative feelings accumulate and create separation.

Another common way of displacing our anxiety or frustration is by taking it out on an object. An example would be throwing the hammer after hitting your thumb. It's obviously not the hammer's fault, but the gesture of throwing it releases some of the pain, as well as your anxiety about making a mistake.

The father who gets angry at his son for not getting a good grade on a school exam might think that he's motivating his child to perform better, but he's mainly discharging his anxiety. He's fearful that his son might not do well in school, with consequences for later in life. He's also fearful that he might be seen as a bad father.

Not only is our use of blame a way to discharge anxiety or frustration, we also use blame to maintain our social status, and its use is deeply intertwined with our biology.

THE BIOLOGY OF BLAME IS LINKED TO OUR SOCIAL STRUCTURE

Previously, I briefly mentioned the role blame plays in maintaining our social standing. This topic requires a bit more discussion.

Every tribe, racial group, political party or nation readily uses blame to discharge its emotions onto other groups, tribes or nations as a way to enhance its social or political position. In politics, national leaders often divert attention from domestic problems by declaring that another country is the source of the problem. We've all heard the cry "Foreigners are meddling in our affairs!"

If the meddling is deemed to be severe enough, then the other country must be violently attacked. They're at fault so they *deserve* to be punished. National pride (or political expediency) demands it.

World history is littered with examples of a nation blaming another country for a particular act, which it then uses as a reason to declare war. President Lyndon Johnson used the Tonkin Gulf incident in 1964 as justification for escalating the Vietnam War. He blamed Communist aggression for the need to intervene. Today it's believed that most of that incident was fabricated.

Similarly, racism and sexism are still used to motivate people to act because of the fear that the other group (or gender) will become dominant and the first group will lose their autonomy. Using blame to defend one's autonomy is pervasive. Therefore, the other group must be contained or even eliminated. Finding fault with that group through criticism and accusation—making them wrong—is a predictable part of the persecution.

There's one last issue about blame's role in our personal lives and our society: *Blame is primitive and inefficient.* It's the communicational equivalent of parchment and goose quills. Blame no longer has any legitimate role in our intensely interconnected world of the iPhone and the BlackBerry. From the most basic viewpoint of efficiency, our society needs a far more effective method of dealing with relationship problems and conflict than blame.

To help us move toward eliminating blame from our lives, let's dig deeper into the roots of blame and explore its specific components.

CHAPTER FOUR

■ ■ ■ ■ ■

Blame Is More Than Just a Single Incident

Whenever you see the word "blame," in this book or elsewhere, I want you to think of it as a *series of emotions and behaviors*, not just a single incident. While we may think of blame as simply assigning responsibility to another person, it's much more complicated and dangerous.

Here's a list of what we do when we blame:

- Shift responsibility to someone or something else
- Criticize and condemn by finding fault with someone, including ourselves
- Accuse of being responsible for a mistake, problem or issue
- Punish and/or humiliate through criticism

So when we use blame against someone else (including ourselves), we are using the powerful, highly charged and negative *actions of criticism, condemnation, accusation, punishment* and *humiliation.* Often blame includes *shifting responsibility* to someone or something else— but not always. Sometimes blame involves only the first three types of attack: criticism, accusation and punishment.

This is an intense list of negative actions. If one of them doesn't get you, another one will.

HUMILIATION: The last action on the list requires a few extra words because humiliating another person is *the most destructive* of all human behaviors. Humiliation attacks that person's value. The emotion of humiliation is so powerful that it can take away a person's desire to live because he or she feels worthless and defective. It can lead to severe depression and even suicidal behavior.

A parallel and highly destructive approach is the use of contempt. Contempt means that you feel disgust, that the person is detestable, and is not worthy of your time and certainly not your love. When contempt or disgust infiltrates any relationship, it cannot and will not endure.

The reason contempt and humiliation are so intensely damaging is because when you are on the receiving end, there's no effective way to protect yourself. **Contempt and humiliation are the emotional equivalent of being burned with fire.** If someone says or does something to you that's so strongly negative as to show contempt, or the behavior humiliates you, it ignites anger to the point of rage or violence. Alternately, you slink away in utter defeat.

I've found that most people don't usually consider humiliation and contempt (along with shaming, disgracing or mortifying) to be part of blame. But they are. And, to make matters worse, these behaviors can be subtle.

■ ■ ■ ■ ■

REORGANIZING YOUR THINKING ABOUT BLAME

The test of a blame statement is whether it provokes a reaction of anger, resentment, anxiety, pain, fear or humiliation. If you feel any of these emotions, then you've just been blamed. Any comment that *implies* that you are in error, or lacking in some way, fits firmly into blame's vast repertoire. The most important concept about blame is that it's NOT a neutral concept or attitude. It's a behavior with one primary purpose: to find fault with another person.

Here's a story to illustrate how all of the components and emotions of blame (including a minor but nevertheless damaging example of humiliation) can quickly create a highly destructive Blame Cycle. This incident starts over a trivial issue but rapidly spirals outward, and downward. Neither party feels capable of doing anything other than responding with blame.

Judd and Samantha Have Been Married Six Years. They are in their early thirties, and both work at stressful jobs. It's Saturday morning, and Judd wants to take their dog for a walk after sleeping badly and waking up grumpy.

"Where's the dog leash? I left it here yesterday." His tone of voice is critical and accusatory. He's certainly not criticizing himself. Didn't Samantha put it away?

"It's not hanging on the hook?" Samantha asks, trying to ignore Judd's accusation.

"Jeez, I'm not blind! If it was hanging up I'd see it!" Judd snaps back. His response is demeaning. He's accusing his wife of asking a stupid question.

"Hey! Don't look at me!" Samantha responds. She's upset and wants to fight back. "You're the one who's always losing things."

"I lose things? Yesterday we spent an hour looking for your purse! You're the airhead!" Judd has not only returned the criticism but escalated into name-calling, ramping up the criticism and humiliation.

Now Samantha's really angry. How did the dog leash escalate into misplacing her purse? How dare he call her an airhead? She is not defective! Now she wants to punish Judd, to *retaliate*.

"Really! This from a guy who lost his keys last week and I had to drive to work to rescue you! Not to mention that you forgot your report and your boss chewed you out. You better get a grip or they'll fire you!" Even though she's hitting way below the belt, attacking Judd's competence at work, she believes she's fully justified.

Judd is furious and storms off without the dog. He doesn't understand how not finding the dog leash turned into such a nasty fight. Samantha is so bitchy! He's going to *teach her a lesson*; he leaves for the whole day and won't answer her calls.

What's going on between Samantha and Judd? Answer: They don't know how to express feelings of frustration, anxiety or distress without using blame.

Meanwhile, the leash doesn't get found, the dog doesn't go for a walk, and most important, the flurry of blame wreaks serious damage on their level of trust. Why is *trust* an issue? Because we need to trust that our partner won't explode over a minor issue.

We need to trust that a mildly critical statement doesn't erupt into a blowup.

The above is an example of how blame ignites an endless series of attacks.

Next we need to examine the emotional energy that provokes the first criticism, and then *endlessly* fuels the process.

■ BLAME ALWAYS GENERATES A SERIES OF NEGATIVE EMOTIONS

What does it feel like to be criticized, accused, punished or humiliated?

Certainly *you won't feel good!* You definitely won't feel eager to get closer to the other person. On the contrary, you'll feel upset and consumed with a series of intense and overlapping emotions. Let's examine this more closely.

Here's a list of the six most common negative emotions generated by blame:

- **anger**
- **resentment**
- **anxiety**
- **pain**
- **fear**
- **humiliation**

Just *one* of these powerful emotions can be devastating to your well-being. Depending on the severity of the blame, you can actually feel *all six at the same time*. When you are under assault by these emotions, it's virtually impossible to maintain a positive, loving attitude. All you want to do is strike back, to get even. That's what blame does.

And as the previous section on the biology of blame explained, you're deeply programmed to fight back when attacked, whether physically or emotionally, or to run and try to escape. Either way, your heart is racing, your blood pressure zooms and your body is pumped up with adrenaline. That's where the power of anger and fear come in.

The inevitable result is that your thinking becomes reactive and primal. Your thinking is now being driven by a more primitive part of your brain, the limbic system, which controls your emotions. Your ability to reason is overwhelmed by the impulse to defend yourself. At the very least you'll fight back verbally. These reactions are entirely predictable.

Now let's review how these six negative emotions—anger, resentment, anxiety, pain, fear and humiliation—affect us in some real-life situations. When a person is being blamed, how many emotions will that person feel?

■ TYPICAL REACTIONS WHEN YOU'RE ON THE RECEIVING END OF BLAME

The following examples start with a criticism or accusation. Keep in mind how much more injurious they would be if their tone was sarcastic or irritated.

- "Do I have to remind you of everything?" Carrie says to Don, her husband, who's just turned sixty-five and retired. "Maybe you need to see your doctor." What will Don feel? At the very least, he'll feel *anger* at being criticized. He'll also feel *pain* at being reminded that his abilities might be waning, and also *fear* of mental impairment.

How might Don respond? He might remind Carrie of her own lapses, or if he was really angry, call her names or make a threat. Or he might withdraw into sullen silence. He surely wouldn't feel like being kind, considerate and loving.

- "Bobby, I already told you! Can't you get it?" the teacher berates the third-grader. What will Bobby feel? I believe he'll feel all *six* negative emotions; *anxiety* and *fear* about keeping up, *anger* at the teacher for being so mean and *humiliation* that it's happening in front of the class. Since he knows that everyone makes mistakes, he'll also feel *resentment* at the injustice of being singled out. Then also *fear* and *pain* that he really might be stupid and defective.

How will Bobby respond? He might try to find a way to get even. Even worse, his attitude might be so impacted with negative emotions that he'll give up on trying to satisfy the teacher.

- "You know, Kim, I wouldn't be staring at women if you were sexier," Bill says to his girlfriend. Bill is blaming/criticizing Kim for not being sexy enough. What will she feel? *Humiliation* and *shame*, and, of course, *pain*. Her body and sexuality are being shamed, and the humiliation makes her feel unworthy of love.

How will Kim react? She might feel so humiliated that she would believe that she doesn't deserve any better. Kim might become more submissive, or find solace in alcohol, substances or addictive behaviors such as compulsive shopping or overeating.

- "Frank, you got the figures in this report all screwed up. Ask Rick to help you," the boss sighs in exasperation. How will Frank feel about being so harshly criticized? He'll feel a lot of *anxiety* about his job, as well as *pain* and *humiliation*, especially if he's worked there for years and Rick is fairly new.

How will Frank react? He'll probably wait for a chance to get even, or look for another job. Either way, his response won't benefit the company.

- "Good grief, can't you do anything on your own?" the father says to his seven-year-old daughter. "Your brother could do this at your age." These two sentences not only criticize but also *humiliate* the child by telling her that she's incompetent and doesn't measure up. How can she respond other than feeling defective and shameful? Why even bother trying since she's obviously so incapable? Result: Her self-esteem plummets.

These are some of the typical reactions people experience when on the receiving end of blame. No matter what form the criticism or accusation may take, Blame Attacks all provoke a negative reaction. At this point, you're probably asking yourself: "Okay, maybe blame really doesn't help, but am I supposed to just stuff my feelings and tolerate abuse?"

So let's briefly address this question.

■ ADDRESSING THE FIRST OBJECTION
TO NOT USING BLAME

So far I've described *some* of the most destructive negative consequences of blame. But I've not provided any alternative. That's
because the solution to blame requires its own section of the
book. The solution is called Positive Accountability and will be
described in detail in Parts Two and Three.

The exclusive purpose of Part One is to make sure that you
understand how criticism, accusation, punishment and humiliation (aka blame) *cannot* and *will not* achieve any of your goals in
communication.

**Blame will not bring you closer to happiness and fulfillment
in any relationship.**

Only when you're solidly convinced of this fact can we move
on to the solution.

In the meantime, there are other problems with blame that
we need to explore. Namely, blame doesn't have a single source,
and can masterfully disguise itself so we sometimes aren't even
aware that we're being blamed.

■ ■ ■ ■ ■

CHAPTER FIVE

Blame Comes from Many Directions at Once

AN ESSENTIAL PART of understanding the complications of blame is that there are three distinct types, and they come at us from three directions. In order to stop its noxious effects, you need to recognize what type it is, and where it's coming from. This issue becomes especially important with the last type: when you are blaming yourself.

THE THREE TYPES OF BLAME

1. I blame others (when I'm angry, hurt, disappointed, feeling anxious).
2. They blame me (when they're feeling the same way).
3. I blame myself (when I'm angry at myself, or hurt, frustrated, sad and so on).

These three categories can also overlap and double up into a free-for-all of multiplying and intertwined incidents of blame. Here's how one very upset patient put it:

> My boss blames me for a mistake. I blame myself for screwing up. My coworkers blame me for being incompetent. I blame my parents for not supporting my education. My parents blame me for not studying hard enough, and for not following their advice. I blame my spouse for pressuring me. My spouse blames me for not taking my work seriously enough, or taking it too seriously. My children blame me for being too strict, and not providing them with enough things. My sister blames me for not understanding her issues in the family. Finally, I blame myself for not meeting everyone's expectations, including my own.

Doesn't that sound exhausting? And that's just the surface. There are layers of blame above, below and even *inside* these obvious ones. No wonder life can feel so stressful!

I call this being stuck in a three-ring Blame Circus. Too much blame coming from too many directions, and—most important—*none of it accomplishes anything positive*. And yet the impulse to blame continues without letup.

■ HOW BLAME HIDES BEHIND THE SHIELD OF GOOD INTENTIONS

One of the many disguises blame takes on as it infiltrates our lives is that of so-called "good intentions." We might think we're correcting a problem, but the criticism embedded in blame only makes matters worse. And while we might not *intend* to criticize or accuse, that doesn't change the consequences.

When I'm working with two patients and one of them says something that irritates or offends the other—and that comment starts an argument—that person typically defends the comment with one of the following excuses.

1. **Helpful advice**—"I'm only trying to point something out to you," he says. After getting an angry response to his excuse, he tries again, "I'm just trying to be helpful."

    Few of us take the time to think about the impact of our comment. Beneath the act of offering advice, we are, in fact, often finding fault and criticizing.

2. **Sharing a feeling**—"I'm so pissed that you forgot the reservation!" he says angrily. When his girlfriend shuts down, he explains, "Hey, you told me that I should share my feelings!"

    Aren't we told to communicate our feelings? Isn't one of the biggest complaints that we don't share our emotions? Yes, but . . . when the vehicle of blame is used to communicate, the recipient ends up getting a dose of criticism and accusation. This kind of sharing doesn't do anything to bring people closer.

3. **Setting excessively rigid limits**—"Your sister doesn't even care enough to remember my birthday, so I don't want to go to her party," you tell your partner.

    Being excessively sensitive to other people's mistakes is a way we use blame to criticize and accuse. In this case, the sister not remembering a birthday is not treated as an ordinary error. Rather, it's a sign that there's something seriously wrong with her, and that she must be punished. Remember, punishing (and humiliating) another person is one of blame's primary functions.

4. **Maintaining high standards**—"*How could you have gotten this so wrong!*" you say to your son in exasperation. "Do it over!" To yourself you say, "I care about quality."

   Demanding that the paper is done over criticizes and punishes your son for not being a good enough student according to your standards.

   "Let's not ask Beverly to come. She wouldn't quite fit in." This critical statement accuses Beverly of not being good enough. Your standards are set so high that people who don't meet them are accused of being inferior.

The four justifications above are all variations on the same theme: denial of basic human fallibility. They deny that we all have personal limitations and we all make mistakes. We justify each use of blame as necessary and serving a purpose; we're just correcting an error, assigning responsibility or expressing an emotion or a need.

What we're not addressing is the effect of a Blame Attack. After being criticized or accused, the other person is not going to say, "Gee, thanks for showing me how incompetent, lazy or stupid I am. Now that I know, I'll do better."

No, their response will be resentment, anxiety, anger, pain, fear and humiliation, which will inspire them to fight back.

Clearly, these responses *are not constructive!* They don't solve problems, build trust or bring people together! They do nothing to build our personal happiness and success.

And yet the people who are (1) offering helpful advice, or (2) sharing a feeling, or (3) setting firm limits or (4) maintaining high standards do not *intend* to stir up a hornet's nest of negative emotions. They're doing what they think they need to do, and feel entirely justified in their behavior.

In my experience, rarely does a person *deliberately* use blame to inflict pain or to settle a score. Almost always the intention behind a Blame Attack is a misguided effort to communicate; either to share an emotion or correct an error. However, the "good intentions" of the person using blame are no comfort to the recipient.

At this point you may be thinking, "But, Dr. Alasko, what am I supposed to say? Seems like every comment I make will offend someone else's feelings."

You would be right to ask: "What can I say instead?"

To which I reply, be patient a little longer. Part Two explains exactly how to live Beyond Blame by using Positive Accountability. In the meantime, we need to continue to explore the many variations of blame in action.

■ BLAME DOES NOT HAVE TO BE PART OF OUR LIVES

Blame does not have to be part of our daily interactions. Our tendency to use criticism and accusation is not a permanent structure in our personalities—even though it may seem so.

I learned an early lesson about criticism in a college freshman English class. My professor sported a bushy white moustache and resembled Mark Twain. His way of teaching was as unique as his looks. He would review a paper and mostly ignore the mistakes. When he liked something, he'd circle the sentence or phrase and write a compliment in the margin. I worked hard to get a "good," and was thrilled to see an occasional "excellent!" His teaching method inspired me to focus on what worked, the positive part of my papers. I learned more from seeing a "good" than from being told that something was written poorly.

At the time, of course, I had no idea that his teaching strategy was "blameless" because it did not rely solely on pointing out errors, the most typical teaching technique. What's even more important is my *positive emotional connection* to the professor and to the class. I remember it as one of the high points of my education.

Yet such an enlightened approach is rare. If you look back on your own school experiences, teachers who focused on your good points were probably the minority. But those are the teachers you will remember with fondness.

Along these lines, what would you guess would be the most reliable predictor of success in grade school? Most people believe that it's intelligence, self-esteem or parental support. In fact, the best predictor of success is the "perception" that the teacher likes the student. If the student believes that the teacher likes her, the child will have a *positive emotional connection* to the teacher and will strive to please, and therefore be more successful.

Another way of looking at this is that when a child is not criticized, when the negative emotions of blame are not present, the child flourishes. Sounds entirely logical.

But as the earlier episode between Ben and Mario demonstrated, children themselves use blame frequently in their interactions. In fact, criticizing others seems to be part of their emotional structure. It's very painful when a peer finds fault with us. Being criticized, accused or humiliated by our school friends really hurts.

If you hear a classmate say, "Eww, why are you bringing *that* in your lunch?" that's the last time you'll bring that item—unless you're really tough or you have no choice. If you hear, "That shirt looks weird," you'll not wear that shirt again. Or if someone says, "No, you can't play with us!" you'll probably slink away in a painful cloud of humiliation.

These criticisms add up, and can make school life an ongoing misery. **Episodes of criticism and accusation can make anyone's life miserable.**

In school we learn how to develop a thick skin, to not feel so hurt when we're blamed for being less-than-cool, out of style, not the "popular" kid; for being too much of one thing or not enough of another. We also learn that if we can't fit in perfectly, criticism is relentless.

Maybe by the time we get to college or get a job, we've developed a thicker hide and have learned that being more resistant to blame is indispensable to our survival. And yet, virtually none of us can defend ourselves from a sharply pointed arrow. If the blame is strong enough, it will always hurt.

And it's a different matter entirely in our private life, especially in our most intimate relationships. To begin with, in our most precious relationships, it's NOT possible to be insensitive to criticism. It depends entirely on how it's delivered, or if contempt or disdain is mixed into the blame. Then it can draw blood, or feel like a flaming arrow in the heart.

That's because we expect our best friend or sweetheart to understand us and our intentions, to always give us the benefit of the doubt, to assign our mistakes and sudden acts of selfishness not to a malign intent, but rather to ordinary forgetfulness. To our human fallibility.

Above all, we expect to be treated with respect, affection and love. And when we're criticized and accused, the injustice of being unfairly treated can result in strong anger, or intense anxiety.

In essence, *criticism and accusation within any trusting, intimate and precious relationship feels like betrayal and disloyalty.* If we don't feel respected and loved, if we find ourselves on the receiving end of even subtle blame statements, the criticisms and accusations build up and create unhappiness. If the blame happens within a relationship that we cannot easily change (between siblings, married with children, or parent/child), or in any relationship where there's a lot at stake, the accumulated effects of blame can be devastating.

Keep this point in mind as we continue to explore the structure of blame and the many variations of this destructive behavior, and how it creates unhappiness.

■ ■ ■ ■ ■

RETHINKING THE SUBTLE EFFECTS OF BLAME

You don't need to be harshly criticized in order for blame to do serious damage to your relationships, or your self-esteem. Even subtle, covert messages have a negative effect on your happiness. The emotional response may not be as strong or direct, your body may not be flooded with adrenaline, but the effect can still provoke confusion and distress, and lead toward lack of trust and unhappiness. Every episode of blame counts, no matter how subtle or indirect.

The endlessly fascinating disguises of blame require further discussion. Think back to how your parent's squinted eye, tightened lips and arched eyebrow could instantly wipe out your best argument and be utterly devastating. All types of nonverbal communications, from frowns, sneers, sighs to grunts, are all part of blame's vast repertoire of slings and arrows.

■ BLAMING WITH THE FLICK OF AN EYEBROW

Insulting words are not the only way to offend. We've all experienced—and delivered—criticism and blame using a broad range of subtle, nonverbal techniques. Disrespect and contempt can be communicated in dozens of ways.

Amy, a high school freshman, knows all too well how a classmate can ruin her day with a simple shrug, roll of the eyes or twist of the lips. She feels instantly criticized by any of these silent putdowns. She's being told that something about her is *wrong*. Is she wearing the wrong shirt, shoes, hairstyle? Maybe there's something intrinsically wrong with *her*! Maybe other people can see that she's fundamentally defective.

The intention of a message is carried in the inflection, the pauses, the circumstances and context, as well as the facial expression that accompanies it. The accent on a word can determine whether it's a compliment or a criticism.

If it's blame, you will *feel* criticized, accused or punished. And your reaction will be any of those six negative emotions: anxiety, anger, resentment, pain, fear or humiliation.

In Amy's case, her most common emotional reaction to a sarcastic comment from one of her friends is *fear*, and its cousin, *anxiety*. She's constantly afraid of being ignored or humiliated. If she wears something that's even a little unusual, she'll be embarrassed. Sometimes she can't put into words what's wrong, but she knows that she's being *criticized* for not being cool, or *accused* of being too . . . something. She knows for sure how it feels. It feels bad.

"Don't you look *fantastic!*" can mean your outfit is wonderful.

"Don't *you* look . . . fantastic" means you're a total disaster.

The statement "Oh that's *great!*" can mean you really did well, or it can mean that you're a total screwup, as in: "Oh, *that's* . . . great." These inflections are part of sarcasm—saying one thing while meaning another.

And just as inflection can turn a compliment into a criticism, a facial expression such as pursed lips, a frown, a sneer, raised eyebrows or rolling eyes can also imply disapproval.

In many of the stories throughout this book, you'll see words emphasized in italics to show the negative inflection. For example, the sentence "I'd like to be your friend" totally changes meaning if it's framed as a humiliating question: "I'd like to be *your* friend?" Now it implies that being your friend is the last thing in the world I'd want to do.

Other nonverbal behaviors also imply criticism or disapproval. One of the most common (and most destructive in relationships) is "stonewalling." This behavior means to remain silent and not respond when someone's talking. A variation is checking your cell phone while talking with someone. You're giving the message that the other person isn't worth your undivided attention.

Social snubs fit into this category. Silvia was invited to attend a networking event put on by a real estate broker. When she arrived she was greeted by the broker and introduced to several veterans in the business. After a perfunctory greeting, they ignored her. One of the men even turned his body slightly so she was cut out of the group. Silvia felt devastated, and her ability to focus on her job was compromised for days.

Ignoring a person when he walks into the room is a variation of blame because it communicates that he's not worthy of your attention. The snub criticizes his value as a person. "High-value" people are never snubbed. Shunning may be subtle, but it's an effective criticism that will inevitably generate negative emotions.

To this point we've explored the "cause and effect" dynamics of blame: you've said or done something, or failed to do so, which triggered a Blame Attack; or someone else's behavior has prompted you to criticize and accuse. But there's another dynamic of blame that is equally damaging, yet doesn't spring from incidents and actions. In fact, the blame attacks something that is unchangeable and constant: your *state of being*.

■ WHEN YOU'RE BLAMED FOR BEING WHO YOU ARE

There's no more destructive form of blame than being criticized for being who you are because there's nothing you can do to change your state of *being*. You can modify your behaviors, your attitudes and your ideas, but you cannot alter who you are!

You can change your hairstyle, your wardrobe, even your level of education, but no one can change their fundamental physical being, or their core personality and temperament.

Even today, despite our great strides in social progress, women are criticized simply for being female. Racial groups are criticized for their origins, simply for being different. People of faith are blamed for their religious beliefs. The poor are blamed for being poor—because they're lazy, of course. The nerdy-looking guy is blamed for being nerdy. And the list goes on and on.

Within families, children are blamed for being needy and

immature, for making mistakes that they're not developmentally able to control. Teenagers are regularly criticized, accused, punished and humiliated for being distracted and self-centered, moody and forgetful, sloppy and selfish. In other words, for being immature adults—although there are plenty of adults who have all these same traits.

Why would parents criticize a child for a developmental state of being? The basic reason is that when they feel anxiety about their child's performance, they don't know how else to express their anxiety. What else can they do?

- "Why are you so clumsy?" the parent says angrily to the seven-year-old who's just spilled his milk. The boy lowers his head in shame and resentment.
- "Did you see how he was looking at you? Those people are all the same," the mother cautions her daughter when she believes the non-native clerk is being overly friendly.
- "Don't even think about hiring a woman for this job. We need someone tough." As though an entire gender is not capable of toughness.

Blame is so embedded in our thinking that we quickly and easily criticize others for either their innate human characteristics, or what we *believe* those characteristics to be.

Now we come to a series of behaviors that are intrinsic to blame. Namely, interconnected and repeating actions that keep us locked into blame. I call this a Blame Trap because it keeps us trapped in an escalating vortex of criticism and accusation.

■ SETTING UP A BLAME TRAP—YOU'RE CAUGHT NO MATTER WHAT YOU SAY

A Blame Trap is a situation in which *anything* you say or do keeps you stuck in a communicational cycle of criticism and accusation. If you reply or try to explain yourself, you're just letting yourself in for more blame. If you don't, you must be guilty, and therefore deserving of the accusation. You're damned if you do . . . or don't.

In a Blame Trap, one party is really saying: "Go ahead and try to show that you're not stupid, or not guilty or lazy. . . . I'll bet you can't." You won't be able to prove that you're okay because every effort you make will be criticized.

Another variation of the Blame Trap is the communication that "You don't really love me. Try and prove that you do." Of course you can't prove your love because every effort will come up short.

If you take the bait and the jaws snap shut, your fate is sealed. Once you're caught in the Blame Trap, all your efforts to prove that you're not stupid (or that you really do care) just pull the trap tighter. The alternative is to not take the bait, which I'll discuss shortly.

Why do people set Blame Traps?

We trigger a Blame Trap out of frustration and anger. Remember that the primary reason we use blame is that our needs are frustrated, or we want to vent a feeling. Our intention may not be to be mean or malicious, but when we're angry, resentful, anxious, fearful or in pain, we say terrible things to each other. We *do* behave badly.

But we simply don't know how else to express our feelings or correct an error! A core thesis of this book is that we use blame because we're just doing what we've always done.

The Single Most Common Blame Trap—the "Why" Question

Blame Traps most commonly start when someone asks a question never intended to be answered because it's *really a criticism*, either subtle or harsh. The blame effectively disguises itself within a so-called "innocent question."

The tone of voice of the person asking the question intensifies that person's feelings of irritation, frustration or contempt. And it also intensifies the frustration and reaction of the person being asked the question.

The following questions all begin with "Why," and all of them are Blame Traps. Imagine hearing them said angrily or sarcastically.

Try to imagine answering these questions in a way that isn't reciprocally critical and sarcastic. It's virtually impossible. That's why it's a trap. You get sucked in deeper and deeper.

Following each one of the questions is a possible reply. Notice that each reply is itself critical and sarcastic, which is more blame!

- "Why didn't you put the orange juice away?" Answer: Because I'm too stupid to remember! Do you feel better now that you know that I'm brainless?
- "Why are you changing lanes so abruptly? Do you want to get us killed!" Answer: That's exactly the reason I'm driving this way, to get us killed.
- "Why can't you remember a simple thing like calling your mother?" Answer: Because I really don't care about my family. I'm not a loving person.
- "Why is it so hard for you to understand? I already explained it." Answer: Because I'm too dumb to understand your instructions.

- "Why do I even bother talking to you?" Answer: Obviously I'm hopeless.

The clear implication in each of these false "Why?" questions is that you're incompetent, stupid, irresponsible or uncaring. When I'm working with couples whose communications are laced with blame, I'll sometimes suggest a simple change: Don't ask any question that begins with "Why," especially when there's any emotional content attached. Just this one small change will stop a lot of the unthinking use of blame.

We'll discuss this intervention in a later chapter on Positive Accountability.

Rewriting the Blame Trap into a Simple Statement

How can you deal with these situations without setting a Blame Trap? The best way is to form them into a direct statement. Asking directly for what you need—and doing so without anger or sarcasm—will communicate your need and not risk a negative reaction.

- "Why didn't you put the orange juice away?" becomes "Please remember to put the orange juice away."
- "Are you trying to kill us . . . ?" becomes "Please drive more slowly. Changing lanes so quickly really scares me."
- "Why can't you remember a simple thing like calling your mother?" becomes "I'd like you to call your mother. I worry about her."

- "Why is it so hard for you to understand? I already explained it" becomes "I'll explain it again when there aren't distractions."

In all of these examples, imagine hearing the second statement rather than the first. Each is cleaner, more direct and, above all, more caring.

A typical reaction to the above suggestions is: "But if I don't show how angry I am, nothing will change!" But has that worked for the last thousand times? Haven't your Blame Traps just triggered a lot more resentment and arguments? Of course they have. Because no one enjoys being attacked, either directly or indirectly.

But what about all those situations in which the other person utterly refuses to cooperate? Yes, living beyond blame applies even then.

THE MOST COMMON QUESTION ABOUT BLAME: What to Do When the Other Person Refuses to Change?

What to do when all your criticisms and accusations only create more tension and escalate into destructive arguments? What to do when your partner continues an irresponsible behavior? What to do when your demands are met with obstinate silence? Or there's an initial agreement but the same old behaviors resurface a day later?

There are many variations on these core questions. The answers, however, are covered in Part Two, when we discuss Positive Accountability.

In the meantime, your homework assignment is to come up with your own answer. Here's a hint: The way to stop using blame is to eliminate all forms of criticism and accusation from your communication. Yes, it's possible. It means to phrase all your comments into a basic request (or demand) that does not criticize or accuse.

But before we get to the solution, we need to continue exploring Blame Traps.

Five of the Most Common Blame Traps—and How to Avoid Them

Here's a list of five phrases and watchwords that can warn you that someone is setting a Blame Trap and inviting you to step inside the snare. Of course not *every* use of these words will be a setup for blame, but they can act as an early warning system.

The following are either false questions—they don't really ask a question—or they're statements laced with sarcasm. None of them completely mean what the words say. What they all have in common is that they're a criticism or accusation *disguised* to sound like the questioner is really interested in resolving a problem, or learning something useful.

IMPORTANT NOTE: As you're reading these questions, remember that the speaker's tone is irritated or frustrated. The tone of voice makes all the difference between an actual Blame Trap and a sincere but misguided or poorly presented question.

1. "Why don't you ... ?" or "Why did you ... ?": This is probably the most common false question that's actually a setup for blame. Criticism, accusation and punish-

ment are either embedded in the question or about to follow.

2. "How come you didn't [or don't] . . . ?": This question is a variation on the above. The words "How come you . . ." are really *telling* you that you didn't do something and the reason is that there's something wrong with you. Obviously you're too dense to figure it out. Or you don't care enough; your love and devotion are in doubt.

3. "Didn't you know that . . . ?": The implication is that you didn't know something because there's something inherently wrong with you. It couldn't be an ordinary mistake because then it could be handled without using blame, and everyone could move on.

4. "I'm just trying to find out why . . .": This apparently innocent question is usually a Blame Trap because its criticism is camouflaged within the good intention of just wanting some information. You know in your gut that the person is trying to disguise criticism, which makes you feel even more trapped.

5. "It would help if you'd just . . .": The implication of this statement is that you don't know what you're doing and the person is going to tell you everything that's wrong with your approach.

What to Do When Confronted with a Blame Trap

The Blame Trap is one of the most devilish communications to deal with because it disguises its message within worthwhile intentions: "I'm only trying to . . . !"

Because Blame Traps can be complex, we'll explore them in

greater depth in Part Two, where we'll use the process of Positive Accountability to work toward a solution.

For now, however, the most important thing to remember is *not to take the bait*. Because neatly disguised inside the bait is a vicious hook.

Here's how it would work in an actual dialogue using one of the above Blame Traps:

Myrna just found out they don't have a babysitter for the weekend. She says: "Jacob, how come you didn't remember to call the babysitter?" She's upset and uses blame to get Jacob to be more responsible. Jacob takes the bait and tries to answer her question.

Jacob: "I was about to but I got involved with something at work." He's squirming and trying to justify his forgetfulness. But this weak excuse doesn't satisfy Myrna.

Myrna: "You *always* have something at work. Too busy with your own projects to make a simple phone call? Now I've got to straighten things out."

Jacob: "Well, remember last time . . . uh, the babysitter canceled and . . . uh, you . . ." Now he's really squirming to defend himself.

Myrna: "What does her canceling have to do with your call? I can't believe it! You'll make up any kind of excuse just to get out of . . ."

The Blame Cycle has begun, and the accusations are flying thick and heavy. As it typically does, the exchange has degenerated.

What would it look like if Jacob didn't take the bait? Let's replay it.

Myrna: "Jacob, how come you didn't remember to call the babysitter?"

Jacob is paying attention and hears the words announcing a possible Blame Trap: *How come you didn't . . . ?* He also hears Myrna's irritated tone of voice and knows he's on the receiving end of blame. So he stays calm and responds only to the issue of forgetting to make the call. He refuses to answer the false question of "How come?" (The false question could also be "Why didn't you . . . ?")

Jacob responds: "I meant to but I forgot. I'm really sorry." That's all. But Myrna's not satisfied because she's upset. She believes that if she accepts his apology he won't know how upset she is and he won't learn the lesson. Also, she wants to discharge her irritation.

REMEMBER: We use blame whenever our needs are frustrated or we want to vent a feeling.

Myrna: "Is a phone call such a difficult thing to remember? I can't *even* trust you to do a simple thing like that." Myrna is piling it on.

Jacob stays on message and does not take the bait that pulls him into the Blame Trap. He does not try to answer Myrna's false question because he knows he can't really provide an answer beyond "I'm sorry."

If he did continue with more excuses in an effort to prove to Myrna that he's right, that's he's a good person, he'd just dig himself in deeper.

Let's hope she gives up, but if she doesn't, Jacob's next move is to exit the discussion.

Jacob: "I've already apologized. You want something more, but I can't give it."

It's utterly essential that Jacob's tone of voice remains even and not inflected with anger or sarcasm. (As we continue through the book, the importance of tone of voice and controlling emotions will be discussed in many situations.) But there's no guarantee this will mollify Myrna because her intention may be to inflict pain and that's all that matters to her. At that point, Jacob may need to physically leave the room.

As this story illustrates, when someone sets a Blame Trap and you're about to be caught in its unforgiving snare, slipping out of the trap takes focus and effort.

In my clinical practice, I've worked with couples whose entire relationship is based on setting reciprocal Blame Traps. Almost every comment is an accusation, criticism or false question embedded with blame.

Learning to recognize a toxic Blame Trap is the first step in avoiding it. In later chapters we'll be examining how to deal with not only Blame Traps, but also the Blame Spiral, the deadliest form of blame within a relationship.

■ ■ ■ ■ ■

CHAPTER SIX

Blame Is a Three-Part Syndrome Initiated by a Blame Attack

■ **PART ONE OF THE BLAME SYNDROME:**
The Blame Attack

"Oh, no, Blame Attacks! Sounds like sci-fi battles. How about telling me what I can *do* about all this blame."

My sister Elaine (my tireless advisor) made this comment after she had read the previous chapters. She was raring to go with the solution, to wipe out blame.

"But," I explained, "I can't start with Positive Accountability until the reader understands how the three parts of the Blame Syndrome work. They're an essential part of Accountability!"

In the end, I reached a compromise with my sister. I'd suggest to the readers to skip ahead to Part Two of the book if they were anxious to read about Positive Accountability, the ultimate solution to blame.

But blame is really complicated. That's why I suggest you persevere and read the next three chapters to get a clear idea about how the entire Blame Syndrome works.

An example of a syndrome in medical terms would be a stress headache. Stress and tension cause a headache. The headache triggers reactions that increase stress. With added stress, the headache becomes more painful.

Similarly, blame is a series of actions and reactions having at least three discrete parts, but with each part *seamlessly* connected to the other. They all work together to generate the Blame Syndrome. The three parts are:

1. **The Blame Attack** (the initial criticism—no matter how minor)
2. **The Emotional Impact** (negative feelings caused by being blamed)
3. **The Reactive Response** (blame is fired back)

Typically, the time span between these three parts is only a few seconds. It usually happens so quickly, one overlapping the other, that the entire cycle is a fast-moving blur.

■ DEFINING THE FIRST PART OF THE SYNDROME: The Blame Attack

A Blame Attack is any statement or message (spoken or unspoken) that criticizes, condemns, accuses, punishes or humiliates—to any degree.

There's virtually no such thing as a trivial Blame Attack,

because when you're on the receiving end of criticism, you'll always feel a negative emotion. Even a minor amount of these emotions—anxiety, anger, resentment, pain or fear—can be damaging to your well-being, or to a relationship. The effect is stronger when provoked by someone you love and trust.

For instance, Mickey brings home a drawing from school. His father barely glances at it and says, "Is this how you waste your time? No wonder you're behind." Mickey's father is directly critical of his son's creativity. Mickey feels humiliated. He loves to draw but is told by the person he's supposed to trust, his father, that his efforts are a waste of time. He's also angry at his father, who doesn't understand Mickey's individual need to be creative. If similar criticisms continue, their relationship will suffer and Mickey might suffer lifelong negative consequences to his self-esteem.

The more powerful the Blame Attack, the stronger the impact, the stronger the reaction, the longer the syndrome lasts and the greater the negative effect.

The husband who sits down to dinner and picks at his food, barely suppressing a frown, is expressing criticism of his wife's cooking. Or he might be overtly critical. "Why did you make this? You *know* I hate it!" Her Emotional Impact would be resentment, which could provoke wider consequences. Later that evening, the husband tries to be amorous and she rejects him. That would be her Reactive Response. But then he launches another Blame Attack and accuses her of being cold and unloving. His attack provokes another Reactive Response from her. And on and on and on.

Let's begin looking at the reasons why we launch a Blame Attack. What's our motivation? Remember, there's always a *reason* for using blame.

■ WE ALWAYS HAVE A REASON TO LAUNCH A BLAME ATTACK

In our own minds we always have a reason for using blame. Our motives seem practical: something wrong needs to be corrected; an emotion needs to be expressed. But just because a behavior seems reasonable at the time, or you don't know what else to do, blame is no less destructive to relationships.

Here are some reasons and justifications we use for initiating a Blame Attack.

a. We want to inform others about their mistake or problem.
b. We want to express an emotion such as anxiety or anger.
c. We want to get others to change their behavior so it fits our needs.
d. We want to protect ourselves from someone else's behavior.
e. We want to shift responsibility onto someone or something else.

Let's examine these reasons and justifications one at a time, starting with the most common:

a. *We use blame to inform others about their mistake or problem.* Our friend, spouse or coworker is doing something wrong and we feel the need to let them know about it.

■ "Why can't you keep your iPad charged like I do?" You're upset and frustrated because sometimes your friend doesn't keep her electronics working. But criticizing her and setting yourself up as a better person creates more irritation and resentment.

■ "You'd think I'd be more important than your friends. But then . . . I'm just your wife!" This statement criticizes the husband for neglecting his wife, and also uses sarcasm to criticize his loyalty. Using a Blame Attack to try to get the husband to be more attentive forces him to defend himself, increasing the resentment of both parties.

■ "It's not that hard to figure out! Just use your brain!" the dad says to his daughter doing homework. The dad's upset and worried that she'll fall behind and dumps his anxiety on her. Humiliation will just make her feel worse about herself.

b. *We use blame to express an emotion such as anxiety, anger, pain or fear.* Whenever we feel anxiety, we try to offload it onto someone. Sometimes we'll use the excuse "I'm just venting!" Or, as many of my patients are fond of saying, "I just need to be myself! I have to express my real feelings!"

All too often the feelings are anger or discontent or frustration. What else are we supposed to do when someone else "causes" us to be angry, or feel anxiety and frustration? Without role models to teach us how to communicate our feelings and needs respectfully and without criticizing, it's no wonder we bundle our own anxieties and resentments into a Blame Attack.

■ "It pisses me off that you can't get anywhere on time! You're so irresponsible," you say angrily. Your partner has shown up half an hour late, and you're really upset, so it feels only natural to discharge your feelings onto him with a Blame Attack.

- "You're pregnant! How could you have been so stupid? Now what are you going to do?" Your daughter is in college, she's pregnant and you're furious that she's made such a tremendous mistake.

- "Oh my God, did you just buy that?" the wife says to her husband who's returned from the mall with a new jacket. "Maybe you thought I'm too dense to notice!" She's been worried about piling up debt and her stress over money is keeping her awake at night. This outburst is just going to add to her stress, because now she'll have to deal with her husband's anger.

c. *We use blame to get others to change their behavior so it fits our needs.* People in your life will inevitably irritate you, or frustrate you or even make you furious. How can you get them to change? If you don't know about Positive Accountability (which we'll cover in Part Two), you'll believe you have no other choice.

Here are some examples of using a Blame Attack in a futile (and destructive) attempt to get someone to correct a behavior.

- "Kevin, you think you're so smart, but why can't you even remember to lock the door?" You have a right to want the door locked, but criticizing and insulting your son has now complicated the process; both of you will now have to deal with the negative feelings created by this Blame Attack.

- "Is it too much to ask that you apologize just once in your life? Just once!" Brianna is intensely frustrated with her partner's argumentative and self-righteous style, but using a Blame Attack to get him to change his behavior will only create resentment.
- "You said you wanted to lose weight. Why did you order cheesecake? Or do you expect some kind of miracle to . . ." Michael knows his wife is gaining weight. But using a Blame Attack to criticize her behavior only gets her angry and reinforces her wish to overeat.

d. *We use blame to protect ourselves from someone else's verbal assault.* Sometimes the best defense is an offense. But if the tactic involves the criticism and accusation of a Blame Attack, the results will be predictably destructive.

- "You made the stupid reservation so don't get upset with me!" You and your partner get to the hotel and find it's in a terrible location. Neither of you knows how to express your disappointment without criticizing the other.
- "Wasn't it your idea to have sex, and now you're having a problem?" When she initially agreed to have sex, she didn't realize she was too tired. Now she makes a negative comment about her partner's performance as a way to protect herself from possible criticism.
- "I was going to get you something for your birthday, but I know how fussy you are." This statement criticizes the other person for being too difficult to please and therefore deserving of nothing.

e. *We use blame to shift responsibility onto someone or something else.* At the beginning of the first chapter, I used the example of Mario taking one of Ben's crayons to illustrate a simple use of blame to shift responsibility to someone else. Yet Mario accused Ben of taking his crayon first, so he feels justified to throw a pencil.

Shifting responsibility to someone else for one of our own errors is an inherent part of our behavior. The psychological term for this behavior is "defensiveness." In essence, you're saying, "The problem isn't me, it's *you!*" Within all relationships, and especially couples, defensiveness escalates the conflict, because it bounces the culpability back to the other person.

- "If you wrote things on the calendar then maybe I could keep track better." As though the reason you don't keep track of things is that your spouse doesn't write them down. Even when she does, you still don't pay attention.
- "No matter how much money I made, you'd find a way to spend it all." The husband blames his wife's spending as the reason for their increasing debt, ignoring his own spending on golf, sailing and a fully stocked wine cellar. Nor is he willing to sit down and work out a budget.
- "Well, if your brother's coming to the party, don't expect me to stay sober." As though the reason you drink excessively at parties is the fault of your wife's brother.

As you can see from this barrage of Blame Attacks, there's a wide assortment of ways to shift responsibility for our behaviors onto someone else.

In these examples, each person always feels he or she has a good reason to launch the Blame Attack. But once the communication turns into a criticism, accusation, punishment or humiliation, the negative emotions always take over. Maybe the intention is not to create anxiety, anger, pain and fear, but it does!

There's one last technique for shifting responsibility to someone or something else: blaming a greater entity such as destiny, fate, karma, Divine Will or God.

■ THE ULTIMATE BLAME ATTACK:
To Accuse Destiny

I'll never forget a couple named Walter and Suzanne. Both were very successful, in their early fifties, and had recently divorced their respective spouses in order to marry each other. Both had children by those previous marriages and were seeking my assistance in dealing with the vindictiveness triggered by their surreptitious love affair and the abruptness of their subsequent divorces.

Amazingly, Walter and Suzanne cited a series of external reasons for their problems. Suzanne explained, "The moment I met Walter I knew he was my soul mate. I waited all my life to meet him. I'd make any sacrifice just to be with him."

Walter tried to muster the same enthusiasm. "Fate wanted us to be together. It's corny, but I believe it."

Neither Suzanne nor Walter wanted to accept responsibility for throwing their families into chaos. From their point of view, they had no choice but to act immediately on their passion because a Greater Power *compelled* them to follow their heart. They had no choice. Because their spouses and children and friends did not automatically support their love, Suzanne and

Walter actually saw themselves as *victims*. Everyone else was too small-minded and selfish, and incapable of understanding the dictates of destiny.

> **THE POINT: Blaming our behavior on destiny or a Greater Power denies personal responsibility and avoids resolving an issue.**

Walter and Suzanne's story is not all that unusual. Their drama illustrates how we can illegitimately use an external force such as destiny or a Greater Power to shift responsibility and justify behavior that can have serious life-changing consequences.

There are, however, smaller instances of Blame Attacks that shift responsibility onto a hidden purpose, destiny, or an isolated event. Here are some examples:

- "Nothing I do to lose weight works, so I might as well enjoy myself." Saying that calories you eat are not relevant to weight gain shifts responsibility onto some mystery factor beyond your control. Since a magical power controls your weight, you might as well give up.
- "My vote doesn't mean a thing; everything is decided by the banks and politicians." Denying your responsibility to participate in your government allows you to shirk civic responsibility by using cynicism (criticism) to justify nonparticipation.
- "My dad smoked cigarettes and drank all his life, and it never hurt him." Using an isolated example to reinforce an illusion of invulnerability shifts responsibility for dangerous behavior onto a magical reality. In other words, the smoker will not experience the consequences of smoking because a miraculous exception will save him in the end.

These typical justifications are part of the wider problem of how blame has seeped into so many of our attitudes and behaviors. Some of them may sound trivial, but because we use them over and over again, they eventually build an extensive web of blame that always pushes us away from resolving a problem in our relationships, or assuming full responsibility for our behaviors.

■ ■ ■ ■ ■

CHAPTER SEVEN

Part Two of the Blame Syndrome

The Emotional Impact

■ THE EMOTIONAL CONSEQUENCES OF BLAME ARE ALWAYS THE SAME

While there are numerous variations within the single behavior we call blame—everything from a raised eyebrow to a scathing attack—the *Emotional Impact* and *emotional consequences* are always similar. A Blame Attack *always* provokes negative emotions. These negative emotions are anger, resentment, anxiety, pain, fear and humiliation, and all their variations. For example, frustration, irritation and resentment are a variation of anger. Being upset, nervous, anxious or uncomfortable is a variant of anxiety or fear.

Within relationships, the passage from the initial thought (for instance "he's being unfair") to the feeling of anger is so rapid that it can hardly be measured. The emotion can hit you like a freight train so you don't have time to think about controlling your emotional response.

Blame does that. Being criticized can trigger an instantaneous Emotional Impact.

■ ■ ■ ■ ■

ANGER IS AN IMPORTANT AND VALID EMOTION

Anger serves a valid and important role in our lives. Anger is an appropriate response to the perception of unfairness. Its job is to help us tell people to back off, or to not cheat us. Not for a second am I suggesting we shouldn't feel anger when we're being treated unfairly. That's the problem with blame. Whenever we're being criticized, accused, punished or humiliated, it seems so unfair and arbitrary that it *feels like* the most reasonable response is anger.

Margaret took special care in preparing a meal for her visiting in-laws. She had everyone sit down and then brought the salad to the table. Her mother-in-law looked at the salad, pursed her lips and said, "Oh, dear. Apples in a salad?" Margaret didn't have time to *think* about her mother-in-law's ridiculous and critical Blame Attack. Instead Margaret *instantly* reacted as though she'd been stabbed with a knife. The emotions of anger and shame exploded inside her before she had a few seconds to think. She angrily left the room.

Her mother-in-law then had a chance to twist the knife. "My

goodness, Margaret's really on edge these days. Has she seen a doctor about being so stressed?"

After the dinner, Margaret's husband downplayed his mother's comment. "Honey, you know my mom is difficult to please. She's not being mean just to you."

What could Margaret have done to temper the Emotional Impact of her mother-in-law's Blame Attack? The following sections will present strategies and tactics to deal with any Emotional Impact, and thus protect yourself.

▣ REORGANIZING YOUR THINKING ABOUT EMOTIONS

My clinical experience teaches me that most of us have scant knowledge about how our emotions function and the dominant role they play in our lives. It's even more of a stretch for people to accept the idea that blame is really all about emotions. It's not actually about seeking justice or punishing the guilty. That's the purpose of Positive Accountability. In contrast, blame's purpose is to discharge anxiety, express irritation or anger, seek revenge through humiliation, increase your status through intimidation and so on. Blame plays an intrinsic role in all these *emotional* activities.

▣ OUR EMOTIONS DOMINATE OUR BEHAVIORS

It's an accepted psychological fact that emotions strongly influence and often dominate our behaviors. Therefore, because blame is essentially an emotional process controlled by our feelings, in order to not use blame, we must actively control our emotions.

In fact, countless experiments have demonstrated how our

emotions can be easily manipulated, resulting in a change in our behaviors. In one experiment, one group of people who are shown violent movies will afterward choose more aggressive solutions to a problem. The other group who watched comedies will engage in nonviolent, more collaborative solutions.

Even exposing a person to a few emotion-laden images prior to an experiment greatly influences the outcome.

Similarly, people who grow up in a home with a lot of arguing and violence tend to argue and fight as adults. Or the opposite: they avoid conflict entirely and don't stand up for themselves. Their behaviors are conditioned by their level of exposure to intense emotions.

Our everyday behaviors and decisions are also highly influenced by our emotional state in each moment. While we occasionally engage in thoughtful consideration about a decision, almost always our emotions dominate, often in subtle or non-obvious ways.

Here are three brief stories to illustrate how emotions influence behavior:

- Donald bought a new car that severely stressed his monthly budget. He explained, "I went to the showroom just to check into the rebate, but once I took the car on a test drive, I just had to have it." Vanity and desire pumped up his ego; clear thinking was thrown out the car window. (Donald used blame to justify his decision: he shifted the responsibility to an *emotional necessity*.)
- Peggy returned from a weekend trip to Las Vegas with her new boyfriend, who happened to be married. She explained, "He's having such a hard time with his wife. He needed to have some fun." The lure of passion and lust trumped ethics

and reason. (Peggy used blame to justify the sexual encounter by shifting the responsibility to her boyfriend's need for comfort since his wife was unavailable.)

- Ron got into an argument with a coworker and fumed about it all day. The next morning he confronted the coworker and it escalated into a shouting match. His actions were written up into a formal reprimand. He still thinks he had a right to be pissed off and it's not his fault if he loses his job. (Ron shifts responsibility for his loss of control to his coworker, who provoked him, and also wonders why the world is against him.)

It's so easy for us to shift the responsibility onto something else when our emotions are in change of our thinking, whether it's buying a big-ticket item, or going on a weekend fling with a married person, or venting rage at a coworker and endangering our employment. From the perspective of blame, we're really shifting responsibility onto our "feelings."

Emotions rule!

THE POINT: We also use blame to shift responsibility to an emotional need or because our emotions overwhelm our ability to think clearly.

Emotions also control issues on a national scale. Just about any appeal to fear (our most primitive emotion) can push ordinarily rational people to make rash decisions.

Since the terrorist attacks on the World Trade Center on September 11, 2001, the most powerful emotion in American politics has been fear . . . of more terror attacks. Politicians emphasize this frightening emotion and blame terrorists for the need to act preemptively.

■ THE EMOTIONAL IMPACT OF BLAME TRIGGERS DESTRUCTIVE BEHAVIOR

Being criticized, accused, punished or humiliated is painful. Blame hurts!

Let's again go over our typical emotional reaction when some-one hurts us. Because we feel hurt, we fight back. We want to punish the person who hurt us. Or, if in that moment we're not ready to do battle, we slink away and plot revenge. This reaction to blame is wired so tightly into our emotional structure that it will take quite an effort to reroute the wires so the feelings caused by a Blame Attack don't do as much damage.

The Emotional Impact caused by a Blame Attack involves very powerful feelings:

- anger/resentment
- fear/anxiety
- pain/humiliation

I've lumped anger and resentment together because resentment is a brooding form of anger. Likewise, the effects of anxiety and fear on our behavior are similar, as with pain and humiliation. Let's examine these emotional pairings and their effects on our behaviors.

■ THE MOST COMMON EMOTIONAL IMPACT IS ANGER

Anger is one of our two most primitive emotions. The other is fear. But anger is the most dangerous because it's so tightly con-nected to rage. Unchecked rage can kill.

In a previous section I discussed how the amygdala, a primitive part of our brain structure, triggers the fight/flight syndrome. But this same syndrome is also responsible for the slightest rise in body temperature, constriction of blood vessels, accelerated heartbeat and the host of other physiological reactions activated to help us confront a physical threat.

Amazingly, this syndrome is even activated when we *perceive that there's a threat* to our standing within any relationship, when our "rightness" is challenged or when a loving connection is endangered.

So anything that lessens our status or diminishes our feelings of belonging will likely receive an angry response.

> **THE POINT: It's a biological and behavioral fact that
> we'll respond with anger to defend our position of
> being right, as well as our connection to others.**

Despite the damage of triggering these emotions, I am continually amazed at how little attention has been paid to our *biological reactions* within our relationships. It's as though we know that anger shuts down our ability to think but don't want to directly confront the problem because it's too big a challenge.

Here's a story about a family so steeped in blame and the Emotional Impact of anger that almost every interaction produced irritation, resentment or defiance. But they wanted to be happier and closer. Fortunately, with concerted effort on their part, they managed to change old behaviors and achieve their goals.

Tom and Isabel Wanted Their Teenage Children to study harder and be more respectful to them as parents. But when they brought their two teens into therapy, it was clear they hadn't a clue about how blame had saturated their lives. The negative emotions of anger and resentment were off the charts.

Here's how Tom, the husband and father, described the situation. "I put everything I've got into my family. I work really hard, and I get really upset when no one shows any gratitude!"

Isabel had a similar complaint. "I work part-time but I'm home every afternoon to make sure there's a hot meal on the table. I do the laundry, cleaning . . . and all I get are complaints."

Their seventeen-year-old son, Matt, sat slumped in his chair. He said, "Everyone's so pissed off all the time, what do they expect? They start all the fights."

Rita, their fifteen-year-old, mimicked her brother. "My mom and dad are so stressed that just being around them is a bitch. No wonder I'm never home."

All four of them used a lot of pseudo-questions setting up Blame Traps. Such as, "Why aren't you doing your homework?" "Why can't you make mac and cheese for dinner?" "Why are you always on the phone?"

Every comment was a variation on a Blame Attack, and no one in the family was able to see how their own behaviors contributed to the family's problems.

THE POINT: When blame takes over, nearly every communication is a criticism, accusation, punishment or humiliation—and anger dominates relationships.

Because the family was committed to improving their situation, I began educating them about blame. Specifically, I pointed out how almost everything they said was tinged with criticism, accusation, punishment or humiliation, *which always provoked an angry response!* Their homework assignment was in two parts: (1) *Ask* no *Why questions.* (2) *Say nothing critical about anyone that triggers an angry response!* And I included sarcasm as a form of criticism.

To help them keep track of their progress, I suggested they keep a notebook open to everyone. Whenever anyone was caught saying something critical, the other person could put an X next to that person's name. Having a visual expression of negative behavior really brought the message home.

I had to do a lot of coaching, but over the next sessions spaced out over three months, they started to understand the destructiveness of criticism and accusation.

The ultimate result for Isabel and Tom's family was a significant reduction of anger and resentment. When the family realized they did *not* have to communicate by criticizing and accusing each other, their natural feelings of caring and closeness greatly increased. Now let's examine the Emotional Impact of anxiety and fear.

■ ANXIETY AND FEAR PROVOKE POWERFUL IRRATIONAL RESPONSES

Living with anxiety and fear creates unhappiness and despair in all our relationships. So reducing the anxiety and fear caused by blame is one of this book's primary goals.

As Tom's and Isabel's family story illustrates, first comes a Blame Attack, then there's the Emotional Impact—and the emotions generated in that exchange dominate the relationship. While the main focus with this family was resolving anger and resentment, everyone also felt a great deal of *anxiety* because anger causes instability. The family worried about their inability to be happy, and that their individual needs for support and closeness would never be fulfilled.

Research supports the idea that all of us live with a lot of anxiety and fear. Much of the anxiety is just part of being alive: Our awareness of death, our fragility and vulnerability create a constant "existential" anxiety.

Within our relationships, however, most of us suffer from too much anxiety and fear primarily because our communications provoke these destructive emotions through criticism, accusation, punishment and humiliation.

The goal of living Beyond Blame is to live without criticism and accusation.

Imagine what it would be like if all the important people in your life stopped criticizing and accusing you! Imagine that the only things they said were positive and supportive! And when conflict arose (as it must) it was handled respectfully, with hardly any anger, fear or pain.

Wouldn't that feel wonderful?

It's entirely possible. But you'll have to wait until we get to the chapter on Positive Accountability to find out how the process works. And it does work, splendidly!

In the meantime, we need to dig a little deeper into the debilitating emotions of anxiety and fear, and how they're connected to blame.

Aaron Teaches High School and Shares Custody of his ten-year-old son, David, who has a learning disability. Aaron's ex-wife is studying nursing and also works, so she has little time to follow David's studies. Aaron blames a lot of David's problems on his ex-wife. Aaron is constantly in the grip of all six negative emotions, but his primary emotion is anxiety: he worries about his son's academic success.

Aaron teaches science and he believes his son should shine in that subject, despite his disabilities and interest in art and reading. Aaron is completely unaware of how his anxiety over David's lack of ability in math and his ongoing criticism affect his son.

During a recent shopping trip, Aaron popped a quiz about the bill. "David, the total was $17.21, and I gave the clerk twenty dollars. So how much change should he have given me back? Go on, do the math in your head."

David mumbled an answer. Aaron snapped, "It's simple! Just think! David, you've got to do something other than read books if you're going to support yourself."

Of course the boy was humiliated and anxious. Why was reading silly? He wasn't naturally good at math and it seemed that unless he was, his father wouldn't love him. Sadly, Aaron's comment was part of a pattern of criticism that eventually created a great deal of anxiety in the boy. He felt increasingly incapable in all his studies. This anxiety made his study of math all the more problematic. In other words, he did a lot worse because of his father's criticism.

Criticism is the main source of anxiety in relationships and threatens the stability of the connection because it communicates that we're not okay, that our performance is substandard.

■ AN OCCASIONAL CRITICISM
IS NOT THE PROBLEM

I'm not saying that an occasional minor criticism destroys relationships. A snappy, "Why did you do *that?*" will not be a problem. Nor will occasional disapproval cause harm.

The problem is the constant flow of messages with a negative emotional charge that tell you that you are *not* good enough. The consequence of living in such a critical environment is a tremendous amount of anxiety about the stability of the relationship.

Our sensitivity to criticism and accusation goes back to our earliest days as children with our parents. We know that their approval is essential to our happiness and all children do their best to please their parents. Unfortunately, too many parents (even in this more enlightened era) still use generic forms of blame and criticism as a means of expressing disapproval. The *intention* might be to improve the child's behavior, but the criticism just makes children feel bad about themselves, anxious about their relationship and especially anxious about their self-worth.

The dynamics of pain and humiliation are similar to those of anger and fear because they typically produce anxiety. For this reason I won't provide a special section about these negative emotions.

Now let's move to the last part of the Blame Syndrome: the Reactive Response and its role in propelling the highly destructive Blame Spiral.

■ ■ ■ ■ ■

CHAPTER EIGHT

The Third Part of the Blame Syndrome

The Reactive Response and the Blame Spiral

WE'VE LOOKED at the first part of the Blame Syndrome—the Blame Attack. And we've examined how each attack provokes an emotional response—the Emotional Impact.

At this point, we know that blame hurts. And we know that because we are hardwired to fight back when we're attacked, we do fight back! We're essentially slaves to our programming.

This back-and-forth battle of blame occurs because no one knows how to do anything other than criticize, accuse, punish and humiliate. Each person is suddenly caught up in the most destructive of Blame Cycles, which I call the *Blame Spiral*.

Earlier in the book I described the Blame Cycle, which is the reciprocal use of blame. A Blame Spiral is essentially the same, except that each Reactive Response becomes more accusatory and vicious, leading downward toward greater chaos.

◼ THE BLAME SPIRAL TEARS
APART RELATIONSHIPS

Falling into the Blame Trap and then having it devolve into a
Blame Spiral creates a toxic situation that's very difficult to
escape.

It's important to know that blame is *designed* to operate within
a particular format, and that the format is a downward spiral (see
figure on page 94).

The Blame Spiral feeds on itself, dragging everyone down
into greater unhappiness and separation. The shape of the spiral
can be broad or narrow. It can be a single explosive event that
provokes a series of vindictive responses. It can consist of dozens
of reciprocal criticisms that go on for years, or even decades. In
the case where ethnic groups are involved, the Blame Spiral can
last for centuries.

> **THE POINT: The first Reactive Response to a Blame
> Attack begins an exchange of Blame Attacks that
> can cause a downward spiral of reciprocal criticism
> and accusation.**

My first experiences with the Blame Spiral were in my extended
family. Many of my family members were cantankerous individuals
who thrived on blame. My aunts and uncles held grudges for years,
often based on a single incident that degenerated into a Blame
Spiral. One of my aunts would declare another sister to be an out-
cast from holiday gatherings. The reason was always a perceived
offense. Decades ago I remember visiting my mother during a holiday and casually inquiring about her sister, my aunt Jule. My mother

would give me a look of stern disapproval and declare, "I'm not talking to *her*." She made it sound like Aunt Jule had joined a satanic cult. The standoff between them involved mutual accusations of disloyalty, or some other form of criticism. Then, months later, it would be miraculously over . . . until the next Blame Spiral. The highly dysfunctional methods my relatives used to deal with their conflicts were the beginning of my education about the unhappy consequences of blame. The best way to describe the toxic nature of a Blame Spiral is to observe it in action.

Bill and Janet Have Been Married for Eighteen Years. Sadly, the last dozen years have been increasingly unhappy. They can hardly say a word to each other without getting caught in a destructive exchange that escalates into more fierce attacks. Because they have grown so used to hearing criticism, judgment, accusation, punishment and humiliation in so many of their communications, even a simple comment seems to carry an inflection of blame.

Here's a replay of their last therapy session. They arrive separately; Bill comes in about five minutes late. They are both obviously upset. In the following dialogue, seven statements and accusations make up this particular Blame Spiral. If I hadn't stopped them, I can only imagine how long it would have gone on.

1. Janet to Bill: "Why didn't you tell me you'd be late?" (*accusation*)
2. Bill: "Well, you weren't on time either!" (*defense and attack*)
3. Janet: "You forgot to make the bank deposit so I had to go out of my way." (*criticism*)

4. Bill: "That was *your* mistake! You said you were going to do it. Jeez, can't you even keep *that* straight?" (*criticism escalating to attempt at humiliation*)

5. Janet: "Me? If you hadn't bought that stupid truck, we wouldn't be so stressed. You didn't need it." (*criticism, condemnation, accusation, humiliation*)

6. Bill: "Such crap! You know, every day you're getting to be more like your mother." (*revenge, punishment, threat*)

7. Janet: "The biggest mistake I ever made was marrying you!" (*vindictiveness, threat*)

If this exchange weren't so painful, it would sound like a pathetic comedy. And yet, numerous couples get caught up in a highly destructive Blame Spiral, throwing ever more negative criticisms and accusations back and forth, resulting in ever more intense threats.

On the following page is a diagram of the Blame Spiral between Bill and Janet. This illustration shows how the communication between them quickly degenerated into punishment and vindictiveness.

Illustrating the destructive effects of this downward spiral makes it clear that once the spiral has gained strength, it quickly takes on a life of its own.

It then becomes part of the couple's "toxic memory," the accumulation of interactions that ended badly. This toxic memory is like a bed of hot coals always ready to flare into flames when any amount of new fuel is added.

This analogy—the quick ignition into a flaming exchange—is typical of Blame Spirals.

There is, however, another variation, which I call the swamp of depression and hopelessness. If there's a long-standing pattern

A TYPICAL BLAME SPIRAL

Every communication between Janet and Bill is blame:
criticism, accusation, punishment or humiliation.

Janet: "Why didn't you
tell me you'd be late?"
(accusation)

Bill: "Well, you weren't
on time either!"
(defense and attack)

Janet: "You forgot to make the bank deposit,
so I had to." *(criticism)*

Bill: "That was your
mistake! Can't you even
keep that straight?"
*(criticism escalating to
attempt at humiliation)*

Janet: "Me? It was your stupid
idea to buy the truck. You didn't
need it." *(criticism,
condemnation,
accusation,
humiliation)*

Bill: "Such crap! You
know, Janet, every day
you're getting to be
more like your mother."
*(revenge, punishment,
threat)*

Janet: "The biggest mistake I ever made was
marrying you." *(vindictiveness, threat)*

of shame and humiliation in the relationship, the slightest hint of a Blame Attack can thicken the swampy feeling of hopelessness.

For instance, Robert says to Jessie, "Oh, let me do it. You're completely useless." Because Robert has been making critical and humiliating comments for a long time, Jessie already believes that she's useless. This Blame Attack pushes her deeper into depression. In this case, the Blame Spiral turns *inward*, and Jessie spirals downward into a more profound feeling of hopelessness.

"Can't you do anything right?" is another comment that can trigger an inward Blame Spiral.

> **THE POINT: A Blame Spiral can be either like a tornado that keeps building in intensity and destructiveness, or an inward process, pushing you deeper into hopelessness.**

One of the most destructive Blame Spirals often begins when a couple is separating and beginning the legal process of divorce.

Here's a story about how years of tragedy were averted when the downward spiraling energy of blame was interrupted by an act of courage, generosity and, ultimately, enlightened self-interest.

Max and Susan Were the Perfect Couple who had two wonderful children. Max would tell everyone how he fell in love with Susan in high school and waited until after starting college to start dating her. They were a very popular couple on the university campus. They both earned advanced degrees and good positions teaching at a university. Their children were both in gifted programs at school.

Then Susan began an affair with one of Max's colleagues. Not only was Max devastated emotionally, he was furious at being betrayed. He felt so deeply wounded that he could only think of hurting Susan as much as she was hurting him. His humiliation at being "cuckolded by his friend" cut deep.

His anger pushed him to file for divorce and full custody of their children. Because Susan was infuriated at his attempt (futile as it might be) to take her children, she responded with an angry fight at his university office witnessed by several colleagues.

Max now felt justified to respond with even greater vehemence. In the divorce documents he made greatly exaggerated accusations about Susan using alcohol and drugs, and even accused her of plagiarizing her master's thesis.

They finally came to therapy during a lull in their fight. Both sensed that they had gone too far. During the session, I questioned Max separately about why he would want to destroy the mother of his children. Did he consider how much stress and turmoil he was creating in his children's lives? At first he brushed aside my objections and focused only on his own pain, and his mistaken belief that attacking Susan would give him relief.

Susan, for her part, had started circulating rumors that Max was sexually abusing their ten-year-old daughter. When confronted about the consequences of her charge, she backed off. But some of the damage had already been done because Max reciprocated by telling lurid stories about Susan to their children.

THE POINT: One of the most powerful effects of a Blame Spiral is its ability to bring out the worst in people.

Let's track why their tragic situation is a Blame Spiral.

The following list traces the sequence of the Blame Spiral.

1. Susan's affair is discovered.
2. Max files for divorce, demanding full custody.
3. Susan provokes an angry fight at his office in front of colleagues.
4. Max makes exaggerated accusations in divorce documents.
5. Susan retaliates with accusations of sexual abuse.
6. Max tells lurid stories to their children about their mother.
7. Susan responds with more accusations.
8. Max withdraws his demand for full custody, ending the Blame Spiral.

In the following figure, notice the contrast between this Blame Spiral and the previous one that involved Janet and Bill. Specifically, this spiral starts out with a much heavier initial attack.

Max and Susan soon realized that they had not dealt with serious issues in their marriage, and that those issues had actually instigated Susan's betrayal. When her affair became known to Max, he responded exactly as if he were the target of a Blame Attack. He felt criticized and accused (in his position as husband) as well as punished and humiliated (as a man).

In my clinical practice, I've observed that men have an extremely low tolerance for humiliation, either perceived or actual. Whenever blame edges toward humiliation for either gender, the consequences can be tragic.

Finally, both the university and their friends confronted Max and Susan and told them they were both in danger of losing their positions unless they stopped behaving badly.

Max brought this information to therapy and began to show the first glimmer of remorse. A realization of how he had contributed to their marital problems also began to take hold. In a courageous move, he withdrew his petition for full custody and wrote a

Susan's affair is discovered.

Furious, Max files for divorce; demands full custody of children.

Susan provokes an angry fight at his office.

Max accuses Susan of child neglect.

Susan accuses Max of sexual abuse of children.

Max tells children lurid stories about Susan.

Susan makes more accusations.

Max comes to his senses; withdraws demand for full custody. Blame Spiral ends.

formal apology to Susan, not to reconcile with her, but to stop hurting their children.

I consider Max's move courageous because it takes courage to resist going along with the momentum, staying stuck in old patterns. It takes courage to apologize, just as it takes courage to say nothing when provoked.

Fortunately, Susan did likewise. They both met in my office and we worked out some basic ground rules about sharing custody, agreeing to never again say anything negative about each other to anyone, especially their children.

Once both Max and Susan came to their senses, while they could never return to an intimate relationship, they could function as co-parents to their children. Their resolution acts as a preview of Positive Accountability coming up in the next chapter.

As if the dangers of Blame Spirals weren't enough to contend with, there's an even more covert form of blame that takes the squishy form of a Mutual Blame Trap. This type of blame is difficult to diagnose because the individuals involved deny that they are, in fact, using blame.

■ THE MUTUAL BLAME TRAP:
The Tyranny of "We"

This variation of the Blame Spiral is found typically in couples relationships, but can also occur in emotionally enmeshed families. I call it the "Tyranny of We." In fact, it's a Mutual Blame Trap because both parties are completely immobilized by the belief that the "we" is all-powerful, and the individual person doesn't have much to say about what happens.

It's not easy to discover if a couple is caught in a Mutual

Blame Trap because no one wants to take responsibility for anything. The result is that the relationship stays stuck.

Oscar and Irene Were Very Unhappy and Didn't Know Why.
I'd seen the couple for three sessions and progress had been slow. I asked how things had gone since the last time we met.

Oscar says, "Well, not too good." When I ask him to describe what happened, he blames everything on "we" or "it." He says, "Last week we got into a really bad argument. It went on for a couple days."

I ask, "What triggered the argument?"

"I don't know how it started." He turns to his wife. "Do you remember?"

Irene glares at him. "It started about you playing golf."

"It did?" Oscar says. "No, I played golf Saturday. The argument was on Sunday."

"It started on Saturday, after you came home."

I break in. "Can either of you recall how the argument began?"

Irene says, "You came home late and we began to fight about that."

Oscar says, "I can't remember . . . but pretty soon we're both going at each other. We both have short fuses, so when we get worked up . . ."

"So, neither of you is certain about why you started arguing?" I ask.

Each of them continues to shift responsibility to a vague and slippery "we." This is a particularly toxic kind of blame because its source can't be clearly identified. As individuals, they were not responsible. The *couple* had all the problems. They did, however, criticize each other for not being able to stop it.

Both found it difficult to separate their behaviors from the overall argument. Once they started fighting, their problems took over. I tell couples that if the individual doesn't know how arguments begin, then they won't know how to stop them. Both parties will remain hostage of the amorphous WE or the IT.

> **THE POINT: A Blame Spiral can also make it seem that no one is responsible for anything because the individual is not in charge.**

The Previous Eight Chapters Have Explored in depth the nefarious nature of blame and how it shows up in our relationships under a countless variety of guises. Now it's time to grapple with the solution, how-to part of the book, Positive Accountability.

The next section, Part Two, describes how Positive Accountability can be used to resolve problems. Part Three goes much further. It presents an actual method to profoundly change your *relationship* to blame by changing your attitude about your errors and mistakes. I call it the Law of Personal Limitations. Understanding this process can liberate you permanently from the need to use blame in any of your relationships—especially your relationship with yourself.

PART TWO

■ ■ ■ ■ ■

Blame Busting

■ ■ ■ ■ ■

**Learning to Use Positive
Accountability Instead of Blame**

CHAPTER NINE

■ ■ ■ ■ ■

What Do I Use Instead of Blame?

In the previous pages we've explored blame in depth. We know it's not just a single behavior, but a three-part syndrome: the initial Blame Attack triggers an Emotional Impact, which creates a Reactive Response. And it takes multiple forms, such as the Blame Cycle, the Blame Trap and the especially deadly Blame Spiral. And that blame always involves criticism, accusation, punishment or humiliation.

Now we need to focus on what to do about it.

The answer is found within the antidote to blame, the solution that works all the time, in all situations: Positive Accountability. But why *Positive* Accountability? Isn't all accountability the same?

I call it *Positive* Accountability in order to emphasize the constructive, positive aspects of the term. And especially to separate it from the negative way that we often use it. Typically, we use the word "accountable" within the phrase "to hold someone accountable," or "to be accountable." I do not use these phrases in this book because in actual practice they are usually disguised as blame. When you are *holding someone accountable*, or wanting someone *to be accountable*, you are often criticizing, accusing and punishing. The term Positive Accountability completely separates it from the negative effects of blame.

FACT: **We can't *hold* people to do something against their will.** Only the police or military can do that, because we give them the necessary authority. Even parents, who seem to hold ultimate authority, are often frustrated with how little power they really have in forcing their children to comply with their wishes.

Because accountability involves accepting some form of responsibility to correct a mistake, it always works best for *everyone* when the person is engaged in a *voluntary* effort to accept responsibility and modify a behavior. This voluntary effort can occur only when the demand to change is presented in a respectful, thoughtful and compassionate manner. That is, without criticism and accusation.

This fact is intrinsic to this book's argument.

Our needs and emotions must be expressed *respectfully*, *thoughtfully* and *compassionately* so that the other person is not intimidated, overwhelmed or provoked through criticism and accusation. Otherwise we'll create a negative response.

Positive Accountability does exactly that.

The definition of Positive Accountability is unique because it describes a series of very ordinary *behaviors*. These behaviors lead to *engagement*. Force, coercion or criticism is not used. The behaviors acknowledge the intrinsic dignity of others and their right to be fallible—to make a mistake without the fear of being blamed. Of course, the definition absolutely acknowledges the same rights for yourself.

■ DEFINING POSITIVE ACCOUNTABILITY

When you engage Positive Accountability, you are practicing two *behaviors*:

1. To thoughtfully acknowledge an error, your own or another person's, and consider how to repair it, if necessary.
2. To express an emotion, or a need, without using criticism, accusation, punishment or humiliation, with the goal of not triggering negative emotions.

These two behaviors create Positive Accountability. They focus on engaging, involving and interacting with the other person *respectfully* in order to produce a positive result. Also notice how the definition emphasizes the need for objective thinking.

Let's examine these behaviors more closely.

BEHAVIOR ONE: *To thoughtfully acknowledge an error, your own or another person's, and consider how to repair it, if necessary*, means you don't ignore the mistake or problem, whether you caused it or whether you are the recipient. Everything you say or do is focused on repairing the error—if necessary.

If necessary is key. Sometimes repairing a mistake is *not* necessary. Many errors are minor and can be ignored. Not every tiny issue must be discussed and resolved.

Or perhaps the error *cannot* be settled because it's too complicated, or there are too many players and so on. As a baseball fan might put it, you don't have to swing at every ball thrown at you.

The decision to repair or to let go is usually a matter of personal judgment (or generosity of spirit), and is an important part of the process.

**THE POINT: We labor under the Mistaken Belief that
every offense must be addressed, every mistake corrected and every emotion expressed. And until then,
we cannot let anything go.**

BEHAVIOR TWO: *To express an emotion, or a need, without using criticism, accusation, punishment or humiliation,* means that when you've
decided that you need to express a feeling, or discuss a problem,
you do so without using criticism, accusation and so on because
criticism and accusation ignite negative emotions.

The entire purpose of Positive Accountability is to express emotions (tell someone how we feel) and deal with difficulties (solve
problems) without using blame, thereby eliminating the Blame
Syndrome. Whenever we don't use blame, the emotional environment of the relationship remains more positive and affirming.

That's the challenge.

And it's a lot more straightforward than it might seem.

■ POSITIVE ACCOUNTABILITY IS A PROCESS

A process refers to something that's more than a single specific
behavior. While Positive Accountability is made up of the two
primary behaviors listed above, the process is not an invariable
formula. Rather it's a flexible *process* you can adapt to a wide variety of *situations* without *losing its effectiveness*. In the following
chapters all these processes will be described in detail from multiple points of view.

Integrating Positive Accountability into your life does take
some effort. The effort requires, above all, *thoughtfulness*: the abil-

ity to think about what you're doing and whether your behaviors will get you what you want.

However, every bit of energy you put into practicing Positive Accountability will produce rich rewards in happiness and satisfaction in all your relationships.

■ WHY POSITIVE ACCOUNTABILITY IS SO EFFECTIVE

Hold on to your psychological hats because I'm about to make a dramatic claim:

> During my twenty-five-year career as a therapist, I have never come across any system of communication or behavior that works better than Positive Accountability. It's effective *all* the time, in *every* situation, for *every* problem and can be adapted to multiple conditions, from the most subtle to the most blatant. Its positive results are immediate and measurable.

Wherever an individual or couple begins to use Positive Accountability in all their interactions, even the most minor, they report an immediate sense of relief, which then leads to greater connectedness and happiness.

IMPORTANT CAVEAT: There's only one objection, and it's important: *Anyone can sabotage anything.* That is, if the other person is determined to act unethically and undermine the relationship, if their *intention* is to be uncooperative or vindictive, there's no plan on earth that will change that objective. If someone is slashing at you with verbal machetes, and is determined to inflict harm, your only recourse is to get out of the way. However, even in such an extreme situation, Positive Accountability can be used, and it will provide greater safety by not provoking the verbally abusive person to escalate.

Learning Positive Accountability will require you to learn new behaviors. You will have to let go of some old behaviors, especially the ones connected to the Blame Syndrome.

You will have to train yourself to be less reactive.

At every step of the process, however, you will gain priceless skills that will immediately transform your interactions into more positive connections. These skills will be yours to use for the rest of your life—and will benefit everyone with whom you interact.

At the same time, *the impulse to blame is difficult to change*. We all need an effective technique that helps us stay focused on our primary goal, which is to always be in control of our emotions and reactions, so we can enhance and build our precious relationships.

Everyone needs to avoid being *controlled by* volatile and dangerous emotions. That's where the Question of Intention comes in.

■ THE "QUESTION OF INTENTION" THAT BEGINS POSITIVE ACCOUNTABILITY

When we're confronted with a problem, we need to carefully *choose* how we're going to react. *Choosing is the opposite of engaging in knee-jerk blame.*

The Question of Intention about Positive Accountability is:

What do I want to accomplish right now?

What is my goal? What kind of relationship do I want? The variations on this question go to the heart of choosing how to react because it asks you to clarify your intention. Do you intend to make things better? Do you intend (plan, propose, have in mind) to draw closer to the other person, to build trust? Or is your intention seeped in vindictiveness and the desire to punish? Are you so filled with resentment and distrust that all you want to do is inflict pain?

The Question asks you to clarify your intention, your purpose, your objective—right now! It asks you to *think*, to use reasoning, which is the opposite of getting caught up in the Emotional Impact of a Blame Attack.

The Question of Intention is very profound. Asking yourself "What do I want to accomplish right now?" demands that you have some idea what you *intend to accomplish*, what you want, and what you need, from this interaction. How can you fulfill that need? Which choice will allow the greatest benefit to come to you? Will your next comment bring you closer to your sweetheart, family member, friend or coworker, or will it drive him or her further away? Will your behavior build your integrity, ethics and standing, or the opposite?

Asking yourself the Question of Intention gives you a chance to *choose* how you're going to deal with a problem or satisfy a need. Choosing requires thinking—as opposed to just feeling. By definition, to choose means to weigh the benefits of each behavior and the possible outcomes of each.

Allow me to repeat this crucial fact: *To make a choice requires thought*. Some common examples:

When Marion's eight-year-old son calls a friend a bad name, Marion has a choice about how to respond to her son's behavior. She can criticize and humiliate her child, or she can think about what she wants to accomplish, and what she wants to teach her son about being respectful toward others. However, Marion might need to take a few moments of thinking to come up with the best way to deal with the situation.

When Betsy buys the wrong item at the store, Harriet is tempted to say, "For God's sake, Betsy, you'd think you'd have learned better by now!" Harriet, in other words, *could* respond to her distress about Betsy wasting money by blaming her for making a mistake. But Harriet *has a choice* about how she's going to respond. She *can* ask herself, "What do I want to accomplish with my response?" Her goal: to avoid triggering a Reactive Response of more negative emotion.

The question of intention applies to dozens of interactions every day.

Wait! What about those situations when the other person isn't into any of this? Suppose you're dealing with someone who refuses to control his or her emotions? That's when we need an ultimate escape clause. In simple terms, you can't negotiate with someone who refuses to follow any basic guidelines, or has an entirely different agenda. The following rule covers those situations.

■ THE RULE OF PERSONAL SABOTAGE

Anyone can sabotage anything—if that's the actual intention.

This means that if someone is absolutely determined to not cooperate, if his intention is to make sure nothing works, and inevitably blame the bad outcome on you, then this rule takes over: Anyone can sabotage anything.

So many times I've heard a patient say, "Oh, we've tried that and it doesn't work." Of course it won't work if one person is set on making sure it doesn't work.

The basic fact that people can have a divergent intention must be considered at all times. And it also reinforces the reason why your comment must contain virtually no criticism or accusation. If you are critical or accusatory, the other person may decide to make himself right at all costs.

The message of this book is aimed at two people or two groups who share a common intention of wanting to improve the relationship. Proving themselves right or winning the power struggle at all costs cannot be their goal.

At this point I want to introduce another fundamental concept that is crucial to a successful communication without blame. The following formula will make it simpler to understand the constant interplay between our thinking and feelings, and which process needs to be principally in control.

■ EFFECTIVE COMMUNICATION REQUIRES AN IDEAL RATIO OF FOUR PARTS THOUGHT TO ONE PART EMOTION

After thousands of clinical hours helping patients resolve problems, I've worked out a general rule that helps assure a successful outcome for every communication within relationships. This ratio is especially important for the success of Positive Accountability.

Positive Accountability requires FOUR parts thinking to ONE part feeling.

As a percentage, this would be 80 percent thought to 20 percent emotion.

In business interactions, where one's personal emotions have no place, the ratio is more likely to be 95 percent thought and only 5 percent emotion. When emotions take over, bad things can happen.

In this context, when I use the word "emotion," I'm referring either to the negative emotions of anger, anxiety, fear and pain, or to the equally dangerous feelings at the other end of the spectrum: euphoria and excessive enthusiasm. These can also be dangerous. Excessive enthusiasm leads to bad business decisions, as well as overly emotional romantic choices.

Of course this ratio can vary, somewhat. But if these proportions swing too much toward emotion—even half emotion and half thought is too risky—the quality of the communication deteriorates rapidly because the fight/flight syndrome is easily activated. Your body can be instantly flooded with adrenaline and you're ready to fight!

In the case of euphoria or excessive enthusiasm, your body could be flooded with hormones that push you toward having inappropriate or dangerous sex.

And yet, amazingly, so many of us continue to throw ourselves into a discussion or behavior when we're already upset or furious (or giddy), when our heart is pounding and our thinking is confused. That's when the encounter can instantly flare into a fight (or a dangerous liaison). Why do we do this? Because we're laboring under another Mistaken Belief about communication.

■ TWO MISTAKEN BELIEFS ABOUT TALKING IN A LOUD VOICE

We make two very common mistakes about tone of voice and loudness when communicating, especially with people close to us.

■ ■ ■

The First Common Error Regards Yelling or "Getting Emotional." This error is linked to similar misunderstandings about communication. In Chapter Two, I described a series of Mistaken Beliefs about communication that creates chronic problems in our relationships. Here are two common beliefs I have heard:

"Criticizing another person's behavior, ideas or even feelings is the way to get that person to change." *Wrong! Mistaken Belief.*

"Defending ourselves by counterattacking another person will stop that person's accusations and criticism." *Wrong! Mistaken Belief.*

We also assume that talking louder and even shouting will somehow get our point across, despite all the evidence to the contrary. We cling to the Mistaken Belief that yelling or getting really angry will force the other person to hear us.

- Teresa says, "I get so frustrated with James that I start yelling so he'll hear me!"
- Gary says about his teenage son, "He doesn't listen unless I get in his face and bellow! That gets his attention."
- The owner marches into the workshop and starts talking angrily at his employees. "Once they know that I'm really mad, then they pay attention."

These are all Mistaken Beliefs. In fact, research amply demonstrates that a loud, threatening voice instantly accelerates heart rate and blood pressure in both the speaker and person listening. The *inevitable* result is that our ability to listen and comprehend is compromised.

The goal of Positive Accountability is to lower everyone's emotional temperature. The method is to insist on a 4:1 ratio of thought to emotion. Only when *thoughtfulness dominates a discussion* can we replace excessive negative emotion with calm deliberation.

The Second Common Error Is That NOT Yelling Implies We Don't Care. Some people believe that putting a lot of volume into our voice conveys passion and caring. If you're not shouting and "getting emotional," you're cold and distant.

This concern is absurd. If this were true, then powerful meaning could be conveyed only if it were shouted. What about poetry, or any passionate speech delivered intensely but calmly?

Men are especially guilty of the Mistaken Belief that anger must be accompanied with a loud voice. A great paradox about anger is that it's most effectively communicated in a calm steady voice, backed up with authentically felt emotion.

Here's a personal story that remains burned into my memory. When I was about sixteen, I was visiting a friend's home. His father collected and restored old guns. On this memorable afternoon, one of the guns, an old revolver, was being assembled. I picked up the revolver and playfully pointed it at my friend and said "Bang," actually pulling the trigger. Of course the gun was empty. But my friend's father saw me. Very slowly he came toward me. In a quiet, hissing voice reminiscent of *The Godfather*, he said, "You will never point a gun at a living person ever again. Is that clear?" To this day I can still feel the power of his quiet anger. His message has stuck with me. So, the idea that yelling is necessary to convey concern or emotional attachment is a myth.

But what about the times when you are too angry, too upset to practice Positive Accountability, or the *other* person is losing control? What do you do when you know you're feeling far too much anger, resentment and anxiety, and can no longer think clearly?

This is where another vitally important rule comes into the discussion.

■ EXITING THE SCENE WHEN YOU ARE TOO AGITATED TO THINK

Whenever you can feel yourself becoming too agitated, when your ability to think clearly is compromised, one of the most effective ways to make sure you don't launch a Blame Attack is to *exit the scene*.

You physically leave. You say, "I need to go!" and you do. Ideally you don't storm out, slamming doors. But even that is preferable to escalating the conflict into a destructive battle. Staying engaged in a conflict when your ability to think is overrun with anger, and you're about to blow your top, does not build trust, either within the other person or within yourself.

This strategy is not the same as stalking off at the first sign of conflict. It's a fail-safe tactic used only to prevent dangerous escalation.

Another possible response—but one that's much more difficult—is to remain silent and consciously calm yourself, saying nothing.

The response of silence is common in a work situation. A coworker does something that upsets you. Because you know that your paycheck is dependent on not exploding, you stay silent. You might consciously try to calm yourself. Or maybe you stew about it and try to think about the best way to deal with the issue.

However, if you *allow yourself to become agitated* and start a verbal battle with your coworker, you know that you'll create even bigger problems. You might even jeopardize your job. For this reason, successful business meetings and encounters between coworkers are ideally 95 percent thought and 5 percent emotion.

In business, taking things personally and engaging in destructive negative emotions can end your career.

Then why don't we practice the same restraint and maintain a more thoughtful position within our intimate relationships? Why do we so often engage in a verbal conflict when our ability to think clearly has been obliterated by anger or pain?

Because we have not learned alternative, effective behaviors. This issue brings us to what I consider to be an astounding contradiction concerning our relationships. Namely: *We don't apply to our closest relationships the rules that govern every other important activity!*

In every *other* activity, we expect ourselves to stay calm, focused and thoughtful as we do our job or engage in our profession. When we're in school, we control ourselves and study. When we're working—waiting tables, driving a truck, repairing equipment, teaching students, treating a patient—we control our emotions. Likewise when we drive a car. If we don't, the consequences are clear.

I'm remembering Roy, a successful trial attorney. Several times a week Roy would stand in front of a judge and jury and question witnesses. He was very skilled. He never allowed his emotions to dictate his behaviors.

But at home with his wife and teenage children, he indulged his passions. He'd yell and call names. Open conflict was common. During a therapy session, I asked him, "Roy, what would happen if you behaved this way in your profession? You'd have no clients and probably be disbarred. So just pretend that your family is your client. Use your professional skills of self-control at home. That would help a lot."

This blunt advice caught Roy off guard. He tried to defend his actions, blaming his volatile reactions on his family's problems. I kept reminding him of how his behaviors were creating ongoing problems. Finally Roy looked at me with the kind of sober and sincere expression that meant he finally got the message. He said, "This may sound crazy, but I've never stopped to think about it. My dad yelled at me. Everyone in my family shouted and called names. I hated it! I've never really thought about changing it."

Remember, the goal of Positive Accountability is the deliberate, disciplined focus on thoughtfulness. The goal is to prevent a Reactive Response, which often leads to the dangerous Blame Spiral.

One of the most common objections I hear from patients is that Positive Accountability is too hard to practice in the heat of the moment; that the responses I describe sound way too calm and deliberate. As one of my patients told me, "That's not how people really talk! When I'm angry or frustrated, I have to express myself. I've got to let my husband know how I feel!" This attitude is summed up in the sentence, "I've got to be myself!"

To which I respond, "When that *self* is destroying your happiness, you'd better get your*self* back under your control."

Another common objection is that I'm suggesting people just "stuff" their feelings. This implies accepting abuse, tolerating domination and disrespect, or even being falsely conciliatory, and stuffing your anger just to get along.

Not at all.

The answer to this objection is found in the two behaviors of Positive Accountability. Every need, every emotion, every issue can be dealt with a hundred times more effectively when criticism and accusation are eliminated.

All that needs to happen is to recognize fully and completely that controlling emotion and tone of voice is *essential* to communicating our needs effectively.

Why do we resist this basic fact? First, because we don't want to recognize that communicating effectively is a skill that must be learned. You're NOT born with it. Second, an entirely new set of skills sounds so demanding. Just one more darned thing to do! Third, we delusionally believe that in intimate loving relationships, love will take care of everything, including communication.

Yes, it is a skill, and something to be learned. And you cannot expect long-term success and happiness until you learn how to communicate without using blame.

This point is so important that I'm repeating below the two essential BEHAVIORS that are the core message of this book. These two behaviors make Positive Accountability possible:

1. **Controlling your emotions and tone of voice.**
2. **Using words and phrases that do not blame; that don't criticize, accuse, punish or humiliate.**

These behaviors are fundamental in improving our lives.

And there's an added benefit: *Opening space* in your relationships for something positive to happen.

OPENING SPACE: AN INTEGRAL PART OF POSITIVE ACCOUNTABILITY

Do you know of any personal relationship that's not infused with emotion? Even friendship can generate powerful feelings.

In order for a more positive atmosphere to emerge within any relationship (especially one that's emotionally charged), there has to be some neutral "empty" space. We need some unused bandwidth, some pauses not filled with emotion. Within these empty spaces, more positive and nurturing emotions can grow.

A basic technique that a skilled therapist uses to create this neutral space is to either remain silent or ask gentle, noncritical questions. Neutral comments *tend to not provoke* a defensive or angry Emotional Impact. If a patient feels pressured, judged or attacked, the therapy will not go well.

Commenting on every mistake is *not* necessary. In the earlier discussion about Positive Accountability, I state, "Sometimes many errors are minor and can be ignored. Not every issue must be discussed and resolved."

Often in relationships, each person instantly questions every word or gesture of the other person. There's no "space" for something else to happen. **The emotional energy is consumed by one defensive reaction after another. If feels terrible.**

Sharon and Leonard were a long-term couple that seemed emotionally tethered to each other. As they sat on the couch in my office facing me, their peripheral vision was so acutely tuned that each of them would pick up when the other made the slightest shoulder shrug or barely audible sigh. Leonard would turn to Sharon and question. "What? Am I'm saying something wrong?"

Sharon would purse her lips and try to appear innocent. "I didn't say a word."

Leonard would be instantly irritated. Neither of them was able to allow the other to say or do anything without a comment or nonverbal gesture of criticism.

When we challenge every comment or gesture, allow ourselves to feel resentment at every perceived transgression, attempt to repair *every* mistake and discuss *every* problem, we rarely spare even a few seconds to think about the possible positive intentions and goodwill of the other person. Practicing silence, or limiting ourselves to neutral comments, can be very helpful in opening space between two people. It also works wonders in a group.

Which leads right to the question of our intentions and intrinsic goodwill as part of our discussion of Positive Accountability.

The Question of Intention asks: *Do you have positive intentions and goodwill toward your partner?*

◼ POSITIVE ACCOUNTABILITY NURTURES OUR ESSENTIAL GOODWILL

Whenever I ask individuals in therapy about their intentions regarding the other person they're discussing—their child, spouse, boyfriend or girlfriend, sibling—they almost always say that they really want to be helpful, to be loving and supportive . . . and . . . if the other person would only stop their selfish, stupid behavior, then everything would go much better.

In other words, virtually no one *intends* to deliberately hurt another person through criticism, accusation and punishment. **Everyone has a justification for their actions.** Either they've been provoked by a harsh Blame Attack, or they're so offended that they have no choice but to resort to blame.

When they feel attacked, their goodwill evaporates faster than dew in the desert. *That's the Blame Syndrome in action.*

I'm assuming that since you're reading this book, you fundamentally have goodwill toward others in your lives, just as they have the same toward you. However, your basic good intentions are difficult to keep in mind when your partner is angry and spouting accusations.

Therefore, when you learn how to substitute Positive Accountability for blame, the positive interaction *nurtures the other person's essential goodwill.* This process opens up some "neutral space" in which everyone has a chance to be their best selves, to respond with cooperation rather than anger. From that opened space good things can come forth.

The best way to see how Positive Accountability works is to use a series of stories. We'll begin with a seemingly trivial, everyday event: a domestic scene over spoiled milk. As we continue, the incidents will become more serious. With each story we'll examine how using the process of Positive Accountability can avoid the typical Blame Syndrome.

> **THE POINT: Learning Positive Accountability puts you in control of your responses. You do not allow your negative emotions to make the choice.**

■ USING POSITIVE ACCOUNTABILITY TO DEAL WITH SPOILED MILK

Here's the scene: It's a warm summer morning and you're getting ready for work. In the kitchen you find the milk has been left out. Darn! It's gone sour! You check the refrigerator—no more fresh milk. Just then your spouse, the guilty party, walks groggily into the kitchen. You don't have milk for your cereal and you want to express your feelings.

How will you deal with this situation?

Using A TYPICAL BLAME ATTACK TO DEAL WITH SPOILED MILK: You're upset at not having milk for breakfast, and it's the second time this month! When will your husband ever learn? So you launch a Blame Attack that sets a Blame Trap:

"Gary, why can't you remember a simple thing like putting the milk back? Is that so difficult?" You brusquely pull open the refrigerator door and shove the milk container inside. "See? Is that so hard to do?"

Gary responds to your harsh attack. "Hey, you don't have to bite my head off! Like you never forget anything, Little Miss Perfect?" The Emotional Impact of your harsh Blame Attack triggers a Reactive Response. Now you've got a fight on your hands. A lousy way to start the day.

USING POSITIVE ACCOUNTABILITY: Now let's try the more enlightened method of Positive Accountability. Just as you're about to nail the guilty party, you ask yourself the Question of Intention: *What do you want to accomplish?*

Your answer? Well, you know you don't want to start an argument. Yes, you're upset and you want to teach Gary a lesson, but not at the cost of going off to work angry. Besides, your experience teaches you that approaching Gary with anger will trigger a harsh Reactive Response.

So you walk to the cupboard where you have taped a printout of the definition of Positive Accountability and you read it:

ACCOUNTABILITY INVOLVES THE FOLLOWING TWO BEHAVIORS:

1. To thoughtfully acknowledge an error, your own or another person's, and consider how to repair it, if necessary.
2. To express an emotion, or a need, without using criticism or accusation, to avoid triggering negative emotions.

Darn, you think, using Positive Accountability really limits my actions! How can I possibly discharge my feelings without criticizing and accusing him? After reflection, you decide that expressing anger about the milk is not really necessary. You can, in fact, rise above it. All you need to do is acknowledge the fact that Gary made a mistake. So you say to Gary, in a calm, even voice:

"Gary, the milk was left out last night and it spoiled. I needed it for my breakfast." This is a declaration of fact. Your tone of voice is calm and mostly free of criticism and accusation. At the same time you're also telling him that the spoiled milk has caused an inconvenience to you.

Another variation could be: "I'm upset that I don't have any milk for breakfast."

These statements work fairly well because you haven't given Gary a target, which would be your anger or disapproval of him personally. You haven't set yourself up for an attack by dumping negative emotion into the relationship. And you've bypassed a Blame Spiral in which Gary could use more blame to avoid acknowledging his error.

This is the paradox of Positive Accountability. When you make a statement without criticism, accusation or punishment (when you do not blame), the other person *can't focus on your Blame Attack* as a way to wiggle out of admitting error.

■ ■ ■ ■ ■

This issue is crucial and bears reinforcing. Namely, because criticism and accusation are so inflammatory, the Reactive Response to them dominates the discussion and overwhelms any possibility of working on the solution. This fact must be kept in mind as we explore Positive Accountability.

Let's hope Gary says, "Oh, darn. I'm really sorry. I forgot again." That would be the end of it, we hope. Trying to rub it in—arguing over spoiled milk—is not a good idea. *It's not what you want to accomplish. Your primary intention is not to have a fight.*

Let's assume Gary is unaware of Positive Accountability, and has not yet learned about asking himself the Question of Intention. So he has no idea about what he wants to see happen with this interaction. He also doesn't know how to control his emotions. Despite your effort to not trigger negative emotions, he gets defensive and fires back: "You should talk! Last week, you left the butter out, and forgot your keys, and you . . ."

But you are still determined to avoid the Blame Syndrome. So you review in your mind the Question of Intention and realize that you've already accomplished what you intended. Your strategy for that morning is to get to work unruffled. So you *do not reply* to the Blame Attack. You say, "I'll pick up some breakfast on the way to work. See you later tonight. Bye."

THE POINT: One person can defeat the escalation of a Blame Spiral by calmly walking away from the conflict. Positive Accountability can be effective only in an environment of cool feelings.

Despite Gary's intention to attack, you walk out the door feeling good about yourself because you remained in control of your emotions. You didn't allow yourself to get dragged into a fight. You can give yourself a big gold star for an excellent job.

Yes, you left Gary irritated. The situation might dissipate on its own, or you might return home and find that Gary's still upset. We'll deal with these possible outcomes in upcoming examples. For now, however, you can be proud that you accomplished what you intended to without triggering a Blame Spiral.

Plus, there's a bonus. Gary might be grateful that you did not respond to his Blame Attack. What a great lesson! This gives you the opportunity to bring up the idea of living Beyond Blame as a part of all your communications. But that discussion can happen only when he's in a calm and receptive mood.

I have found that people greatly appreciate not being criticized and accused, and eventually catch on when they're not being blamed. They feel better. Eventually they, too, are willing to learn about Positive Accountability.

Let's look at another couple's issue that's handled first with a typical Blame Attack.

You Want to Go for a Walk with Your Girlfriend because you've been cooped up in an office all day and it's a beautiful summer evening. And you need to get some exercise. You come in and see Suzie lying on the couch. You say, "Wow, it's been a tough day. How about taking a walk?"

Suzie doesn't move. "I'm so relaxed right now. I just want to veg out."

You're instantly irritated because she's already been home for a couple hours. You feel that she's being really selfish. So how are you going to deal with your frustration?

TYPICAL BLAME ATTACK: You say, "What do you mean, you're tired? You've been home for hours already." You frown and think about how unfair she is. You say to her, "You know, Suzie, when it comes to something I want, you're always too tired. But if you want something . . ."

Your critical attack, of course, provokes a Reactive Response from Suzie. "You come in here and didn't even ask me about my day. I just have to follow orders! It's always about *you!*" Now the Blame Syndrome has been triggered, and she really doesn't want to go anywhere.

Let's see what else you could do; what other choices are available.

USING POSITIVE ACCOUNTABILITY: You ask yourself the Question of Intention about *what you want to see happen*.

Yes, you'd like to convince Suzie to take a walk with you, but, above all, you do not want to start a fight. But first you have to deal with your disappointment and irritation. Accountability involves *acknowledging an error, your own or another person's, and considering how to repair it, if necessary*.

But there's no mistake or error to be corrected! In this situation, only part 2 of the definition applies: *To express an emotion or need without using criticism, accusation, punishment or humiliation in order to avoid triggering negative emotions*.

You're definitely disappointed and upset. You think she's being unfair. How are you going to express these feelings without a Blame Attack?

Just as with the spoiled milk in the previous example, *you make a declarative statement expressing your feeling and your need*.

"Suzie, I'm disappointed that you're not up to walking. But I really need to get some fresh air so I'll go on my own." In saying this you're not blaming her for wanting to stay home, and you're taking care of your essential need for exercise.

Or you might also try to negotiate a solution. "Do you think you'll be up to it a little later?" If you suspect that she's upset about something, you could also say, "Is there something going on that you need to talk about?"

While you are expressing your disappointment, or taking care of your needs, you have to be careful not to set up a Blame Trap in which Suzie feels compelled to defend herself.

■ ■ ■

A Vital Report Is Due on Monday and you want to make sure that Josh, your employee, gets the report done on time. Josh works well and his reviews are good, but you're under a deadline and anxious about his performance. Plus, you've recently been promoted and you want to look good to your boss. What's the best way to guarantee the report will be finished on time? Because this is a business environment, emotions need to be kept to a minimum. Notice, however, that when blame is used, feelings (all negative) become instantly aroused.

TYPICAL BLAME ATTACK: You call Josh into your office and say, "Josh, I hope you know how important this report is. You'd better have it on Monday. No excuses and no screwups! Is that clear?" You raise your voice at the end for extra emphasis. Even before Josh has had a chance to succeed or fail, he's being accused of failing or making up excuses!

Josh looks at you with his mouth open and walks out. For the rest of the day he's sullen and looks distracted. Should you call him back into your office and give him another lecture? A trusted friend comes to you and says that Josh is really pissed. You wonder why. You're just doing your job, making sure that everyone performs at his best. Now you're angry at Josh for being too sensitive. Does he think this is grade school?

USING POSITIVE ACCOUNTABILITY: Before you talk with Josh about the deadline, you ask yourself the Question of Intention, which begins Positive Accountability:

What do I want to accomplish right now?

Clearly you want to make sure the report is done on time, and you *also* want to maintain the best relationship with your employee because you depend on his goodwill and performance. And during a recent seminar on leadership skills you learned that demeaning a person dissipates goodwill and doesn't help efficiency. You also know that everyone already feels anxiety because of the deadline and adding more tension will not be helpful.

Again, part 2 of the definition applies here. You want to *express an emotion or need without using criticism or accusation, to avoid triggering negative emotions*.

You can express your anxiety about the report without criticizing. "Josh, I gotta tell you I'm really anxious about the report. I just need some assurance it's going well and it will be ready by deadline." Josh says, "Yeah, I know it's important. I'll definitely have it ready on time." Then you might add, "Great, and if there's anything I can do to help, let me know. Okay?" You might even add with a smile, "I'm counting on you to make me look good with my boss." This last comment conveys your anxiety but without criticizing or accusing Josh. It also expresses faith in Josh.

This interaction is completely respectful because it's devoid of criticism or accusation. You're really discussing your own anxiety and directly enlisting his support to achieve a specific goal. The intention is not to build emotional closeness, but rather an effective working relationship.

Your Teenage Son Comes Home Smelling of Beer. Nick's been at a party and was just dropped off by a friend. You smell his breath and you're furious. Your son just turned sixteen and expects to get his driver's license soon. You see visions of him driving while drunk and crashing the car. You're afraid of him getting hurt, and you want to ground him for a month to teach him a lesson. Nick clearly needs to learn a lesson about alcohol, but which lesson? And what's the best way to teach it? And how can you best share your fears?

TYPICAL BLAME ATTACK: You're so angry that you scowl at Nick in disgust and say, "I know you've been drinking! And don't even think of denying it. Do you think I'm stupid? You're grounded! And you know that driver's license? Well, forget it!"

Nick curses under his breath and stalks off, slamming the door to his room. You didn't ask what happened at the party or the relevant circumstances; you instantly focused on *punishment*.

Now you'll have to deal with his anger at you for launching a harsh Blame Attack. All those negative emotions will make it far more difficult to work out an appropriate consequence. Even more important, loading up the event with negative feelings erodes the emotional connection between you and your son. His resentment, justified or not, will push him away and make it more difficult to focus on changing his behavior. You've just complicated your job of parenting.

Often, a teenager's Reactive Response is simply rebellion, either active or passive. Their Reactive Response can be especially dangerous if it becomes part of a power struggle linked to their need for independence. The teen says to himself, "You think you can order me around, and make my life miserable? Well, I'll show you!" The power struggle and Reactive Response become fused into something that takes on a life of its own, and takes you far from your initial intention to be a loving parent with a close and lifelong relationship with your child.

USING POSITIVE ACCOUNTABILITY: Because this is an unexpected crisis (the most difficult kind), it's essential to use the Question of Intention to avoid launching into a Blame Attack. What's a productive answer to the Question of Intention? Above all, *what you need to accomplish* is maintaining your emotional connection to your son. You need to act wisely so your relationship isn't damaged. Any damage always has to be repaired. If there's too much injury to your emotional connection, your moral authority as a parent is weakened.

Keeping in mind the core purpose of Positive Accountability, which is to control your emotions and tone of voice, and use words and phrases that do not blame, that don't criticize, accuse, punish or humiliate, you say to your son, "Nick, you've been drinking. Go to bed and we'll discuss this tomorrow, when I'm calmer."

These sentences clarify the infraction and communicate that you're upset, but they are not punishing or humiliating. They're far less likely to elicit a surge of negative emotions.

The next day when you sit down with your son, you take your time working out an appropriate consequence, engaging him in the discussion. At age sixteen, if he's not part of the solution, he'll lose respect for the process of holding him responsible for his behavior. When you have both agreed on the consequences, it's now your job as parent to enforce them. In the meantime, you've used the incident as an opportunity to teach your son about how to work toward solutions.

Just as You're Getting in the Mood for Love, your boyfriend turns over and says he's really tired. Before dinner you had mentioned getting to bed early, and he seemed to agree. You developed an expectation that something would happen. It's equally natural that when it doesn't happen, you feel disappointed, frustrated and maybe even angry. These emotions can lead to a Blame Attack.

You worry that his behavior is becoming a pattern and you're concerned about the long-term health of your sexual intimacy. Isn't the guy the one who's always after sex? And here you are begging for attention.

TYPICAL BLAME ATTACK: You sit up in bed and nudge his shoulder. Your voice is heavy with sarcasm. "So what's happened to you? You hit the pillow and lights out? Aren't you kind of young to be having sexual problems?"

He's caught off guard and tries a weak defense. "I'm just tired, that's all."

"Yeah, well you're not too tired to play video games!"

Your boyfriend now feels attacked on two levels: you're questioning his ability to perform sexually (and therefore doubting his masculinity) and also accusing him of preferring video games to spending time with you.

Angered by your Blame Attack, he says, "You know I'm not some kind of machine. Maybe if you weren't so damn demanding!"

He's accusing you back, and now you're hurt. "I'm tired of begging for sex. In fact, I'm tired of you. Why do I even bother?" The series of Blame Attacks has quickly descended into a destructive Blame Spiral.

Sadly, this is a common way we address serious problems. Not only is the moment (just before sleep) inappropriate and the issue deeply serious, but this Blame Spiral has left no space open for resolving the issue. Every drop of nurturing has been contaminated.

USING POSITIVE ACCOUNTABILITY: Your boyfriend has turned away and you're angry. You ask yourself the Question of Intention and remember that you don't want to harm the relationship. You're both having a problem with sexual intimacy that needs to be resolved.

So you say, "Honey, I'm upset because I had the impression we'd make love tonight. Tomorrow we need to find some time to discuss what happened. But not now. Good night."

This may not be the end of it, especially if there's a history of frustration. But at least you're not dousing the last of the smoldering embers.

Yes, your response is strong, but it's not personally critical or accusatory. You are directly expressing your upset and that you feel cheated. Your calm expression of what you need (talking about the issue the next day) allows space for creating a time when you can both discuss this important issue.

Most important, by not launching a Blame Attack, you haven't created a powerful Reactive Response that would have left both of you fuming with anger or shaking with anxiety.

These last two examples illustrate situations in which passions are too high to allow reasonable discussion of the issue. We'll continue exploring Positive Accountability in the next chapter with situations outside the range of established relationships. We'll examine how even the very first moments of meeting another person provide a rich arena for the use of Positive Accountability, and all its components.

This is the troubled, anxious and yet wonderfully dynamic process called *dating*.

CHAPTER TEN

■ ■ ■ ■ ■

Dilemmas of Dating

Using Positive Accountability in New Relationships

THERE'S PROBABLY NO AREA of relationships that induces more powerful and sometimes overwhelming emotions than dating.

After all, meeting a like-minded stranger for coffee might be the beginning of a lifelong relationship, the opening act of a connection spanning half a century, the birth of children and even grandchildren.

Or it could be the beginning of a disastrous union that creates years of remorse and despair.

We all know that dating is very important, which means that it provides ample opportunities for blame. One thing's absolutely certain: Dating is an activity for which Positive Accountability is indispensable! Specifically, the 4:1 ratio of thinking to feeling is especially vital—if you want to avoid heartache and future tragedy.

But wait! Isn't dating all about romance, the heart-stopping joy of being rapturously in love? Of course it is. All the more reason to use Positive Accountability and some well thought-out guidelines to protect your heart from unnecessary aching. Perhaps at no time in your life is it more important to stay on track and pay attention to issues, especially the use of blame.

Let's start with the most powerful influence on the dating process: our biological programming. Here's a fact: The chemical structures of our brain and hormonal system do not necessarily work in our favor. Our reproductive drive is not interested in our personal happiness. The goal of our reproductive instinct is to make as many healthy babies as possible, not create decades of conjugal happiness.

■ THE CHEMISTRY OF ATTRACTION: OUR HORMONES ARE IN CHARGE

Human beings are innately attracted to personal beauty. Fortunately for the continuation of our species, each individual interprets beauty according to very personal tastes. "Beauty is in the eye of the beholder" describes this perfectly.

When we recognize beauty, when we experience "she's gorgeous" or "he's cute" and our sexual desire is triggered, biology takes over. Romance blossoms, often with the emotional power of a rocket booster. Our body floods with powerful compounds: epinephrine (aka adrenaline), testosterone or estrogens, dopamine, serotonin, endorphins, vasopressin, norepinephrine and oxytocin.

Just as anger or fear triggers our amygdala to initiate the fight/flight syndrome, an even more complex series of chemicals trigger our desire to have sex, and make babies. These same chemicals create romance and the desire to form a bond with another person.

These hormones and neurotransmitters create the energy to stay up all night talking about our inner feelings, inspire us to write poetry, take great personal risks, buy extravagant gifts and make outrageous promises.

In fact, when romance is in charge, it's all but impossible to figure out what love really is. Without these chemicals racing around our bloodstream, would we feel love? Philosophers have been debating the meaning of love for centuries, and recently biologists and psychologists have weighed in.

In previous chapters, we've discussed how our emotions easily overwhelm our good sense. This fact is especially true when two people are in love. That's when the ratio of feeling to thinking oscillates wildly, and can easily be 95 percent emotion and 5 percent thought. For example:

- Dan's girlfriend unexpectedly becomes pregnant. Only then does he question the wisdom of his erotic entanglement: "What was I thinking?"
- Denise starts to date a sexy guy who also happens to smoke, and drink and keeps losing jobs. After months of increasingly angry arguments over his smoking, drinking and lack of money, she wonders: "Was I out of my mind?"

What happened is that neither Dan nor Denise had done much thinking at all. Their bodies were under the influence of powerful chemicals. That's exactly how we're programmed.

Even though we like to think of romance as glorious and beautiful, all too often it brings us misery, or even disaster. Shakespeare's tragedy about Romeo and Juliet is an archetypal drama about how a forbidden romance leads to the death of both lovers.

> **THE POINT: The less rational thinking you put into the dating process, the more likely you'll blame both the other person and yourself if things don't work out.**

Before we begin exploring how Positive Accountability applies to the dating scene, I want to present three basic guidelines about dating.

These three guidelines are aligned with this book's basic argument, that success in relationships requires a strong component of thinking. Whenever the ratio of thought to emotion moves away from the ideal of 4:1 (80 percent thought to 20 percent emotion), you put yourself at risk because you might make a too-hasty decision about . . . anything.

I call the following principles the Three Basic Guidelines for Dating because they emphasize the BASIC need to remain thoughtful. The guidelines ask you to thoughtfully and carefully evaluate every piece of information you receive from the person you're dating.

Remember when you're dating someone, you are *accountable to yourself*. You are the *only one* who can take care of your interests. No one else will! You are, in fact, dating a stranger, and you cannot know if that unknown person will behave ethically.

By emphasizing the cognitive function in dating, you'll be helping yourself avoid heartache, or even catastrophe. This is especially important in these days of Internet dating, when you're meeting a complete stranger who can present any kind of facade.

◼ THE THREE BASIC GUIDELINES FOR DATING

Guideline One: Everything Counts

Every gesture, word, smile or grimace, every fact about the person's history and detail of his or her life, is important and must be part of your consideration. Be aware, however, that to assess the value of that information—or to notice that the red flag flapping in front of you is really a red flag and not a few carnations—your thinking cannot be clouded with rhapsodic emotions. You must maintain a high ratio of thinking to feeling. You can't allow your emotions to dominate your good sense.

Now, I recognize that asking someone to be thoughtful when having just met someone wonderful might be asking a lot. Which is why it's so vitally important to ask it.

At the same time, your analysis must fit your personal needs. Not everyone who dates is looking for a lifelong relationship. They're just out to have fun. Then things develop and . . . they find themselves saying: "What was I thinking?"

Guideline Two: Show Me the Proof

Words and gestures are wonderful but so are the facts. You need to check everything out to see if it's true.

This is especially important when it comes to the three deal break-ers of relationships: availability, finances and addictions. Is George really divorced, or just thinking about it? Does Hanna still have strong feelings for her ex? Why does she still spend time with him? Is George's income sufficient for his lifestyle? Does Hanna go from living off a credit card to living on money she borrowed from her parents? Does George smoke pot only occasionally, as he claims, or does he use it every day? Does Hanna like to have a glass of wine with dinner, or does she first have a few ounces of vodka? Most of this information is right in front of you (if you choose to see it), or you can learn the facts with a little thoughtful probing.

The bottom line is that you need to know about these three core issues in the other person's life before you give your heart away. Whatever claims he or she makes, you need to see the proof. I'll explain more about what I mean in the following stories.

Guideline Three: One Date at a Time

It's so easy to start mentally galloping ahead and begin planning the honeymoon after the fourth date. You've just met the most wonderful guy and you can't believe how lucky you are! Wow, this guy's perfect! Flashing neon sign: *No one is even close to perfect.* Everyone has limitations, different styles of communication, dissimilar goals in life and a complicated personal history— including yourself! All these differences will need to be worked out in your relationship. Going slowly, one date at a time, allows you to figure out if all these inevitable differences can be negotiated. The answer can save you a broken heart, or worse.

■ THE AVERAGE TIME BETWEEN THE FIRST DATE AND SEX

One of my favorite questions to an audience during a lecture about dating is, "How long usually passes between the first date and having sex?" The general consensus is two weeks. Two weeks!

This is a shockingly short period of time to know someone well enough to become sexually intimate. Once sex has been introduced into the relationship, the powerful hormones that whip up the passions of romance really take over. These energies absolutely overwhelm the ability to think clearly and make solid, thoughtful decisions.

■ PUTTING INTO PRACTICE THE THREE BASIC GUIDELINES FOR DATING: Taking Care of Yourself Without Using Blame

Tonight will be Sheli's fourth date with Tim, and she's really excited. Tim works in another department at her company, and she was thrilled when he finally asked her out. Tim is outgoing and friendly; she describes him as "hot." He shares custody of his four-year-old daughter and says he's interested in a long-term relationship with a woman who could get along well with his daughter. Sheli definitely wants to get married and start a family; having a stepchild is no problem. Already Tim has told her that she's the kind of person he needs in his life.

So far they've only kissed, and she thinks that tonight (it will be her fourth date!) she'll spend the night with him. She finds herself having fantasies about marrying him.

While at dinner, Sheli goes to the restroom. She returns to find him laughing with the waitress. As she's taking her seat she notices Tim slipping a note into his pocket. Did he just get the waitress's phone number? At the movie, Tim answers his phone, then leaves and stays away for ten minutes. He explains that it was a good friend who's going through a divorce and needed to talk. When she asks about the friend, Tim becomes evasive, then says, "Why are you interrogating me?" Afterward, Tim gets romantic and invites her to spend the night with him.

Sheli starts to think about the Three Basic Guidelines. First: *Everything counts.* She realizes that Tim's behaviors did not make her feel very trusting of his intentions. And flirting with the waitress and the absence during the movie and his irritation over her question bother her.

She listens to her intuition and declines his offer to spend the night, saying she wants to get to know him better. He suddenly becomes silent and grim. He drops her off, barely saying good night.

His rude behavior also counts. Really counts! Hardly the actions of an emotionally mature man looking for a permanent adult relationship.

That Monday, back at work, Tim barely says hello to Sheli. She sees him leaving work with another female coworker, laughing. Tim does not return her calls.

HOW SHELI USES BLAME TO DEAL WITH THE PAIN OF REJECTION

Sheli is hurt—and furious. And why not? She calls Tim and leaves angry, accusatory messages. She calls two female coworkers and tells them Tim's a liar. The next day after work, she confronts him in the parking lot. Soon she's yelling at him, calling him names.

But that night, at home alone, Sheli criticizes herself for being too rigid. Maybe if she hadn't been so uptight and had sex with him a relationship could have developed. So what if Tim was "overly friendly." She'd be able to convince him to stay loyal to her—if she tried hard enough. Once Tim got to know her, he'd want to stay. Damn, why had she played so hard to get?

So now Sheli is blaming *herself*. There must be something *wrong* with her! The night after the scene in the parking lot, Sheli is so angry at herself that she drinks far too much. The next day she can barely function and considers quitting her job just so she doesn't have to see Tim flirting with all her coworkers. She'll never get married!

■ HOW SHELI CONFRONTS THE SAME SITUATION USING POSITIVE ACCOUNTABILITY

How can we apply Positive Accountability to Sheli's situation with Tim?

First we need to review the two-part definition of Accountability:

1. To thoughtfully acknowledge an error, your own or another person's, and consider how to repair it, if necessary.
2. To express an emotion, or a need, without using criticism and accusation in order to avoid triggering negative emotions.

It's clear that the second part applies most directly to Sheli. But let's also look at the first item. Did anyone make a mistake? Sheli herself made the mistake of allowing romantic euphoria to make her see Tim as ideal before she knew anything about him. She too willingly believed his line about her being the right woman for him.

Now she wants to express an emotion (her anger at being

misled), and her need (for a long-term relationship), but without criticizing, accusing or punishing Tim. Above all, she does not want to trigger a Reactive Response of more blame. At the same time, she doesn't want to criticize and punish herself. And the fact that they work together demands great care.

But doesn't Tim need to be criticized? Shouldn't she punish him for his unethical behavior? Shouldn't she show him she can't be treated badly?

This is when the Question of Intention comes in. And it's a question that must be answered carefully: *What do I want to accomplish right now? And for my future?*

What result does Sheli want to achieve by confronting Tim and making a scene? She wants to hurt him, to even the score.

Remember, however, that we need to make sure that our decision is based on at least 80 percent thinking and 20 percent emotion. So she really needs to do a lot of thinking about both the *predictable* consequences as well as any *unintended* consequences of her behavior.

Specifically, she must consider how her actions will reflect on *her*. How will people regard her if she does make a scene in public? Certainly, it will not enhance her reputation. Nor will it bring her closer to her long-term goal of developing a fulfilling relationship with another man.

Fortunately, a friend advised her to consider Tim a lost cause, a chronically selfish, immature SOB, and move on. Her friend also told her that Tim already had a reputation of using his charm and good looks to have sex with as many women as possible. Apparently, he'd even had affairs while still married.

CONCLUSION: Sheli decided to say *nothing* to Tim. And she stopped complaining about him (criticizing and accusing) to other people.

Nor did she use blame on herself, punishing herself for being naive, stupid or uptight. Actually, she complimented herself for not using any variation of blame.

These decisions did not come easily. She had to constantly refer back to Tim's offensive behaviors when she'd refused to go to bed with him. Over and over, she had to return to her *reasoning*, the thoughtful part of herself that told her that Tim had clearly shown that he was not really interested in a long-term relationship. The episode also pointed out that she needed to address her tendency to attach too hastily whenever she felt attracted to a man. To help her understand her behaviors, she started individual therapy.

■ STAYING CONVINCED ABOUT THE TRUTH OF YOUR BELIEFS

Sticking to the facts about a sparkling new relationship is always a significant challenge. That's because lust and desire easily distort our perception of reality, and therefore our beliefs. These emotions are always ready to enlist our ability to create delusional realities. "He doesn't have a problem with alcohol; he just drinks to relax." "She's not a flirt, she's just naturally friendly." "He's generous with his money, but not irresponsible." What can you believe about each phrase?

In Sheli's case, whenever she indulged in fanciful ideas about "what might have been if . . ." her mood fell off the cliff. Her emotional swings were dramatic and painful. Her desire for a relationship with Tim would take over her thinking. When these negative emotions took over, she'd go back to blaming herself, criticizing herself for being too rigid, stupid, demanding—everything negative.

To counteract this self-blame, she'd found it necessary to

review her memories about Tim's selfish and insensitive behavior and his history of multiple sexual partners, and then she would force herself to rise above useless and destructive self-blame.

To help herself stay anchored in the facts, she wrote them down on three-by-five cards and stuck them on her refrigerator, and kept one taped to the dashboard of her car. She even wrote out a poster that said in large letters, "Tim is a liar." These messages served as reminders about her own perceptions, her own reality.

Writing down—and frequently rereading your clearest thoughts—is an extremely effective tool to help you stay convinced of the truth of your beliefs.

Self-blame and self-recrimination are very powerful, and it usually takes a significant effort to stay anchored in the *facts as you know them*. Staying true to your beliefs will help you maintain the ratio of Positive Accountability, 80 percent thought to 20 percent emotion, so you don't fall back into the dark sinkhole of criticism and punishment.

Now let's look at another relationship using the Three Basic Guidelines, and look again at how to use Positive Accountability to ask for what you need without using blame.

Fernando Plays in a Band on Weekends and that's how he meets Cindy. They both love music and dancing. Right away they begin having passionate sex, and soon they're inseparable. Fernando finds himself falling deeply in love.

However, after only a few weeks, Fernando notices that Cindy drinks several glasses of wine every night. She always has a reason: it's a celebration, or her job is very stressful. When Fernando asks her about her drinking, she insists alcohol is not a problem.

One Saturday night, Cindy gets so drunk that Fernando has

to help her into his car. The next morning, she apologizes pro-
fusely and explains that she'd had a really tough week at work.
She promises him it will never happen again.

Over the next few weeks, Fernando falls more in love and
wants Cindy to meet his parents. She's all in favor and they plan
a weekend trip. The night before, she drinks heavily, and by ten
o'clock, she's passed out on his couch.

Now he's really worried. He loves Cindy and doesn't want to
abandon her. But should he take her to visit his parents when
she's acting like an alcoholic? Maybe if he sticks by her, his love
would help her to get sober. What should he do?

■ FERNANDO USES BLAME TO DEAL WITH CINDY'S DRINKING PROBLEM

Fernando is angry at Cindy for deliberately sabotaging their relationship. He accuses her of lying to him about wanting to develop
a long-term tie. He criticizes her: "Don't you have any willpower?
Aren't you strong enough to control yourself?" Now whenever
they're together he worries that she might be sneaking a drink,
and whenever they go out he strictly controls how much alcohol
she consumes. The tension between them grows.

■ HOW FERNANDO USES POSITIVE ACCOUNTABILITY AND THE THREE BASIC GUIDELINES

Fernando thinks about his first dates with Cindy and their months
together and tries to organize his thinking *using the Three Basic
Guidelines*.

First he realizes that there were many warning signs about Cindy's drinking that he either ignored or minimized. He never considered that "everything counts" or the need to provide himself with some kind of proof that Cindy didn't abuse alcohol.

Fernando hadn't taken the relationship "One date at a time" until he had solid information about this issue. He'd simply fallen in love and rushed ahead with idealistic ideas about her suitability as a lifelong partner.

Months into the relationship, he's convinced that Cindy's frequent drinking is actually alcoholism; it's too much for him to handle. He accepts the fact that her alcohol abuse will make it impossible to form a long-term healthy relationship because he'll have to devote too much of his time trying to control her drinking.

Now it's time for Fernando to use Positive Accountability. To that end, he *expresses an emotion or need without using criticism, accusation, punishment or humiliation in order to avoid triggering negative emotions.*

Specifically, he tells Cindy simply and honestly that he's not willing to dedicate his life to keeping her sober. He explains that he cares about her and he might consider a relationship if she would enter a treatment program and remain sober for six months.

At first Cindy is very angry and hurt. She unleashes a barrage of Blame Attacks on Fernando. Her drinking increases and she's ticketed for DUI.

The expensive violation finally convinces her that she has a problem. She enters an alcohol treatment center. Several months later, working on her sobriety and attending several AA meetings a week, she contacts Fernando. They cautiously start dating again. He goes to an AA meeting with her, and also Al-Anon (the program for friends and partners of alcoholics), and they both begin couples therapy to deal with their issues.

What's made the difference is Fernando's determination not to get caught up in a Blame Spiral. He refuses to use Blame Attacks to criticize Cindy's drinking. This allows him to stay committed to his own thoughtful understanding of the problem, and eventually find a more solid path toward happiness.

The next story illustrates another common dating problem: meeting a complete stranger through an online dating service. This is where all Three Basic Guidelines of Dating are especially important. You *must* find out for certain if everything the person says about himself is true. Yes, *everything*.

Anita Likes How Brant Has Responded to Her Online Profile. His picture shows him to look his age (forty-seven), and she likes the fact that he's financially secure, running his own consulting business in a city an hour's drive away. Brant has traveled a lot, and is looking for a partner who likes adventure. Anita is forty-five, has an excellent job with a good income and owns her own home. They hit it off really well on the phone, and after several weeks of long phone calls, they meet for coffee.

In person, Brant looks older than forty-seven, more like mid-fifties, and he's heavier than his photo. But he's well dressed, charming, considerate and she really enjoys being with him.

They go out to dinner and Brant talks openly about his past, speaks appreciatively about his ex-wife, glowingly describes his successful adult children and vacations to his condo on Maui. Brant seems like the perfect gentleman. He's also deeply religious but very accepting of other people's beliefs.

They talk every night, and the next date goes equally well. He explains that sometimes he travels for business and is not available by phone because he needs to focus on work. After over a month of dating, Brant begins to appear preoccupied.

Anita tries to get him to talk and he reluctantly describes how his biggest consulting client is going bankrupt and not paying him. But he's very optimistic it will work out. Not to worry.

Brant always brings her flowers, frequently refers to God's blessings and is always interested in her life. He happily shows her photos of his grandchild and can't wait to introduce her to his two children and their families. When they become sexually intimate, Brant is an attentive lover. Anita begins thinking about him as a potential husband.

But as time passes, Brant seems increasingly worried about his client's bankruptcy. One Sunday morning after church she offers to help. She trusts his optimism and business acumen and knows that soon he'll be fine. He refuses her help and insists it's his problem. Caught up in her romantic fervor, eager to show her love and without much thought, she writes him a check for $15,000. With great protestations, he finally accepts the money.

Over the next few days, Brant calls often, telling Anita how God has blessed him with her presence in his life. Then his phone goes dead. Days later, anxious to the point of desperation, she drives to his address—she'd never been to his house because it was "being remodeled"—and finds that he'd never lived there.

For days she refuses to accept the truth that Brant had lied to her from the very beginning. Finally, her anxiety becomes so extreme that she ends up in the emergency room suffering a panic attack.

■ HOW ANITA USES BLAME TO DEAL WITH BETRAYAL AND DECEIT

Anita's story is a classic example of completely ignoring the Three Basic Guidelines of Dating, especially the second, "Show me the proof." But how could Anita question the word of someone so utterly sincere, with such strong religious beliefs? In fact, she'd never made any effort to find out if anything he said was, in fact, true. He lived in another city and she never went to his house because he showed her the pictures of the "remodel." They'd planned several visits but he'd always had to postpone.

Anita gave in to self-blame, punishing herself for being gullible and stupid. Every thought focused on how she was unbelievably dumb and incompetent. Her obsessive self-punishment was so constant that she could hardly eat or sleep. Her performance at work suffered. She swore she'd never trust another man . . . ever!

■ HOW ANITA WORKS THROUGH THE PROBLEM USING POSITIVE ACCOUNTABILITY

Anita's situation is unusual because the person who betrayed her was an authentic scoundrel, a con artist. After his disappearance, Anita turned her rage against herself.

So how can Anita use Positive Accountability to handle her self-blame?

Fortunately, there is a very effective technique that's a major part of Positive Accountability, and that comes into play at this point. I call it the Law of Lessons Learned. It's not really a "law" in the typical sense, but thinking of it that way is extremely helpful in committing to not criticizing and punishing yourself.

The Law of Lessons Learned—a Defense Against Self-Blame

Over decades of clinical practice, I've learned that everyone needs an effective antidote to self-punishment and the damage of regret and remorse. We are *all* gullible *and* skeptical, trusting *and* suspicious, thoughtful *and* impulsive, generous *and* self-centered, forgiving *and* vindictive. We possess all these qualities at all times. In certain circumstances, some of them can become dominant, especially if we're in pain or have been humiliated.

Which means that even the most thoughtful person can sometimes think too much and let slip a wonderful emotional opportunity. Or engage in an act of generosity that puts him at risk. Or be overly suspicious and push well-meaning people away.

In other words, everyone will eventually make an error in judgment. We all make mistakes.

Given that to err, therefore, is human, how can we protect ourselves from self-blame, from punishing ourselves with paralytic levels of regret and remorse?

That's where this highly effective law comes in.

THE LAW OF LESSONS LEARNED

Every mistake contains a lesson. Make a note of the lesson, process the accompanying emotion, and move on with your life.

The reason this law is so effective is that it's based on the simple reality of how people learn: through trial, error and experience. A child can learn how it feels to run and fall only by running and falling. And so it is with every area of life.

Therefore, once you've made the mistake, you figure out how and why it happened, and note the lesson that you need to learn. After you go through the resentment, anger, pain and grief you need to feel, your next step is to consciously *refuse* to allow yourself to continue to dwell in those emotions. You force yourself to *move on* and get ready for the next experience.

In short, you make a decision to stop blaming yourself.

While this process works very well in the physical world (we learn quickly about falling and hot stoves), it's more difficult to learn lessons about relationships. Why? Because of the many intersecting and overlapping emotions that trigger a physiological response, especially when romance is involved.

Let's look at how Anita can apply the Law of Lessons Learned to her situation.

First, she recognizes that she allowed herself to get caught up in Brant's skillful presentation. He'd been both boastful and modest about his alleged accomplishments. He used his religious beliefs to make everything he said seem morally correct. Anita had wanted to believe every word he said. Whenever a voice inside her questioned anything about Brant, or warned about a contradiction, she'd minimized or ignored it.

What are the lessons Anita needs to learn? First, that she needs to *stop being so trusting*. Second, that she needs to *stop allowing loneliness to drive her to ignore important information and make foolish decisions*. She knows that she acted on an impulse when giving Brant the check. In fact, she didn't consult with anybody for fear they wouldn't understand her love for him. She admits to acting secretively. She allowed the joy of being benevolent to overwhelm her thinking.

In order to avoid blaming herself, Anita employs the Law of Lessons Learned:

Every mistake contains a lesson. Make a note of the lesson, process the accompanying emotion, and move on with your life.

She makes careful notes about her mistakes and what led her to make them. She recognizes that being cynical about all men is foolish. And while she paid a heavy price for this lesson, it could have been worse. She was, after all, willing to marry Brant!

Most important, Anita recognizes that her trusting nature is based on her emotional need for a relationship. As she looks back on many of her personal decisions outside of work, where she excels, she realizes she too frequently bases them on anxiety. She can't bear to hurt anyone else's feelings. This pushes her to not think through decisions. More important, this fear pushes her into making decisions that are not in her long-term best interest.

After a couple weeks of feeling really bad about herself, Anita settles down sufficiently to make notes about Lessons Learned, and stops punishing herself. And as she lightens up, her natural good-natured optimism blossoms again.

About six months later Anita meets another man. On their third date, she has a brief talk with him about how, in the past, she has been too trusting. She hopes he won't mind if she asks to check out things as they go along. Because this man really is who he says he is, he has no problem with that.

■ THE NEED FOR VERIFICATION
WITH ONLINE RELATIONSHIPS

When you're dating someone to whom you're *not* introduced by a friend who could verify his or her story, the need to validate the person's history is crucial. If that person (male or female) isn't willing to substantiate a claim or is offended by the request, you should be very suspicious. That person must have a very good reason to refuse. The excuse "That's my private business" is not acceptable because of the nature of the relationship.

This last story about dating involves the problem of having different values and goals for a relationship, another common problem that can be resolved without blame. This time, we'll skip the boulder-strewn path of the Blame Attack and simply use the principles of Positive Accountability to demonstrate how to resolve an issue without criticism and accusation.

Sarah and Chris, Both Single Parents, Have Kids at the Same School. After chatting casually during the school year, Chris invites her for coffee, and after a couple months, they're spending their nights at each other's house. They seem to have a lot in common and Sarah soon finds herself quite attached to Chris. But after the third month, Sarah realizes that Chris would rather be on his computer than spend time with her. And he has a tendency to let chores slide. She's starting to argue with him about fairly minor issues and wonders whether she should just accept his sloppy habits and computer obsession. Sarah also notices that she's beginning to be critical and accusatory as she tries to communicate her feelings and needs.

■ HOW SARAH USES POSITIVE ACCOUNTABILITY TO FULFILL HER NEEDS

Sarah has now recognized that she hadn't followed any of the Three Basic Guidelines when she began dating Chris. She'd moved too quickly into a living-together relationship and did not make sure that Chris's flurry of enthusiasm for her interests wasn't just a temporary thing.

Now, however, Sarah realizes that she needs to take firmer action. She recognizes that using blame doesn't work, that matters would only become worse if she criticized and accused. So she's determined to deal with Chris in a more effective way.

Let's refresh the definition of Positive Accountability:

1. To thoughtfully acknowledge an error, your own or another person's, and consider how to repair it, if necessary.
2. To express an emotion, or a need, without using criticism, accusation, punishment or humiliation in order to avoid triggering negative emotions.

Let's recall, as well, the Question of Intention:

What do I want to accomplish right now? Another way of putting it would be: What do I need from this interaction?

At first glance, it might seem that Part One of Positive Accountability doesn't apply to Sarah's situation. What was the error in the relationship?

In fact, she's made several. Sarah had been far too casual when she and Chris started spending a lot of time together. Initially he would often join her in various activities, but she hadn't noticed that he'd been reluctant to go along. When he starting spending hours in front of the computer, she hadn't said anything. She now accepts responsibility for letting things go too far.

Following Part One of Positive Accountability, Sarah needs to admit her error and correct it. Then in Part Two she needs to ask for what she wants directly and without using blame. But Sarah absolutely hates conflict or arguments! Which is why she has, thus far, avoided confronting Chris over any of these issues.

So again, she asks herself the Question of Intention: What are her intentions? What does she want to accomplish? She believes that Chris is a good person, and she wants to bring him closer, not push him away. Knowing how easily she gets upset—her ratio of thinking to emotion quickly surges to 80 percent emotion and 20 percent thinking—she *writes* her message, editing it down to its essentials. This way she'll be less likely to fall prey to her negative emotions.

She asks Chris for only five minutes of his time. She specifies the time so he doesn't assume it will be an open-ended discussion. She also asks him to not respond while she's talking, just hear what she has to say. Once they're both seated, she reads him her note.

"Chris, I must apologize for not being clearer when we began our relationship. I should have told you exactly what I need from a man. I need some personal conversation every day. Just saying hi, giving me a quick hug, then getting on the computer is not enough for me. I accept my responsibility for not being clear about that. I would like you to think about it and let me know what you'd like to do."

Sarah is stating her needs with virtually no criticism or accusation. Of course Chris could still respond defensively, arguing with her about the contents of the note. If that were to happen, her non-blaming request has not created a backlash of negative emotions. Now Chris can calmly figure out what he wants to do. He may want to cooperate with her, or he may not. At least they can discuss her concerns without heated arguments.

These stories have covered a variety of situations encountered in dating. In the following chapters we'll explore other situations—marriage, parenting and the workplace—in which the principles of Positive Accountability put an end to destructive exchanges and make communicating much more powerful, meaningful and enriching.

CHAPTER ELEVEN

■ ■ ■ ■ ■

Marriage

The Proving Ground of Accountability

THIS IS THE LONGEST CHAPTER of the book. Why? Because blame thrives in environments in which commitment and obligation are crucial, such as marriage—or any long-term committed relationship.

The more committed and obligated our relationship, the more likely that we'll resort to blame. The higher our expectations, the greater the potential for disappointment, frustration and anger. The greater our anxiety over possible failure, the more we'll seek to discharge our anxiety onto the other person.

While reciting marriage vows is ostensibly about love, it's also about commitment and obligation. No matter how we word our vows, both parties accept a *lifelong commitment* to each other that involves multiple and complex obligations.

In contrast, if you're not intensely obligated to each other (as in friendship or business), there's not much need to criticize or

accuse; you can let a lot of stuff pass by. But when you're connected to your spouse for life, you need that person to perform, to
fulfill your expectations and obligations. And if he or she falls
short, disappoints or creates conflict, *that's* when we'll use the
most strident forms of blame.

■ BEGINNING THE RELATIONSHIP
WITH SHARED CORE VALUES

Typically, two people who see each other as lifelong partners agree
on similar Core Values, at least in the beginning of their relationship. In fact, research about satisfaction in marriage concluded
that couples who share the same values and goals for their lives
and families report the highest level of satisfaction with each
other. And their marriages last. (We'll discuss the importance of
Core Values in marriage in a following section.)

Even when a couple fundamentally agrees on their values and
goals, though, they can still get frustrated with each other because
it's impossible to have the same wants and needs at exactly the
same time. So when partners get frustrated, irritated or disappointed, as inevitably they must, they tend to discharge their
emotions onto the other in the form of blame. They attack each
other with criticism, accusation, punishment and humiliation.

Let's suppose that a couple really wants to communicate effectively with each other and avoid using blame. Simply asking the
Question of Intention—"What do I want to accomplish right
now?"—can help focus each person's needs and emotions toward
similar goals.

When partners ask themselves the Question of Intention,
the answer will typically be the same, or at least similar. That is,

each person wants the relationship to succeed in the long term. Each wants the marriage to fulfill his or her own needs. Both need honesty and respect, affection, time and attention, playfulness and fun, and especially *acceptance* of their own peculiarities. All of which add up to love.

In contrast, when two people are dating, each person's goals and values are yet to be discovered. Their ability to commit may be widely divergent, and the answer to the Question of Intention may be different.

But now let's assume you're in a committed relationship. And that you're encountering ongoing problems communicating or having trouble getting your partner to respond to your requests and demands.

We've clearly established that using blame in any of its forms will only make matters worse, and you will be pushed further from your goals. Which is why it's so vitally important to have a thorough understanding about how to use Positive Accountability in marriage.

Before we begin this exploration, though, let's briefly discuss the most powerful emotional source of blame in relationships: fear and anxiety. I've touched on this issue in previous chapters, but now I want to focus specifically on how it affects the committed couple.

■ HOW FEAR AND ANXIETY PUSH US TO USE BLAME

Most people are not very aware of their susceptibility to anxiety and stress. In fact, in one form or another, fear, anxiety and worry run our lives, often in ways we don't realize.

For instance, specialists who study the causes of addictions (from alcohol to food to drugs) recognize that the greater the ongoing stress, the greater the need to self-medicate with drugs or alcohol. The primary purpose of self-medicating is to calm one's anxiety.

Within a committed relationship, we take out our fears and anxiety on the person closest to us through criticism and accusation. "See what you made me do!" "You got me so upset I forgot to . . ." "It's your fault that I'm looking at other women!"

These are common expressions that discharge onto our partner the anxiety we feel when making a mistake. To be seen as ineffective, insufficient, less than capable—even to ourselves—creates stress. So shifting responsibility onto another person seems to alleviate some of that stress. But it comes at the cost of increasing doubt and distrust.

Doubt and Distrust Are the Enemies of Happiness in every relationship. We've already explored the connection between fear and the fight/flight syndrome, which floods the body with cortisol and adrenaline. Cortisol (also known as hydrocortisone) is often called "the stress hormone," and is classified as a cortico-*steroid*. Note the steroid component. One of its functions is to suppress the immune system. Ongoing suppression of the immune system, of course, leads to a higher incidence of illness.

Even small amounts of stress provoked by doubt and distrust increase the levels of cortisol in our blood. Cortisol also depresses a person's mood and suppresses the desire to connect emotionally to others.

In short, there are such strong negative consequences to stress that it's no wonder that we'll do just about *anything* to lessen our anxieties and worries.

And "anything" often involves using blame.

Of course, it doesn't work. Not even close. But we keep using it. Which is why it's so necessary to learn how to replace blame with Positive Accountability.

At this point, it may be helpful to review the two most essential components of blame.

- Blame is finding fault with another person (or group) through criticism and accusation, as well as punishment and humiliation.
- Blame transfers responsibility onto someone else (or group), typically by using criticism and accusation.

It's obvious that using blame in a committed relationship will not develop closeness and trust, because there's nothing even remotely positive or constructive about being *criticized*, *accused*, *punished* or *humiliated*.

However, the question everyone always asks is: "If I can't criticize my spouse, how can I get him to change?" How can you communicate your needs and feelings and get your partner to correct an error or modify a behavior?

The following stories show how to accomplish exactly that. All the elements of Positive Accountability will be involved, beginning with asking the Question of Intention, with special focus on avoiding Blame Traps and Blame Spirals.

These situations may not be identical to your personal problem or challenge, but they're broad enough to apply to just about every difficulty couples encounter.

Let's start by reviewing the most critical element in achieving success: your own and your partner's *intentions*.

A POSITIVE INTENTION IS INDISPENSABLE

One of the questions I ask when I'm working with a couple in therapy is, "Do you believe that your partner *intends* to do the right thing?" Does he *want* to be respectful and loving, even if he often gets overwhelmed with negative emotions and doesn't know what else to do?

If the person responds, "Actually, he really means to hurt me," then we're in big trouble. If you find that your partner sabotages every effort to improve your relationship, the chances of effecting any positive change are about zero. Why would anyone make an effort to get closer to someone you believe *wants* to hurt you?

However, if you believe that your partner really has good-hearted intentions, but just gets overwhelmed with his emotions and lacks the necessary skills to communicate effectively, there's a lot to be done.

IMPORTANT: Sometimes the accumulation of resentment and frustration can make it seem like your partner wants to hurt you. However, within the "safe" environment of therapy, it's sometimes possible to work through the resentments and move the relationship toward earnest effort.

Furthermore, believing in your partner's good intentions can waver considerably, especially from one situation to another. It doesn't have to be 100 percent all the time.

During the process of learning to use Positive Accountability, it's essential to hold on to the belief that your partner is doing as well as he can—that his *intention* is to be loving. (We'll discuss more of this issue in Part Three, when we cover the Law of Personal Limitations.)

Remember that in using Positive Accountability, we must maintain the ratio of thought to emotion at 4:1 (80 percent thought to 20 percent feeling) so you are available *to think* about your decisions.

Now let's look at how Reed and Deanna learned to use Positive Accountability. I'm beginning with a drastic situation—a couple on the edge of divorce—to illustrate how even when a couple is just about to fall into the abyss of separation, they can still pull themselves back.

Reed and Deanna Were on the Brink of Divorce. The couple came to see me in hopes of saving their marriage. Within the first minutes of their initial session, they argued about everything from putting things away in the refrigerator to taking a vacation. Reed owned a retail clothing store, was opening a second and worked long days. Deanna helped with the books and cared for their two children. My first request was for each of them to decide if each partner's *intentions* toward the other were positive or negative.

At first all they could focus on was criticizing each other. Reed accused Deanna of being impossible to please, saying that therapy was going to be useless because she was always so negative about everything, especially him. Eventually, though, he was able to concede that in fact Deanna tried hard and had a good heart.

The same was true for Deanna. First she focused on her husband's sullen attitude, but she also conceded that Reed was a devoted father who worked hard for the family. And even though he didn't verbalize his intentions, they were visible in his devotion to all of them.

Next I asked both to condense their complaints into one primary demand. This required them to focus on what they wanted and needed from each other, rather than just reciting from their list of complaints.

Finally Deanna said, "I want Reed to treat me like he cares about me, at least a little, and not be grumpy and angry all the time."

When Reed heard this he instantly attacked. "How can I? You're always so furious at me that even when I try to be nice to you, you just about snarl at me!" It was easy to see how they were locked into opposing positions that guaranteed a high level of conflict.

Then I asked Reed to come up with his primary need from his wife. It took him a while to say, "I'd like her to realize that I work my butt off for my family—and give me some credit!"

Amazingly, even though they used different words to express themselves, they were actually asking for the same thing: *to be recognized and appreciated and receive affection.*

So I assigned each of them some homework. But for the homework to be effective, they first had to understand exactly why their current way of relating to each other was so destructive. They had to understand how the Blame Syndrome was destroying their marriage.

Understanding how the blame syndrome functions within a marriage is the first step in changing the entrenched behaviors and destructive patterns of blame. Deanna and Reed needed to be able to recognize the three parts of the Blame Syndrome, and how they work together. Now would be a good time to review this syndrome.

1. **The Blame Attack** initiates the syndrome. This could be any type of criticism or accusation, from a loud condemnation to a subtle rebuke. It can be verbal or a frown or rolling of the eyes to imply disdain. A Blame Attack always creates a response, the Emotional Impact.
2. **The Emotional Impact** is the variety of feelings provoked by the Blame Attack, the negative emotions of anxiety, anger, resentment, fear or pain. As soon as these emotions take over, the next part of the syndrome is triggered.
3. **The Reactive Response** is the all but inevitable reaction to feeling anger, anxiety and pain, and usually consists of throwing the attack back—giving as good as we got.

If the two people in a marriage or committed relationship launch multiple Blame Attacks at each other, the situation can quickly degenerate into the deadly Blame Spiral.

Deanna and Reed recognized that the Blame Syndrome had become a functional part of their everyday lives. And that in order to make a positive change, they had to STOP initiating Blame Attacks. A total and absolute stop.

Deanna and Reed Begin to Stop Using Blame. I assigned the couple some homework: to use Positive Accountability in all their interactions and to avoid all Blame Attacks, including using critical body language, snorts or grimaces.

I condensed it into a single sentence:

Say or do nothing in response to the one who criticizes, accuses or punishes.

"How do I do that?" Deanna asked. "What would I say?"

Reed rolled his eyes, as if to say, "That will be impossible for her."

I said, "That's the heart of the problem."

I looked at her husband. "Reed, do you realize that getting angry and snapping at your wife is a form of criticism and accusation?"

"No, it's not! When I'm tired, I'm just trying to keep my distance, to not get attacked."

His comments stunned me. "Really? Well, if you want to pull yourself back from the brink of divorce and rebuild your marriage, you'll have to make some changes. One of which is recognizing that you can be respectful and pleasant even when you're tired."

Reed's next move was typical of someone who's intensely frustrated and angry, and is especially prevalent among men. "Divorce would be easier. I can just move out and live by myself somewhere. I don't need much." It was a desperate ploy for sympathy.

I responded, "Reed, you've worked really hard building up your business. I'd hate to see it all fall apart, selling your house, disrupting your children's lives, just because you and Deanna aren't willing to make some changes in how you behave toward each other. All we're talking about here are changes in your behavior. It's not a personality transplant."

Slowly their mutual frowns softened, a sign that they were willing to change.

When aiming for a breakthrough: the willingness to change is the key to success. The emphasis here is on the word "willingness." No one can or should be expected to change a long-established pattern of thinking, beliefs, attitudes or behaviors at the first try. It takes perseverance. It takes trial and error. With an emphasis on error.

Why? Because errors and mistakes are part of the process. The first attempts at using Positive Accountability may be awkward and faulty, and that's to be expected. But those first attempts must not be criticized! As we've seen throughout our discussions, blame does not change behaviors.

What I'm always looking for with my patients is the first breakthrough. It's especially important with couples, because they tend to support each other's entrenched patterns. How do I spot it when one occurs?

A breakthrough is the first time a person changes a destructive behavior into something positive and constructive. That change initiates a shift in perspective in how each person sees and relates to the other.

Three obstacles commonly stand in the way of breakthroughs.

FIRST, resistance to change is built into everyone's personality. Inertia and the safety of routine play a big part in keeping us stuck, preventing us from trying new behaviors.

SECOND, any two people who live together create a history. Every time Reed fires off a Blame Attack, the emotions generated in the Emotional Impact leave a noxious residue. The accumulation of unresolved negative emotion sits like crumpled pieces of trash piled up between him and Deanna. That toxic rubbish heap has to be cleared away, or pushed to the side.

THIRD is the erosion of trust. It's difficult for Reed and
Deanna to *trust* that their efforts to change wouldn't
be used against them. It's especially important that
both the therapist (if there is one) and the couple
themselves celebrate even the smallest positive
change.

So let's see how Deanna and Reed managed their first attempt at
using Positive Accountability instead of the usual blame.

How Deanna and Reed Stopped Using Blame. Their
homework was to *not say or do anything to each other that involved
criticism, accusation, punishment or humiliation*, an extremely difficult
task. However, these behaviors are the tip of the iceberg. Underneath are all the negative emotions that the other person's behaviors create. Here's an inside look at one incident, and how Deanna
began to incorporate Positive Accountability into her life.

Reed had promised he'd be home at six on Friday to attend a
school event. He showed up at the school at seven, without having called to say he'd be late. In this case, Deanna said nothing
when she saw him at the event. She even smiled at him and acted
somewhat friendly. She did all this even though she was upset
because of his broken promise to be home early.

Deanna's decision to not *show her anger* at Reed for showing up
late was her first attempt to not criticize her husband's behavior.

Let's examine her thinking behind that behavior. She thought,
"What can I possibly say that won't trigger a reaction? Reed already
knows he's late. He's acting guilty. Rubbing it in right now won't
help. Of that I'm certain. So I'll say nothing."

Even when they got home she wanted to ask him why he was

late. But she kept running the Question of Intention in her head. Her answer: She wanted to express her irritation but . . . she *could not come up with a way that wouldn't sound critical or accusatory.* She already knew that he'd been late because of something involving work. And she didn't want to push him away. So, to her surprise, she actually didn't say anything.

To her continued surprise, as they finished dinner, Reed apologized. It was a simple, "Sorry about being late. I really need to pay more attention to the time." Nothing elaborate. To Deanna's credit, she said only, "Thanks." Nothing more. Inside herself, she was very pleased because he'd actually acknowledged his error on his own.

But, you may ask, what about Deanna's feelings? What about her anger at Reed for showing up an hour late? Does Positive Accountability boil down to just stuffing your feelings?

No. But it does mean that if Deanna had to use blame in order to show Reed she was angry, then she could NOT, by the rules of their homework, do it.

Here's the point: If you can't find anything to use but blame, don't say anything! It's called creating an opening, a pause in the action.

CREATING AN OPENING ALLOWS FOR GOOD FEELINGS TO GROW. As we discussed in a previous section, when two people pause . . . and don't attack each other, it creates an opening.

In the situation between Reed and Deanna, both already know the reason Reed was late: his work. Regardless of his best intentions, he allowed himself to be swept up in his work.

When Reed showed up late he expected to be blamed. Even when he was punctual, Deanna would often say something like "It's about time!" She couldn't compliment him because she was in a constant attack posture. She always felt angry.

Asking herself the Question of Intention allowed Deanna to pause and create an opening for a positive experience. At the school, when she said nothing to Reed and even smiled at him, his resentment toward her lessened. The opening between them allowed their emotions to settle down, and then inspired him to apologize . . . later.

As a generation of active people always on the go, we tend to downplay the importance of silence, of saying nothing, of a moment of contemplation. I'm not describing angry fuming silence, but rather the conscious decision (which usually requires a lot of effort) to not speak.

This incident taught Deanna and Reed an important lesson. They had achieved a significant breakthrough. And that was no small thing.

Their next step was to incorporate what they learned from this breakthrough into their thinking. This is where the Law of Lessons Learned comes in. What's the point of learning something important if you don't use what you learned?

Applying the Law of Lessons Learned to their relationship now became the ongoing challenge. To review, this fundamental "law" states:

Every mistake contains a lesson. Make a note of the lesson, process the accompanying emotion, and move on with your life.

Prior to their breakthrough, Deanna and Reed simply hadn't known about the destructive power of blame in their relationship. They'd assumed, like so many couples, that when they felt some anxiety or irritation or resentment, they could criticize or accuse each other and that it was the right thing to do.

Now, however, they were beginning to realize that using blame hadn't come cheap. In fact, launching a Blame Attack is a major mistake. The receiving party feels the Emotional Impact and then launches into the Reactive Response. These are major errors in communication.

Once they "got it," they started to remind themselves, and to remind each other, about the Lesson Learned—that blame makes everything worse!

Here's a scene between Reed and Deanna that demonstrates a Lesson Learned.

"Darn, where are the car keys?" Deanna asks irritably. "I'm already late. Reed, why can't you put them on the hook?" She's using blame to vent her frustration.

Reed stops and says calmly, "Do you want some help in looking for them?"

"Now you're going to make me even later! Where are they?" Deanna is accusing Reed of making her late. Rather than focus on finding the keys, she criticizes and accuses.

Reed looks around and finds them on the kitchen counter. He knows he didn't put them there, but mentioning that fact will not be helpful. He hands them to her.

Deanna glances at him coolly, barely muttering a thanks. A few minutes later she calls from the cell phone. "Thanks for being patient with me," she says.

"You're welcome. See you tonight. Have a good day." That's all he says.

The element that made this interaction so successful—it could have blown up into an argument—was the conscious effort on Reed's part to not criticize his wife for misplacing the keys. His behavior *created an opening*. He allowed Deanna to fuss about and even criticize him, without taking the bait. He consciously resisted giving in to his own Reactive Response.

Over the next weeks, both Deanna and Reed became more

aware of how often they had been critical of each other in dozens of small and not so small ways. As they reduced the number of negative reactions between them, inevitably they started to feel better toward each other. They experienced more moments of closeness and pulled back from the brink of divorce.

It was to be expected, of course, that a new and larger problem would test their newfound ability to avoid blame.

■ HOW DEANNA AND REED NEGOTIATED A VACATION WITHOUT BLAME

Human beings typically learn in a series of plateaus. That is, we try and try, then all at once things come together, we succeed and then move up to another plateau. Any chart illustrating growth and learning is not an uninterrupted line that climbs upward. Rather it's a series of ups and downs. Our goal is to see a steady trend upward, with more up than down.

So it was also with Deanna and Reed as they learned to use Positive Accountability to solve their conflicts, including one over taking a vacation.

Every summer they spent a couple weeks at a mountain cabin owned by Deanna's family, at no cost. This year, Reed said he wanted something different and more interesting. Now that they could afford it he wanted to go to a beach resort in Mexico.

Deanna's initial reaction stunned Reed. "You obviously don't care if our kids get kidnapped or shot at by drug lords." Reed was angry at her extreme reaction. They brought their arguments into therapy. Again I used the same homework assignment. I asked Deanna to state her objections without accusing Reed of being irresponsible. But the negative emotion of fear was overriding her ability to be thoughtful. She was so fearful that she couldn't think of anything to say that wasn't critical.

Reed was doing the same, deriding his wife as overcontrolling and paranoid. I asked Reed to present his argument without criticizing Deanna's fears. He had to think for a moment before he said, "For ten years our vacations have always been the same. I need something different. I also believe that our children need to see some of the world beyond our city and the cabin." He looked at her, then added, "We can't always stay stuck in a rut just because Deanna's so paranoid about—"

"Stop," I said. "That's enough. You've veered into unnecessary criticism."

In fact, as soon as Deanna had heard the word "rut," she'd begun glaring at him. She didn't believe that she was in a rut or that her concerns were paranoid.

They ended the discussion without reaching a resolution, but they did have a clearer idea about how deeply ingrained their tendency was to use blame at the first sign of frustration.

So at the end of the session, I assigned them the homework of using the "5 x 5" listening exercise (described at the end of this chapter) to explore their thoughts and feelings about changing their vacation plans. In the meantime, Reed could do more research about the Mexican resort and safety issues.

For her part, I asked Deanna to think about her fears, where they came from, and what she would need to feel sufficiently safe to travel . . . somewhere. Were there alternative destinations she'd feel comfortable exploring? Both of them were to use the 5 x 5 listening exercise to discuss these issues, because the guidelines of the exercise—to be aware of when their discussion was slipping toward criticism or accusation—help contain the tendency for a conversation to erupt into a Blame Spiral.

Let's quickly review the two essential behaviors that make Positive Accountability a success in relationships:

1. Controlling your emotions and tone of voice.
2. Using words and phrases that do not blame, that don't criticize, accuse, punish or humiliate.

These behaviors are fundamental. If Deanna and Reed could think about their challenge from the perspective of adopting *specifically* these two behaviors, their challenge might become more manageable. So far, at least, they'd avoided escalating into a destructive power struggle.

By definition, a power struggle is always destructive because the goal is to win, to dominate the other, not to reach a mutually satisfying agreement.

Power struggles are dangerous because one power struggle typically leads to another and another. When a series of power struggles have taken over a relationship, the chance of achieving happiness and fulfillment is all but gone.

When Deanna and Reed returned to therapy, they hadn't resolved the vacation question, but they had made progress. Deanna had realized that her husband's expressing desire for more vacation variety was a reasonable request. Not only that, but she saw it as a sign of his greater commitment to their family. Together they had developed alternatives from Hawaii to Cancún.

Above all, they had decided that they would never return to thoughtlessly criticizing, accusing, punishing or humiliating each other.

Now let's explore one of the most intractable problems facing many couples: fulfilling sexual needs. Yes, Positive Accountability can even be of help for a couple dealing with a seemingly chronic sexual problem.

Nothing Worked for Kimberly and Robert in the Bedroom.
After twelve years of marriage, they had developed a very low tolerance for any level of frustration. So when they attempted to make love, the smallest personal problem or reluctance by either of them led to an accusation. If Kimberly said, "It's already kind of late. I think I just want to go to sleep," Robert would say, "It's always too late for you! You never want to have sex!"

Each of Robert's responses is a Blame Attack: both consist of criticism and accusation. When Robert says, "It's always too late for you," he's telling her that there's something wrong with her. When he adds, "You never want to have sex," this is a direct criticism of her sex drive. She must be abnormal. Whereas he, of course, is healthy.

How did Kimberly feel after hearing these accusations? Flooded with resentment and anger.

Alternatively, when Robert has arranged time for them to be alone, Kimberly would retort, "Do you think I can program myself according to your schedule?"

Between them, they had set up a lose/lose situation in which the constant use of blame ruined any attempt at sexual intimacy. The result was deep frustration and despair.

How Kimberly and Robert Turned Around Their Sex Life.
The first step in effecting change in their relationship was education. They both had to understand how the Blame Syndrome had

established itself in many areas of their lives and how it was constantly creating unhappiness.

Once Kimberly and Robert had an understanding of what blame was and how it perpetrated its nasty agenda in their relationship, the next step I prescribed was the same one I recommend to just about every couple and every individual: *Learn how to communicate your feelings and needs without criticism and accusation. And always control your emotions and tone of voice.*

While there may be numerous variations on the theme of blame and thousands of ways to criticize, accuse and punish, the antidote to blame can *always* be found within Positive Accountability. That's the great thing about recovering from the use of blame: One Size Fits All. Accountability always works!

However, the simplicity of the intervention—a total stop to criticizing and accusing—is counterbalanced by the *extreme difficulty* in following its simple demand. Here's a restatement of the reasons it's so difficult to stop using blame:

1. **You don't know what else to say.** You haven't been taught how to communicate without criticism, especially when you're agitated, anxious, angry, fearful and so on.
2. **You're not fully aware of how the negative emotions of anger and fear dramatically influence our ability to think clearly.** This is why we need to use the formula of 80 percent thought and 20 percent emotion.
3. **You believe that blame is necessary!** If you can't tell the other person what's wrong, how can you get him to change?

These three factors are always working against us. We must deal with them directly if our relationship is going to make progress toward greater happiness and connection.

There's one more factor we need to consider: the sense of betrayal caused by blame. The issues of betrayal and disloyalty become all the more important when, as with Kimberly and John, the conflict is around the highly intimate subject of sex.

■ BETRAYAL MEANS: HOW CAN YOU HURT ME IF YOU LOVE ME?

When your spouse or sweetheart attacks you, it feels like betrayal and disloyalty. Love is not supposed to allow for betrayal, but that's exactly how it feels. "If you really loved me, you wouldn't be so critical of my mistakes. If you loved me, you'd see the effort I'm putting into this. You'd see that I'm really a good person." Along with this belief is the expectation that your partner should know you well enough (by now) to know that you're not trying to be purposefully forgetful or inconsiderate. Your behavior is just a mistake!

When you're critical of a mistake, you are, in essence, telling your partner that you don't trust his or her motives and intentions! The Emotional Impact is intensified because this perception powers the reaction.

True, we don't typically think of a criticism or accusation as a breach of trust. But in the context of a committed relationship, it *feels* like it is. It feels unfair because it is. In essence, the criticism is showing a lack of respect for your *intention* to do the right thing. You've made an ordinary mistake and—wham!—you're being attacked!

Now let's get back to Kimberly and Robert as they struggle to get their sexual needs met from each other without using blame.

■ ■ ■

Kimberly and Robert Learn How to Ask for What They Need without criticizing each other. Robert has hurt Kimberly with his accusations, and Kimberly has held on to her resentment, waiting for a chance to get even.

The only way to cut through this kind of power struggle is to rigorously follow the steps of Positive Accountability, beginning with the Question of Intention. Both Robert and Kimberly must stay focused on *"What do I want to accomplish? What do I need from this interaction?"*

At the same time, they need to closely monitor the ratio of thoughtfulness to emotion. The goal is 80 percent thought to 20 percent emotion. Each of them has built up a hair-trigger response that's always cocked and loaded, ready to fire back with more criticism. Which means that most of the time their ratio is reversed: 80 percent emotion to only 20 percent thought, or even less.

Robert takes the lead. In asking himself the Question of Intention, he answers to himself, "I want to be closer to my wife, emotionally and sexually." That's an excellent description of his goal, of what he wants to see happen.

But how will Robert accomplish this? He spends a couple days thinking about it, then asks Kimberly for some time alone to talk. (In fact, he's following the outline of "Constructive Conflict" that I describe in my book *Emotional Bullshit*, published by Tarcher/Penguin.)

Robert asks for only five minutes without interruption. Because he recognizes that he easily gets upset and off track, he writes out his primary message. He has to try writing it several times to make sure he doesn't include any accusatory phrase.

He reads his message to Kimberly: "I admit I haven't been a

considerate lover and I'd like to do better. My attempts at sexual closeness with you haven't worked. I'd like to find a way for us to go back to being wonderful lovers, like we used to be. Can you help me?"

When Kimberly hears this statement, she becomes quite emotional. She can hardly believe her ears. Here is her husband, from whom she was feeling increasingly distant, making an authentically heartfelt statement to her. He's asking for her help! He really does want to be closer to her. How amazing!

■ ■ ■ ■ ■

WRITE AND EDIT YOUR MOST CRUCIAL MESSAGE

I've emphasized several times the importance of recognizing how negative emotions influence our behaviors. Anger and fear push us to say and do things that are critical or accusatory. When there's a vitally important issue in a relationship that must be discussed and resolved, the best way to say what you really mean is by writing out your message. Taking time to edit it carefully helps prevent anger, resentment or anxiety from pushing you to say something that might make matters worse.

Robert's heartfelt opening allowed the two of them to begin sharing their desires and fears. Here's a replay of their discussions. Despite their best intentions, they still drag in something from their past (a criticism), or make a dire prediction (an accusation) about the future.

Kimberly says: "I really appreciate your attitude, Robert. I've been feeling really unhappy about how things were going. *No* matter what I said, you never seemed to hear me." (Blame! She's criticizing Robert for his past behavior.)

Robert winces slightly at hearing this last sentence. "Well, I'd like to focus on now, and the future. Do you have any ideas about how we can spend some special time together?" (He's not responding to her Blame Attack.)

Kimberly: "Of course I do. I'd like you to just hang out with me after work. You know, just kind of chat. *But I know that's really hard for you to do. You'd rather watch TV.*" (Blame! She still can't accept his offer without adding a dig.)

Robert is getting a little upset, but he perseveres. "Okay, I'll try that."

Kimberly: "Well, I don't mean five minutes of chatting and then we go into the bedroom!" (Blame! She's continuing with her critical and demanding tone of voice.)

Now Robert is angry. "You know, Kimberly, I can see that no matter what I do, it's not going to be enough. Why am I even trying?" (Blame! Now he wants to punish her.)

Kimberly realizes that her critical attitude has gone too far. She absolutely sabotaged her husband's efforts to get closer to her. "I'm sorry, Robert. That was really bitchy of me." (She's trying to repair her sabotage.)

Robert: "Yeah, well, it's too late!" Now Robert's emotions have taken over.

Kimberly takes his hand. "I'm really sorry. Can we talk again later, please?" She has suppressed her negative emotions and is trying hard to be thoughtful. Her request is sincere. Robert softens enough to agree. Although this exchange did not solve their problem, it was a significant step forward. Both saw that each of them really wanted to make things better.

▩ BEWARE OF DEEPLY INGRAINED PATTERNS TAKING OVER

As this encounter demonstrates, the tendency to resort to blame is a deeply ingrained part of our communication patterns. Stopping yourself from using blame requires both a rigorous effort and a definite plan.

To briefly review: The reason blame is entrenched in so many of our communications is that it's *our primary way we have learned* to relieve anxiety and anger.

In the above conversation between Kimberly and John, it's easy to see how Kimberly was dumping her accumulated frustration and hurt onto her husband *even as he was attempting to make things better between them!*

This dynamic of criticizing and accusing someone even when he or she is trying to get closer or make a change for the better is extremely common, and one of the biggest obstacles couples face as they try to move their relationship Beyond Blame.

Changing these ingrained habits requires constant effort—at least at first. There isn't a single technique or particular brilliant insight that creates a miracle cure.

Just as many religions require daily prayer and weekly (or more frequent) attendance at a church, mosque, synagogue or temple, so too the goal of living Beyond Blame requires daily attention to the behavioral model of Positive Accountability.

Kimberly and John Experience a Breakthrough! Here's what it looks like when a couple braves their way through the bramble patch of blame. For this breakthrough, they needed to put away old ways of communicating that *had never worked*, and truly dedi-cate themselves to far more effective behaviors.

Several days passed, after the conversation about their sexual life, while both of them put thought into their encounter. This time Kimberly asked to talk with John. She chose a Saturday after John had been bike riding with some guy friends. She asked to sit at their dining room table, the best place to have this kind of talk. Sitting at a table lends some formality to the proceedings.

Kimberly hadn't written out her request, but she did keep it short. (When talking to men about a relationship problem, I urge women to keep the message short and to the point.)

Kimberly says: "Ever since you asked for my help about how we could be closer and be better lovers I've felt really hopeful. And I also saw how my attitude has pushed you away. So I'm going to make a real effort to not be critical. Maybe we can take a shower together after dinner. I'd really like that."

This statement gets the maximum four stars. Kimberly is ex-pressing her hopefulness, which is a positive emotion, and she's doing so thoughtfully, without inserting any hidden criticisms of John. She's also taking on the responsibility of not being critical. And finally, she's making a specific suggestion about something they could do together. **Excellent work.**

And the good feelings that flow out of this Beyond Blame communication begin to build on themselves.

Can a breakthrough be this simple? Yes, it can.

But behind this big step forward must lie a lot of personal effort, a strong desire to change your habitual way of doing things. Habit plays a big role in how we talk to each other. Criticizing each other is very much a habit. Avoiding its use can provide a rapid breakthrough.

■ HOW TO AVOID THE MOST COMMON BLAME TRAPS IN MARRIAGE

The fastest way to stop setting Blame Traps is to eliminate almost all questions that begin with "Why . . . ?" or "How come . . . ?" Asking a "Why" or "How come" question implies the person has a reason for making a mistake. We discussed "Why" questions in the previous chapter about the Blame Syndrome, but we need to review them in more detail as we explore the types of blaming that arise in marriage and committed relationships.

Here are a few of the hundreds of possible examples of such questions:

"Why didn't you put the orange juice away?" Reason implied: "It must be too hard for you to remember," or "You think I'm your servant."

"Why are you driving so fast?" Reason: "You must want to kill us."

"Why isn't coming home on time important to you?" Reason: "Obviously we don't matter much in your life."

"Why can't you just pay attention?" Reason: "You must have sawdust for brains."

"Why are you watching TV again?" Reason: "TV is more important than me."

"How come you didn't call to tell me you'd be late?" Reason: "Everything else is more important than you keeping your word."

"How come you're so slow?" Reason: "You must enjoy making everyone wait."

Being on the receiving end of these questions can't help but feel bad. What can you do if your spouse or partner has a habit of asking "Why" or "How come" questions?

■ HOW TO DEFEAT A BLAME ATTACK
   DISGUISED AS A QUESTION

A "Why" question can be tossed into the air anytime one partner is feeling some irritation, anxiety or frustration. Therefore it's essential to develop a method to stop using them.

This becomes more complicated because of the intense relationship between husband and wife. For instance, Brenda is talking to Sam and he starts glancing at a magazine. She fires off, "Why can't you pay attention? Do you think I'm talking to the wall?" Or, "Would a few seconds of your time be asking too much?"

Brenda's "Why" question is actually criticism. Sam hates being criticized. He hates it even more when Brenda adds her comments about her "talking to the wall." He believes that he usually does pay attention. So he feels an Emotional Impact. He gets all ready to fire off a Reactive Response, but he knows that the ratio of thinking to feeling has reversed itself: he's 80 percent emotion and only 20 percent thought. Maybe even less.

So Sam makes an effort to calm himself. *He does not respond verbally.* He puts aside the magazine. He waits until that afternoon and he asks to talk to Brenda. "I want to discuss our communication," he says. Then he asks Brenda to ask him directly to do something without any "Why" or critical comments. "For instance, just say, 'Please don't read when I'm talking to you.' That's all I need to hear. Anything more is a criticism that just gets me upset."

Suppose Brenda responds, "Why are you so sensitive? Can't you handle a simple question?"

As you're reading this, you might say to yourself, "That's exactly what my spouse would say! My spouse would accuse me of being controlling. It wouldn't work!"

Maybe. At least, however, you'd have the satisfaction of knowing that you are protecting yourself from an escalating situation that *definitely* will make things worse.

IMPORTANT: The first time you can manage to not respond to a Blame Attack disguised as a "Why" question, you will lessen the tension and distrust in your relationship. Not responding to a Blame Attack makes it easier to request that your spouse stop setting Blame Traps.

Couples must always have an effective way of sitting down and discussing an issue with the goal of reaching agreement. I've used the following, which I call the "5 x 5 Listening Exercise," as have many therapists. I've included it in my book *Emotional Bullshit* in the section "Constructive Conflict."

▮ USING THE 5 x 5 LISTENING EXERCISE TO DEFEAT THE BLAME SPIRAL

This exercise simply involves two people taking turns talking for a full five minutes *without interruption of any kind.*

The reason for using the 5 x 5 exercise is to restrain the individuals from giving in to their anxiety and discomfort, which might escalate into an argument.

As I've discussed many times so far, no one likes to be unfairly accused. An unfair accusation provokes either anger or anxiety, both of which are difficult to tolerate. The impulse to reply instantly (without thinking) to your partner's (perceived) unfairness is what drives most arguments and leads to the dreaded Blame Spiral.

Using the 5 x 5 exercise can bypass the (perceived) need to use blame in a couple's *communication* by creating a place where each can safely express thoughts and feelings. This simple exercise is all but guaranteed to stop the destructive back-and-forth of blame that tears relationships apart. Of course, because *anyone can sabotage anything*, if you're dealing with a person who refuses to follow the guidelines, then nothing will help.

But with Liz and Derek, it has changed the entire quality of their relationship.

Liz and Derek find themselves locked into a power struggle over where to send their daughter to college. Derek believes she should spend the first two years at a community college to save them money. Liz wants to send her to a private college, for which they'd have to borrow. This is not, given their finances, a minor issue.

They agree to set aside twenty minutes for their first 5 x 5 exercise. Twenty minutes is the minimum required for each exercise because that allows each person to talk for a total of ten minutes. Talking for that long *without interruption* can be significant.

They sit at their dining room table for the exercise. I always suggest sitting at a table, rather than casually sitting in a chair.

Liz and Derek use a timer so neither person has to look at a clock as he or she is talking. They flip a coin and decide that Derek will speak first. They will alternate speaking and listening in five-minute segments (at least) four times, for a total of twenty minutes. If they're up to it, they've agreed, they can continue, adding more listening and speaking segments.

Both agree to follow these guidelines:

1. Liz, as she listens, must not say *anything* for those five minutes. No grunts, sighs or other sounds that communicate

criticism or accusation. She must practice continual eye contact and NOT use any negative body language or gestures. No grimaces, eye-rolling, shrugs, head-shaking or sighs of exasperation. Staying respectfully attentive is the key to success.

2. Derek, when he's speaking, can say anything he wants, but obviously staying on topic will work better. He must use the full five minutes. If after two minutes, he says, "Okay, I'm done, your turn," he still has to sit there until the bell rings. The reason is that often, after a minute or so of silence, he might think of something else to say.

3. Derek can express any emotion, and use a reasonably elevated level of volume, but there must be no shouting, name-calling or any disrespectful language.

4. Liz must listen during those five minutes but she's not *obligated* to respond to the exact issues Derek brings up. And although discussing an entirely different topic could be seen as sabotage, it's important that neither party be controlling about what the other person chooses to discuss.

5. When the exercise is over, the participants must NOT casually discuss the issues brought up during the exercise. The tendency to lapse back into blame is very strong. Derek might say, "What did you mean when you said . . . ?" This kind of question potentially triggers more blame and can quickly trigger a Blame Syndrome.

To repeat, the purpose of using the 5 x 5 exercise is to *eliminate the use of blame in their communication*.

FAQ ABOUT THE 5 x 5: What's to prevent Derek from using their entire five minutes to blame Liz for all their problems? That sometimes happens, especially during a couple's first experience with the exercise. Which is why I ask couples to go through at least three exercises of twenty minutes each, and allow a day to pass between sessions.

My experience with hundreds of couples has shown me that the parties might use the first one or two exercises to criticize and accuse their partners. However, because each person has a full five minutes to talk without interruption, and then has another five minutes to talk, people tend to not repeat the same old blame messages.

Furthermore, the *purpose* of using the exercise—to discontinue using the some old tactics that have led to distrust and unhappiness—tends to progressively redirect its tone.

In their first attempt at the exercise, Derek begins speaking, and soon he's repeating most of the arguments and criticisms he's used against Liz in the past. Running out of steam after four minutes, he sits quietly for a minute. The bell goes off.

Liz, angry at hearing the same old blame, has a hard time stopping when the bell rings. They both take a one-minute break (the maximum). Derek then continues. He starts to rebut all of Liz's arguments, but after three minutes, he slows down and says something more understanding and conciliatory. Liz, finishing up the exercise, also softens a bit as her five minutes go on.

At the end of their first 5 x 5, they haven't quite achieved a breakthrough, but each of them has had a glimmer of understanding of their own and their partner's dynamics.

Derek and Liz have now begun pursuing the shared goal of learning how much they use blame against each other and have taken the first step to use Positive Accountability instead.

Several days later, they try again. Now they know how the exercise works, and have been thinking a lot about what each other said. This time at the end of the twenty minutes they choose to keeping talking for another five minutes each. They have tapped into some issues that both want to explore.

Two weeks later, by the time they've used the 5 x 5 for a total of four exercises, they've learned the structure so well, and are so pleased with how the effectiveness of their communication has improved, that they continue to talk informally about other issues outside the exercises. They begin to automatically give each other several minutes to talk without interrupting. They have successfully incorporated the guidelines of the listening exercise into their everyday lives.

CONCLUSION: With rare exceptions, every couple begins their relationship with the highest aspirations for togetherness and happiness. Sadly, some couples have such profound differences, incompatibilities and low levels of emotional maturity that they're incapable of making the marriage work.

But for most couples—those with good solid intentions and sufficient emotional maturity—it is indeed possible to learn how to be more effective partners by eliminating blame from their relationships and using Positive Accountability in its place.

Living Beyond Blame is the perennial secret of a happy marriage.

Now let's examine another area of human interaction that is rife with blame: parenting.

■ ■ ■ ■ ■

CHAPTER TWELVE

Parenting and Positive Accountability

SADLY, blame thrives in the parent-child relationship just as readily as in marriage. The more dependent two people are upon each other, the greater the possibility of using criticism, accusation and punishment when either party is under stress.

That children depend upon parents are self-evident. The satisfaction and happiness of parents are closely connected to how well their children perform. So it's little surprise when parents feel anxious and resentful when their children disappoint their expectations.

"Why can't you do something as easy as pick up your toys?"

"If you'd just put in more time studying you could've done a lot better."

"You can't even follow a simple instruction!"

"Well, since you have to cry like a baby, maybe I should put you in a diaper!"

These comments are just a few of the thousands of ways that criticism, accusation, punishment and humiliation enter, and slowly destroy, a loving parent-child relationship.

But what are parents to do when their child does something wrong, or refuses to comply with a rule or follow through on a task?

Again, the answer is to use Positive Accountability. They must control their emotions and maintain a 4:1 ratio of thought to feeling. And they must be clear about what's truly important in their relationship with their childern. Parents need to identify their Core Values and constantly refer to them whenever they are tempted to resort to using blame.

STRONG CORE VALUES PROVIDE A STRUCTURE FOR ACCOUNTABILITY

Many parents lack a firm set of behavioral guidelines that they can refer to—and that they can refer their children to—as they move through the developmental stages of their children's growth. They either discipline their children the way their parents disciplined them, or employ some variation that shifts and changes as each new challenge arrives.

Establishing a firm set of Core Values is important because values act as a constant point of reference. It's like having a compass to guide you to true north. And, when the time comes to enforce Positive Accountability, they'll know just where you're coming from. Core Values will help you guide your child through the two vital steps of establishing Positive Accountability:

1. To thoughtfully acknowledge an error, your own or another person's, and consider how to repair it, if necessary.
2. To express an emotion, or a need, without using criticism, accusation, punishment or humiliation, with the goal of not triggering negative emotions.

In psychology, we define a value as an attitude or behavior that is deserving of time and resources.

For instance, a Core Value as stated in the Declaration of Independence is that *all men are created equal*. While it took a couple hundred years to more fully realize this value (and we're still working on it), the statement nevertheless has served as our national moral compass.

A wide assortment of values can guide a family as it decides how it will spend its time and resources and shape its emotional structure, and how it will enforce its rules.

For some families, a Core Value is education, including reading and intellectual pursuits. For others it's learning a trade, getting a job and working hard. For some, religious beliefs and activities are paramount. Or polite manners and social graces. Or excelling in sports and athletic achievement. Some families focus on a media-free home in which TV is not part of daily life. Other common values are financial frugality, care for the environment and community service.

For a family living Beyond Blame, a crucial Core Value involves refraining from using criticism, accusation (sarcasm, ridicule or contempt), punishment and humiliation as part of your communication.

Then we have everyday *operational* values such as keeping a clean kitchen, putting things away and being organized. One family might place a high value on cooking and eating healthy food, whereas another family is content with prepackaged and fast foods.

The point is this: When parents make a decision about a Core Value, the value itself is not open for discussion because it is an intrinsic part of their way of life.

Simply put, *the parents' values are fundamental and non-negotiable*.

IMPORTANT NOTE: I am deliberately using the term "non-negotiable" to imply that parents need to hold fast to what is important to them, and not be whipped back and forth by the pressure from your child's peers, or the newest media-supported craze. However, using this term does not imply taking an extreme or rigid attitude toward developmental challenges, or a child's essential nature. For example, if your son is not strong in academics and prefers to do practical work with his hands, insisting he go to college rather than learn a competent trade would be an abusive enforcement of a parent's values.

But how can parents enforce their Core Values? Ah, that's the problem! Most of the time, parents' values, beliefs and attitudes are unspoken, and children absorb them into their daily life, much as they would another language spoken in the home.

But as children grow, their *desires* and outside social pressure come into conflict with the family's values, and the friction between them increases. Teenagers challenge either openly or covertly their parents' attempts to restrict their desires.

Some typical conflicts over Core Values are: personal organization and tidiness (clean rooms); study habits involving school (homework); helping out with daily maintenance (chores); controlling where children go and the time they spend with their friends; and especially how to spend the parents' money to buy things.

During the teen years, the areas of conflict become more serious and involve riskier behaviors (alcohol, drugs, sex), staying out late (violating curfew) and other activities such as going to concerts (more potential for alcohol, drugs and sex), driving a car (personal safety) and obeying the laws. And again, there's always the issue of spending money.

Nature has designed our little darlings to constantly challenge parents' Core Values. Most conflicts involve everyday issues: "Why should I have to eat this?" "I already cleaned my room!" "I don't want to wear that." "My friends don't have to come home so early!" "You're so strict and mean!" And when things go badly, the comment: "I hate you!"

In the face of these challenges, the parent often becomes upset, angry, frustrated or even offended. The opportunities to become emotionally reactive are numerous.

That's why it's utterly essential that the parent maintain the 4:1 ratio of thought to emotion. If a parent allows his or her emotions to take over, criticizing in a loud and angry voice and hurling accusations, the stress increases and the relationship degenerates. Most important, the parent gets further away from having the child cooperate and thus fulfill the family's goals.

■ THE THOUGHTFUL USE OF PARENTAL POWER TO ENFORCE VALUES

When children challenge a family's Core Values, the mother or father must be ready to use her or his Parental Power to enforce those values. Above all, this power must be used *thoughtfully* or there's a risk of lapsing into blame or creating a power struggle.

This means that the typical destructive instruments of blame cannot be part of the parent's repertoire. No criticism, accusation, punishment or humiliation.

Attaching the term "thoughtful" to the phrase "Parental Power" immediately separates out the use of violence or forceful coercion. Parents must recognize that they do indeed have power. They do, in fact, control most of the elements in the child's life. So they must use their control (another word for power) in a way that minimizes the Emotional Impact and Reactive Response.

But kids fight back; they want what they want when they want it. So a certain amount of (temporary) unhappiness and displeasure is to be expected from the use of Parental Power.

My clinical experience teaches me that the more thoughtfully the parent exercises this power, the better they'll be able to handle their children's unhappiness. Ultimately, the outcome for both parent and child will be far more positive.

A lot of parents resort to using their raw power to get compliance because it's quicker. *"You'd better do it now, or else!"* Parents resist thinking through a problem and coming up with a more effective solution. While children really do want to cooperate and follow the rules, the desire to cooperate is in constant competition with the child's need for autonomy.

But should the child be involved in reaching a solution?

Paradoxically, discussing a problem with the child and engaging him in the solution, and then following through with that solution, doesn't take away a parent's power. Discussion and engagement strengthens the parent's power because another dimension is added to the child's world: thoughtfully working together toward a result. The parent's function as a teacher is enhanced.

This sentence might trigger a protest: "My kids only want their own way. The last thing they'd do is cooperate with *us*!"

Well, let me tell you a few real-life stories from my own clients. All of them illustrate variations in collaboration between parent and child. As you'll see, using the concepts of Positive Accountability makes every interaction less stressful and more effective. The following story illustrates the intelligent use of Parental Power.

Carrie Establishes Core Values for Playing Video Games.

The scene: A recent therapy session with Carrie as she tries to set limits for Jeremy, her eleven-year-old boy who seems to live for video games. Carrie, who is divorced and whose children spend most of their time with her, also has a five-year-old son, so she's frequently distracted. Here's how she stated her problem.

"Jeremy comes home and dumps his stuff in the hall. I ask him nicely to pick it up, but an hour later he's on the computer playing a video game. I remind him a couple times, then I yell at him. If I yell loud enough, he might pick it up. But sometimes we get into a yelling match. When he finally picks up his stuff, he's really sullen. Then I still have the problem of the video games. I can't get him to just cooperate. I've tried everything!"

Well, actually, she hasn't. I review the definition of blame with her and she realizes that her methods involve a lot of criticism and accusation. She really wants to find a way to enforce limits without alienating her son and triggering an Emotional Impact.

I suggest she start with establishing Core Values for herself as a mother and for her family. Her son would adapt his behaviors into those values since he is part of the family. Those Core Values would be, in themselves, non-negotiable.

This point needs to be reviewed and reinforced. I've found that parents are often reluctant to establish firm, non-negotiable limits with their children. *These days parents worry about being too rigid or demanding.* Or they attempt to establish limits through the use of blame. Neither approach works well. It's an established fact that children thrive in a well-structured environment in which they know the rules and they know that the rules are fairly implemented.

The operative method is moderation. Neither the Core Values nor their implementation can be extreme. So as part of her session Carrie wrote out a "Core Value Regarding Electronic Entertainment."

"In our family, our relationships and personal responsibilities come *first.* All use of media comes after we take care of family relationships and individual responsibilities. This includes cleaning up your stuff, helping out in the kitchen, school homework and also conversation."

This is where the Thoughtful Use of Parental Power came in. She had to acknowledge to herself that she had the power to make sure her child adhered to the Core Value, but had to do it thoughtfully.

I suggested that she sit down with her son and discuss their problem. *Yes, the problem belonged to both of them.* At age eleven, he is fully old enough to get the message.

Of course, he does not have to agree with it. In fact, that would be expecting too much. He is immature enough to want his own way no matter what.

A big part of Carrie's message was: "We can't spend our valuable energy arguing about this. We need to have an agreement and then stick to it."

Because it would be difficult for Carrie to monitor whether Jeremy had completed his responsibilities before plugging into electronics, they set a time limit: No media before 7:00 p.m. Everything turned off at 8:30. To add some strength to this agreement Carrie added, "If this agreement is broken for any reason, media will be off-limits for the rest of the day."

This last part brought forth a strong objection from Jeremy, but Carrie handled it without criticizing her son's ability to follow rules. She just listened to him complain, then said, "Having a specific limit will allow us to stick to our Core Values without more conflict."

It's important to note here that during the discussion with Jeremy, not once did she use blame. *She did not criticize, accuse, punish or humiliate him.* Because there was no negative Emotional Impact, and no Blame Syndrome, their discussion remained relatively calm.

During the following weeks, Jeremy tried to find a way around the agreement. Most children will, especially when their most beloved pastime is threatened. Twice she had to pull the plug on the computer. Jeremy hollered! Carrie listened for a moment, then left the room without saying anything. Later, she invoked the Thoughtful Use of Parental Power. She said, "If we as a family don't follow our agreements, then we won't be able to trust each other. Trust is our most important value."

Jeremy said, "Oh, you and your stupid trust. Who cares about that?" This was difficult for her to deal with because she did not have Jeremy's father to back her up. But she stuck to her commitment to set a Core Value and maintain it.

■ ■ ■ ■ ■

ARTICULATING THE ARGUMENT ALWAYS HELPS

Parents tend to go to extremes in their parenting styles. First they might try to reason with their children, then give up in frustration and shout their commands. The idea behind expressing your Core Values *out loud* is to present your argument so it can be heard. It's not a lecture. Nor are you trying to convince your child that your values are valid. Your goal is merely to make sure that they are articulated clearly. It's important that you say the words and express the significance of your beliefs, and the briefer the better. Eventually the overall message does sink in.

Several months later, Carrie checked in with me about Jeremy and his computer games. Jeremy continued his avid interest in video games, as was expected. Time and again she had to return to the written Core Value and use it as an anchor in her struggles to control her son's behavior. The most positive development was that their arguments mostly disappeared. Without yelling and anger and criticism, their relationship improved significantly. Carrie credited the progress to keeping the schedule firmly in place. The nightly struggles all but stopped.

In the next story, parents address sibling fighting that's become a chronic problem in the family. Yes, Positive Accountability works even for an ongoing issue that seems unsolvable.

■ ■ ■

Judi and Mark's Children Never Seem to Stop Fighting.
The nearly constant conflict between their eight-year-old son,
Darren, and his ten-year-old sister, McKenna, makes most meals
tense. When the family takes trips they often have to put one in
the front seat to separate them. Each child, of course, blames the
other.

Judi and Mark are themselves easygoing and rarely argue—
except about their children—which makes the behavior of their
children even more difficult to understand or deal with. Up until
now, neither had come up with a workable solution they both
could agree to.

The ultimate solution to their problem will be found in establishing strong Core Values and the Thoughtful Use of Parental
Power. During a therapy session involving just Judi and Mark we
worked out a plan of action.

I asked Judi and Mark to write out a statement that described
their Core Value about getting along. Mark was initially reluctant, as he didn't like the formality of putting it on paper.

IMPORTANT NOTE: My clinical preference is to write out Core
Values because I've found that even a single word can make all
the difference. Putting in a conditional "should" or "ought" allows
indecision to creep in. It gives children a route for evasion, and
increases the potential for arguments. However, if a person refuses
to write something down, at least make sure the values are clear
to everyone involved.

So after some editing Judi came up with this:

"Our family uses only kind and respectful words to deal with each other. We do not call each other names, criticize each other or use violence in any form."

"We've been trying to enforce exactly that for years now. It hasn't worked," complained Judi.

I explained that now would be different because they would also bring into the mix their Thoughtful Use of Parental Power. We worked out a plan.

The next day Judi and Mark asked their children to sit at the dining room table and listen for just a few minutes. Mark presented the problem, beginning with an admission that they hadn't done a good job so far in motivating them to treat each other more respectfully. He read the statement describing their Core Value and asked for their ideas. As expected, Darren blamed everything on McKenna, and vice versa.

At that point, Judi and Mark had to use their Parental Power. Mark said, "Well, kids, we can't abandon what's important to us. We must live respectfully, and without violence and criticism."

Again, each child blamed the other, saying, in essence, "Because he won't, I can't." They had developed an entirely self-regenerating Blame Spiral.

Mark continued. "So what we've decided is that whenever either of you get into a fight, everything in the family stops. Everything you're doing stops. If you fight in the house, you'll both lose TV or sports or any activity for that day. If you fight in the car, we go back home."

This sounded horribly drastic to their children. "You can't do that to us!" they protested.

"Not only *can* we do it, we *will* do it," Judi and Mark responded.

McKenna, the oldest, argued, "But what happens when Darren kicks me? Why should I be punished?"

"Since we have no way of knowing whether you said any-thing to Darren and he kicked you in return, and we can never get the truth from you, both of you will suffer."

Both children were very upset at this turn of events. They had grown so used to acting out every irritation against each other. If someone rarely suffers any consequences other than being yelled at, the behaviors become habitual. Why change?

But now the consequences for behaving disrespectfully or violently toward each other were clear. However, a piece was still missing: implementing Positive Accountability.

McKenna brought up the issue. "But, Mom, what *should* I do if Darren kicks me?"

"You come to me. All three of us will sit at the table and talk about it. We'll find a way for you and Darren to talk to each other without saying nasty things or calling names or striking each other." Judi was teaching her children to live Beyond Blame. They were learning to communicate respectfully.

This program required, at the onset, much more dedication from Judi and Mark. They were forced to stop arguing with each other about how and why their children were fighting. They couldn't resort to the usual criticism or accusation. They had to be more thoughtful.

The plan worked marvelously well. Judi and Mark only had to "stop everything" three or four times for the new system to take hold. Darren and McKenna quickly figured out that Mom and Dad were not going to budge from their new approach. Con-fronted with overwhelming but thoughtfully applied Parental Power, they—as do almost all children—changed their behavior. Not surprisingly, the children appreciated being able to sit at the table (the best place to discuss a problem) and work out better solutions. The family was moving Beyond Blame.

Now let's explore how these strategies could be used with a sixteen-year-old when the parents have allowed a very dangerous situation to develop. In this case, the teenager was willing to escalate to an extreme.

Sixteen-Year-Old Allison Wanted to Have a Beer with Her Boyfriend. When Chuck and Bettina found two empty beer cans in their daughter's bedroom, Allison yelled at her parents for invading her privacy. "How dare you search my room?" she protested furiously. Chuck yelled back. Curses were exchanged, and doors slammed.

When Chuck and Bettina came to see me with Allison, she was sullen and resentful. Glaring at her parents, she said, "I'm almost seventeen, for God's sake. I'm not a little girl anymore. All of my friends drink. You can't control me!"

After a few minutes, I asked Allison to wait outside while I discussed the problem with her parents. Chuck started by blaming Bettina for being indulgent with Allison. Bettina fired back that Chuck worked so much that she'd been forced to take over discipline. I spent most of the session getting them to stop blaming each other and accept the fact that what mattered now was fixing the problem. And that to do that, they'd have to work together.

Despite her willful and disrespectful behavior toward her parents, Allison was a good student, but her grades had slipped in the last semester, which worried her parents. I asked, "Who will pay for her college? And her car insurance, and her car?"

"We pay for everything, of course," Chuck replied.

"So that's the source of your Parental Power. Now you just have to use it thoughtfully."

"Dr. Alasko, you have no idea how angry Allison can get. She yells and throws things and makes our lives miserable. She won't let up."

"I do understand. Allison has learned how to use blame against you! She criticizes and *punishes* you for being lousy parents. You accept her accusations, feel guilty and back down. She gets what she wants . . . in the short term, so why shouldn't she continue? These behaviors, of course, will not help her in life. Or at college. And it's seriously damaging your relationship. Right now she believes that she has more power than you do. That's a dangerous Mistaken Belief you've allowed to develop."

I asked Bettina and Chuck to write out a brief statement of the family's Core Values. Both objected that Allison wouldn't give them more than three seconds before she'd storm out of the room. Indeed, when they had tried, she'd blown them off and called them names.

So we discussed the next step. I said, "You have to exert your Parental Power and get her attention. But always using Positive Accountability, which means no criticism or accusation. You know, you really do have more power than she does."

"But how? Short of . . . oh, I don't know. I just don't know." Bettina was desperate.

"Simple," I said. "Not easy, but simple. You'll need to get her attention. To do that, you need to change *your* behaviors. Stop everything . . . until she gets the point. Stop giving her money. Not a penny. Cancel her credit card. Stop filling the freezer with frozen pizzas that she feeds to her friends. When she yells at you, walk out of the room. Keep the car keys with you so she can't just take it. Tell her she can't have any friends over, and if they show up, ask them politely to leave."

"Wow, that's going to be really tough," sighed Chuck.

I nodded sympathetically. "There's more. Also check her room during the day and at night. If there's a lock on the door, remove it. Kids are never supposed to lock their doors. It's not a hotel, it's a family home.

"Above all, stay calm. NEVER raise your voice. In fact, talk more slowly and quietly than usual, and even walk more slowly. That will get her attention. She'll probably think you've been taken over by vampires, which might be kind of cool. It will take at least a week, maybe two weeks before she does finally want to talk. Then put her off for a couple of days. Let her know that there's a price for putting you through all this."

After several false starts, Bettina and Chuck finally got into stride. It took almost two weeks before Allison wanted to talk with them. As I instructed, they did not make themselves overly available, but delayed for a couple days.

Finally, Allison broke down. In tears, she cried, "Why do you guys hate me so much?"

Bettina resisted the impulse to pull Allison into her arms and make it all better. Chuck had rehearsed for this moment. He said, "These last weeks have been very painful for all of us. Are you ready to sit at the table and discuss this situation?"

Calmly, the three of them sat down and Chuck read the statement he and Bettina had written, defining their Core Values as a family. "We've allowed one crisis after another to define our parenting approach. Your mother and I haven't been consistent. That hasn't worked well. From now on, we intend to adhere to our Core Values. Here they are.

"We treat everyone in our family with equal dignity and respect. We discuss conflicts and problems calmly. We make decisions in advance whenever possible, and they involve input from everyone. Our family does not allow illegal or dangerous behavior. We encourage decisions that build future happiness and success of every family member."

These Core Values are both broad and specific. They describe their overall relationships, focus on the needs of every family member and form a basis for bringing emotional outbursts under control. They also identify Allison's illegal and dangerous alcohol use as the entire family's concern. During the following discussion, Allison's main worry was that her parents would be too controlling—the typical objection of pretty much every teenager. So when she again brought up her desire to have her boyfriend over and maybe have a beer with him, Chuck and Bettina recited the last sentence of the Core Values. Chuck said, "We consider you old enough to have a small amount of beer or wine with us during a meal. We don't believe in total abstinence. But we must draw the line with anyone outside of our family."

Allison tried to argue this point with the "fact" that all her friends drink or do drugs. "And a lot more than me. I'm a saint by comparison."

Bettina said, "As your parents we must focus on your future happiness."

Allison responded angrily. "Future! That's all you guys think about! I want to have fun now!"

"We understand that," her father replied. "And it's still our job to think about your future even if you don't want to."

Notice that Positive Accountability is fully in play here. **There's no blame.** Even if Allison initially believes that she's being punished, Chuck and Bettina are not actually criticizing, accusing, punishing or humiliating.

Of course, Allison did her best to get her parents to weaken their resolve. But over the next days and weeks, she realized that they were determined to peacefully maintain a firm position. Whenever she tried to escalate into a shouting match, they remained calm.

They consistently maintained the 4:1 ratio of thought to emotion. Only once did Bettina lapse back into raw emotion, with the result that she and Allison fell back into a Blame Spiral, hurling accusations back and forth. This breakdown served to reinforce for both Bettina and Chuck how vitally important it was to stay calm, deliberate and determined—and to never use blame.

Two months later, Allison had returned to her studies, had dropped the beer-drinking boyfriend and was actively working toward college admission. Chuck and Bettina had weathered the storm, and redirected their family in a healthy direction.

Here's the key to this kind of success: When parents are confronted with the accusation that they're "punishing" their child, their primary recourse will always be to return to their Core Values. They must consistently take the position that *it's their job to raise their children within a structure of firm values*. **If not their values, whose?** This is by far *the most effective way* for parents to remain firm in their efforts to support their children's need for independence.

Here's the final story in this chapter, dealing with an extremely common problem that most parents avoid solving: getting a child to keep a room neat and organized.

■ HOW LEO USED BOTH DISCUSSION AND HIS PARENTAL POWER

Leo's fourteen-year-old daughter refuses to clean her room. Leo shares joint custody of his daughter, Claudia. She has her own bedroom in both parents' homes, and wants to keep her bedroom at Leo's home the way she does at her mom's—a colossal, smelly mess.

"But Dad, that's the way all my friends keep their rooms. I like it that way. And Mom doesn't care. *Why* are you so uptight?"

Obviously, Claudia has her arguments all lined up.

But Leo believes that adopting standards of neatness is intrinsic to developing an orderly lifestyle. Those are his Core Values, and he isn't about to compromise them. In the past, he's criticized, accused and punished his daughter for her continually messy room. But all the criticism, accusation and punishment failed to work for long, and he ended up being far too upset over their frequent arguments.

After consulting with me about his problem, Leo decides to use Thoughtful Parental Power. He knows that above all he will have to stay firmly within the 4:1 ratio of thought to emotion. In practice this means *never becoming reactive or punitive*, and staying completely away from the Blame Syndrome.

Leo has worked out a statement of Core Values and discusses it with his daughter at the dining room table. He tells her, "Claudia, I know you want to do what you please with your room, but here are some issues.

"First, it's not *your* room. You only use it. It's my property. When you leave, I'll still own it. My Core Value is that all property is treated respectfully, especially my own. I won't compromise on that basic principle. Do you understand?"

Of course Claudia argues but Leo calmly sticks to his position. "If you value your room, you will keep it clean. If you value your clothes, they must be kept folded on your shelves."

"But Daaad, that's so much work! And none of my friends do that. Not one!"

Unruffled, Leo responds, "The basics of my values are not up for a popularity vote. I can negotiate around the edges, but I can't give up the basics."

REMEMBER: Dear Parent, once you're clear about your values, they act as the moral center of your relationship and are beyond negotiation. While they will evolve over time, and must take into consideration the essential temperament of your child, they are not subject to fundamental change or ongoing argument with your child. And again, the details of enforcement can vary. For instance, your Core Value is to protect your child. This might mean a curfew of ten-thirty for a fifteen-year-old. The time is a detail. But the value of protecting your child does not change.

So here's what Leo does. He tells Claudia, "On Saturdays, your friends cannot come to visit, nor can you leave with them, until your room is in order. Anything you don't fold and put away will end up in a garbage bag in the garage."

Notice that Leo stays faithful to Positive Accountability. *He is not criticizing or accusing or punishing his daughter.* Putting her things in a bag is not a punishment; it's the pre-arranged consequence (result or outcome) of a certain behavior. Punishment's synonyms are "penalty, chastisement, reprimand, retribution." Leo is doing none of that.

Leo's standards are reasonable, but of course his daughter doesn't see them that way. The next Saturday, Claudia does a quick cleanup, stuffing everything under her bed. Then she leaves. Later, Leo goes into her room and puts everything jammed under the bed into a big plastic bag and puts it in the garage.

When Claudia returns, she screams bloody murder! "Where are my jeans? I need them!"

Leo refuses to be drawn into her drama. He does NOT yield

to the typical parental response of returning his daughter's anger with his own and triggering a shouting match. That would be a parent-child version of a Blame Spiral. Instead he sits down (an excellent tactic that implies determination) and waits until Claudia calms down.

He then says, "I don't expect you to understand my values, but you have no choice but to live by them, since this is my home and you are my daughter. You will keep your room in order. By Saturday morning, it must be done. If you don't clean it, I will. And you'll lose everything you don't care enough about to take care of. I hope that's clear."

Leo is making a simple statement of facts. *Again, there's no blame*. No criticism. No accusation. And no punishment or humiliation. Leo had already established the consequences for nonperformance. Because he's not criticizing or accusing his daughter, Claudia could respond to the loss of her personal items only if she didn't take care of them. The lack of emotional content made it much easier for her to comply. After a few weeks, she automatically began keeping her room in order. Maybe not perfectly, but well enough.

Now let's move to an essential area of everyday life—work and employment. Because the workplace is rife with anxiety and fear, it's a fertile ground for criticism, accusation and, especially, punishment and humiliation. Adding to the emotional complexity of the workplace is the differential in power between boss and employee, and even between coworkers.

CHAPTER THIRTEEN

■ ■ ■ ■ ■

Using Positive Accountability in the Workplace

SIGMUND FREUD IS SAID to have once declared that the two most important issues in life are work and love. He placed work first because work creates money to pay for food, clothing and shelter that support our physical existence. Love, affection, appreciation, even sex, are hardly possible unless we have the things necessary to exist.

Since some type of work, career or profession is a dominant feature of most people's lives, this chapter examines the important question of how it might be possible to function in a work environment without criticism, accusation, punishment or humiliation.

But how can you get an employee to do the job well and on time without criticism? And when an employee makes a mistake, doesn't he deserve to be criticized? From the position of a worker, how can you avoid receiving feedback from your boss that is not in the form of blame? And as a colleague or coworker, how can you maintain your position with your peers without criticizing and accusing them?

In the following pages, I'll use a series of stories to look at the situations we commonly find in the workplace, and demonstrate how the Process of Accountability works effectively even in that highly demanding environment.

Always keep in mind, as you read, that blame functions within the three-part process called the Blame Syndrome. Every Blame Attack creates an Emotional Impact that then triggers a Reactive Response. The only way to avoid creating an outpouring of negative emotions as part of the Emotional Impact, and then the firing back of more criticism and accusation in a Reactive Response, is to avoid the first part—the Blame Attack.

In this chapter we'll focus both on how to take care of your best interests when you're the target of a Blame Attack, and how to avoid initiating one yourself.

First, let's begin with a story that illustrates how positive an environment a workplace can be when coworkers refrain from using blame with one another. This will show how criticism and accusation are unnecessary for any reason.

■ HOW THE ABSENCE OF BLAME INCREASES PRODUCTIVITY AT WORK

My personal friend Lorenzo has a high position at a company known for its enlightened attitude toward employees. Lorenzo was going through a difficult divorce, and one weekend he was involved in a car accident. He was behaving deliriously because he was under the influence of a medication prescribed by his doc-tor. Because of the legal complications surrounding the accident, he missed a plane to attend a work-related conference.

When Lorenzo showed up for work after the weekend, the CEO asked to speak to him. Lorenzo was expecting to be criti-cized. The CEO asked about his missing the conference and Lorenzo told him what had happened. He admitted that he had allowed a personal problem to get in the way of his work. The CEO went on to express his concern for Lorenzo and wished him the best of luck in sorting things out with his ex-wife. He also asked if Lorenzo needed anything from him in the way of support. *That was it.*

There was no criticism, accusation or humiliation. The CEO used the essence of Positive Accountability because it was *not necessary to correct a mistake*. Lorenzo was already fully aware of both the error and what he had to do in the future, and had hon-estly discussed it with the CEO. He admitted to his responsibility and pledged to make sure it didn't happen again. Clearly, Lorenzo already felt humiliated and did not need to have more piled on. The CEO expressed his concern very calmly and professionally. As a consequence, Lorenzo was even more motivated to work toward the company's goals.

This story illustrates a "best practices" case of using Positive Accountability. Would that more companies were so enlight-ened!

However, peers in the workplace often use blame against someone else as a way to enhance their power. And blame can be a very destructive weapon when someone already pos-sesses power, is trying to accumulate power or wants to hold on to power.

■ THE CONNECTION BETWEEN BLAME AND POWER AT WORK

We all want to feel competent and respected at work. Our liveli-hood, our careers and even our happiness depend on it. And yet, every one of us is subject to the negative emotions of anger, fear and pain, especially in the workplace. Even though work is really supposed to be about just doing a job, strong emotions are always bubbling just below the surface.

At work, therefore, fear and anxiety are probably the most potent emotions. We worry about not being recognized for our efforts, are afraid of not being promoted and fear losing our job.

So it's only natural that we can use blame as a handy tool to either defend ourselves when we feel afraid or enhance our own position at the expense of a coworker.

All too often we adopt a Mistaken Belief, namely a zero-sum approach. The term "zero-sum" refers to a fixed or limited amount of anything, such as success or advancement: if you become suc-cessful, it must mean that I'm less successful, because there's only a fixed total amount of success to go around. This Mistaken Belief fosters the use of blame to discredit the competition, inviting unscrupulous rivalry rather than collaboration, to the detriment of everyone involved.

Here's a story to illustrate how this process created a lot of anxiety and misery, and did not turn out well for the person using blame.

Brandon Has Just Been Hired as an Electrician and works under Jerry's supervision. Jerry has worked for the company for twenty years and believes he has special privileges. He often arrives at the job late and is sarcastically critical of Brandon's work, even though Brandon knows he's doing it according to the specs. In contrast, Brandon arrives early and leaves late, which increases Jerry's resentment toward him.

When a serious problem develops with an electrical installation, Jerry accuses Brandon of making the mistake. Some of the wiring has to be torn out and done over, at considerable cost. Another electrician tells Brandon that Jerry has started drinking again but won't admit it.

How Brandon Uses Blame to Deal with the Problem. During the discussion with the owner, Brandon becomes angry at the false accusation and has a hard time explaining his side of the issue. He suspects that Jerry has set him up, and scathingly denounces Jerry. The owner is disturbed at Brandon's outburst and counters that they're not there to discuss Jerry, but to focus on the problem. But Brandon is too angry to hear it and by the end of the meeting, the owner has decided that Brandon has got to go.

From the perspective of blame, Brandon allowed his fight/flight syndrome to be triggered, became overwhelmed with negative emotions that compromised his ability to think clearly and ended up creating very negative consequences.

How Brandon Uses Positive Accountability to Rescue His Job. When he goes to the owner's office, Brandon knows his job is at stake. He reviews the Question of Intention about what he wants to accomplish. He forces himself to put aside his emotions and focuses on his long-term goals.

He must decide how he'll implement the core elements of Positive Accountability. These are: Brandon must thoughtfully acknowledge the error and consider how to repair it, if necessary. And he must express his need without using criticism, accusation, punishment or humiliation in order to avoid triggering negative emotions.

As Brandon works through the two behaviors of Positive Accountability, he realizes that there's not a mistake that he needs to repair, because he didn't make one. But *he does have a need to redeem his reputation*. He must do so, though, without using criticism. Tricky!

Brandon knows that Jerry has marshaled evidence "proving" that Brandon made the mistake. How can he salvage his reputation without counteraccusation? During the meeting, he listens to his boss and asks to take notes. He breathes slowly to control his agitation, and says very little. At the end, he asks to have a day to present the facts. He says nothing to contradict the owner's belief that he's actually at fault.

Brandon manages to get a copy of the blueprints and equipment orders that are supposed to be signed off by Jerry. Brandon carefully works through the specs to show how there were possible lapses in the ordering system. Brandon refuses to accuse anyone, allowing the information itself to argue the case. He does suggest, though, that the company work out a system to avoid having the same thing happen in the future. The boss appreciates this positive step forward, and that ends that particular problem.

Jerry is not happy with the outcome, because he believes Brandon is at fault. He continues to make negative comments about Brandon. Eventually, Jerry is offered early retirement.

Because Brandon does not engage the Blame Syndrome to defend himself, and he maintains the 4:1 ratio of thoughtfulness to emotion (more likely, in this case, 10:1) and stays focused on Positive Accountability, he comes out the clear winner.

■ HOW THE LAW OF LESSONS LEARNED APPLIES AT WORK

We all make mistakes, and whenever we gather in a work environment, we will make mistakes related to our work, and in our communications with each other. The more complicated the job, the greater the frequency of and potential for errors.

The names Lehman Brothers and Goldman Sachs have become synonymous with mistakes of supercolossal proportions. Hundreds, perhaps thousands, of people were—and still are—trying to figure out the lessons from these debacles. Probably an equal number of people are dedicated to NOT allowing those lessons to be applied to their future business practices.

For our purposes, the Law of Lessons Learned applies to both our personal lives *and our lives at work*. Here's the entire law:

> *Every mistake contains a lesson. Make a note of the lesson, process the accompanying emotions and move on with your life.*

Mistakes of any size offer the opportunity to extract a lesson, examine it for its core message and then figure out a way to not repeat the same mistake again. To do this most effectively, a calm demeanor and clear thinking are absolutely essential.

THE POINT: The greater the intensity of the emotions involved, the less you'll be able to take the lesson and use it because responsibility for the error will be projected elsewhere.

The importance of calm thoughtfulness is integral to understanding Positive Accountability.

Now let's consider what can happen when no one uses Positive Accountability, and a blame-storm erupts that affects an entire organization.

■ USING BLAME TO DEFEND AN ENTRENCHED POSITION

Arthur had worked at the municipal government office for twenty years when Janice was hired as a specialist to implement a new computer system. The system required all employees to substantially change the way they worked.

As part of her job, Janice had to interview the most senior members of the city's operations, including Arthur, and instruct them on the new technical regime.

Arthur found Janice's expertise and assertive style to be threatening to his authority, even more so because she was an attractive woman twenty years his junior. During an administrators' meeting to discuss the implementation of the new system, he openly demeaned Janice's expertise and spread rumors that she was incompetent.

In an effort to work out their differences, the city manager brought Arthur and Janice together. In the presence of the manager, one of his longtime colleagues, Arthur directly attacked Janice's competence. He cited several problems and broadened the attack to include personality issues, suggesting that she flirted with her coworkers.

Janice was outraged at the attack, which relied on completely incorrect information. She responded vigorously, accusing Arthur of sexism. Arthur counterattacked with another sexist slur. The argument grew progressively louder.

The city manager said nothing. Janice angrily left the room. Arthur, back in his office, twisted what had happened as gossip spread among the staff. Soon the entire staff was divided. The veteran staffers sided with Arthur. The younger people took Janice's side.

■ HOW BLAME CONTINUED TO MAKE THE SITUATION WORSE

Unfortunately for Janice, the city manager distorted the meeting's events to suit the position of the entrenched staff. Janice felt growing hostility and felt threatened by the senior employees.

Because the manager did not want to invest energy into controlling Arthur, he hired a consultant to counsel Janice on "how to become a better team member." She was furious, and consulted with an attorney about filing a lawsuit.

Ultimately Janice requested, and received, a transfer. However, her abrupt departure slowed the adoption of the new computer system and the city was forced to pay for extended implementation contracts.

It took Janice several months to recover from the disaster. She tried to find a way to explain how it had all happened and extract a lesson for her future. She came away with the realization that she was up against an opponent who was willing to use any tactic to defend his power base.

Janice's story reflects the basic rule that *anyone can sabotage anything if that's the actual intention.* If one party is determined to not cooperate, and is willing to use vitriolic Blame Attacks, nothing will work.

When this dynamic is in play, there's nothing to be done except recognize that you're dealing with a saboteur and get as much distance as possible. Arthur was determined to win at any cost. His lack of scruples meant that Positive Accountability was inadequate.

Janice needed to recognize this fact sooner. If she had, she never would have allowed herself to be in a room with Arthur and the city manager without a witness to record the events. Simply put, she underestimated her opponent's lack of ethics.

■ USING ACCOUNTABILITY TO DEAL WITH BEING EXPLOITED BY A BOSS

Fortunately, many bosses and supervisors operate ethically and in the best interests of the company and the employees.

But what do you do when your boss exploits your desire to do a good job, when whatever you do just isn't good enough? Or when a boss uses criticism and accusation to take advantage of your need to hold on to your job?

To a certain extent, that's the eternal (and never resolved) conflict between those who have power and those who don't.

But the need to be profitable, the need to be seen as an effective manager, or the outright practice of greed leads to unrelenting pressure on employees. The following situation describes a relationship where one party is not willing to come forward and provide something the other person needs; where the situation has reached an impasse or a dead end.

■ ▪ ■

When Abby Joined the Sales Team for a National Company, she worked hard to prove herself. In fact she worked so hard that her boss kept piling on more responsibilities without an increase in pay. After two years on the job she got married and a year later had a baby. Now she's no longer able to work sixty to seventy hours a week.

As she tries to lessen the demands of her schedule, her boss makes sarcastic, critical and accusatory comments about her work ethic. Some of her coworkers make similar comments, a few quite derogatory and hostile. Abby tries to negotiate a way to cut back on her hours and still remain with the company, but her efforts are fruitless.

Abby feels under attack by everyone. And yet, when she attempts to put in sixty hours of work, her home life suffers, particularly her connection to her infant.

Her situation is becoming more and more untenable. Every day she goes to work her anger and feelings of betrayal by her boss and coworkers increase. She believes that she, having poured her heart and soul into the company, deserves some kind of accommodation. The more Abby thinks about the unfairness of their behavior, the angrier she gets.

She's about to launch a series of angry Blame Attacks of her own when she stops to ask herself the Question of Intention: *What do I want to accomplish right now? What is my long-term goal?* Is it just to vent her emotions, all of them negative?

As Abby considers this question, she realizes that she has two goals. One is to advance her career; the other, to take care of her child.

Abby doesn't want to endanger her reputation and put her

earning future at risk. Following the guidelines of Positive Accountability, she recognizes that to use blame in any form would be counterproductive.

So she writes a letter of resignation, explaining that her family needs are incompatible with the company's needs at this time.
She criticizes no one. She also agrees to train a replacement,
always being helpful and pleasant. Ultimately, her positive (non-
blaming) attitude impresses her boss and colleagues. When several months later a part-time position opens, Abby returns to her
company as a consultant. The situation ends up a win for everyone.

What makes Abby's approach work is her determination—
despite the frustration and provocation—to not succumb to using
criticism or accusation. Staying focused on that determination
paid a good dividend.

Our final story about Positive Accountability and the workplace involves an ongoing and difficult merger negotiation between
two companies.

Tarek Has Risen to Senior Vice President at the Bank. He
expects to continue his successful career when, unexpectedly,
the bank announces a merger. Now Tarek finds his job at risk.
He's delegated to facilitating the merger of his smaller bank with
a much larger one. He soon finds himself surrounded by execu-
tives who criticize his previous bank's work ethic. As though he
didn't work hard enough? He finds himself left out of important
decisions.

Tarek is angry that his decades of loyalty have suddenly evap-
orated, to be replaced by suspicion and personal disregard.

One afternoon, Tarek makes a sarcastically critical comment about the bank management. His comment reaches the president, and he hears through colleagues that his loyalty is in doubt.

Tarek realizes the power dynamic between himself and the new bank makes his position extremely unstable. He holds no power except his experience.

He requests a meeting with the president. Tarek keeps in mind the Question of Intention about the outcome he wants to achieve. Even the most subtle Blame Attack would be received badly. He thoughtfully explains his goals and says he will do whatever it takes to fit into the new administration. Over the next few months, he rigorously practices 95 percent thoughtfulness and 5 percent emotions. Eventually the new organization offers him a new position.

This story yields a *paradoxical* outcome. Specifically, because Tarek deliberately focused on thoughtfulness and steered away from the negative emotions of anxiety and resentment, he "opened a space" within this process to come up with an entirely different outcome.

To that end, Tarek decides that he's ready for a new challenge in which he can feel more connected to the outcome. He secures a position as teacher of economics at a local junior college and makes the move. He earns half what he made before but is much happier and works far fewer hours.

In reviewing this story, we see that the new bank used criticism and accusation to intimidate the smaller bank they were taking over, creating friction and stress and a difficult working environment. Eventually, the outcome led him in a completely different direction from what he had expected. If he had angrily resigned, as had several of his colleagues, he might not have gained this insight.

The overriding message in this chapter about workplaces and the use of blame is that the power differential between those in higher positions and lower-status employees makes for a fertile field for the use of criticism and accusation.

We've reached the end of Part Two, and our discussion of Positive Accountability. But before we launch into the challenge of Part Three and the Law of Personal Limitations, I want to answer some of the most typical questions a discussion of Positive Accountability usually brings up.

These issues make up the category of "What do I do if . . . ?"

And, "Suppose my partner won't . . . ?"

The answers will always be found within the description of Positive Accountability.

▪ RETURNING TO THE MOST COMMON QUESTION ABOUT BLAME: SUPPOSE MY PARTNER WON'T CHANGE A BEHAVIOR?

Several times throughout this section I've described situations in which the other person's intentions are not to advance mutual trust and be openly supportive of the relationship. Rather, the intention is to prove the rightness of a position and to "win" the argument at all costs.

In all these situations, the typical response is to return to using blame as the only means of either defense or attack.

Over and over I hear, "What can I do when Gary refuses to come home early like I've asked?" Or, "Debbi never balances the checkbook and we get so many late fees." Or, "David rages and then insists he can't control himself. Am I just supposed to put up with his tantrums?"

This is where the most paralyzing attitude in all relationships comes in:

Because you won't, I can't!

Because you won't stop using blame, I can't stop either!

Because you won't change your behaviors, I can't change mine!

Because you won't buy healthier foods, or not order French fries when we go out, I'll continue to gain weight and risk diabetes and a heart attack!

Because you won't maintain your agreements, I have no choice but to continue to harass and attack you, just as I've always done, and make both of our lives miserable.

The list is endless. And it's an extremely serious problem.

The prescription described in *Beyond Blame* presents **an authentically revolutionary challenge.** This challenge—and its demand—is at the heart of human growth and development. Namely, if both parties continue to use dysfunctional behaviors in their relationships, then both of them will remain stuck. If you return violence with violence, you have constant war.

However, decades of psychological research and decades of clinical experience with hundreds of thousands of therapists have demonstrated that when one person (or one society) changes an entrenched behavior, the entire relationship changes also.

In actual practice—in real life—this means that when you stop using blame, when you stop using criticism and accusation in your communications, you will no longer be under the control of the power of the negative emotions of anxiety, anger, resentment, pain and fear.

This doesn't mean you'll no longer feel these emotions. It does mean that you will no longer be *controlled* by these negative emotions. Anger and resentment will no longer run your life. Anxiety and fear will no longer have you gripped by the throat.

In order to make this claim even more practical and permanent, Part Three of *Beyond Blame* presents an entirely practical and quite radical way of looking at all human behavior, including your own.

The Law of Personal Limitations asks you to reconsider how you look at personal responsibility, and calls for a significant change in your attitude toward human fallibility.

PART THREE

■ ■ ■ ■ ■

Advanced Work with the Law

of Personal Limitations

■ ■ ■ ■ ■

INTRODUCTION TO PART THREE

■ ■ ■ ■ ■

THIS FINAL SECTION of the book is described as "advanced work" for a good reason.

If we were to use a college degree system, Part One of *Beyond Blame* would represent undergraduate work in understanding blame's destructiveness; after a thorough reading, you can award yourself a bachelor's degree in the Psychology of Blame. You're prepared to stop using criticism and accusation in your everyday life.

Part Two of the book, Positive Accountability, is at the level of a master's degree. However, learning how to *consistently* use the antidotes to blame requires skill and perseverance. You'll probably have to refer back to the book many times to perfect your skills.

Now you've arrived at the Ph.D. level. The Law of Personal Limitations and the Paradox of Criticism are not easy concepts to understand, and even trickier to use in everyday life. But the reward of incorporating these techniques and strategies into your thoughts, beliefs and attitudes—and eventually your communications—will generate a magnificent payoff in higher levels of tranquillity, happiness and fulfillment.

So let's embark on your journey to earn a doctorate degree in the Psychology of Blame.

■ ■ ■ ■ ■

CHAPTER FOURTEEN

Dealing with Personal Limitations

Always Start with Your Own

"It seems so pessimistic to focus on my limitations," Catherine said anxiously. "I thought that therapy would help me to think positively, to realize my potential. Focusing on what I don't know—my limitations—seems like wallowing in my own stupidity."

Catherine said this as she sat in my office discussing her recent and painful divorce. She was having a tough time understanding how she could have made the disastrous mistake of having an affair with Bryan and then quickly marrying him.

"How could I have been so stupid?" she kept repeating. Catherine was in her mid-thirties, and really wanted a family. Bryan was in his early forties, worked as a computer engineer for a large corporation and was the father of two boys. When they had met four years ago, Bryan told her he had just separated from his wife.

And so she believed.

The night of their first date, they had torrid sex. But just a few weeks later she learned that, in fact, Bryan was not separated; he still lived at home. When Bryan's wife found out about their affair, she filed for divorce. *Then* Bryan moved out. The drama began. Catherine, feeling guilty about being a "home wrecker," devoted herself to helping Bryan get through his divorce. She even lent him money for an attorney, and bought a town house with Bryan, putting up the down payment herself.

Within a year of their wedding, Catherine was devastated to learn that Bryan was having an affair with one of her close friends! Then she found out that Bryan had also been having extramarital sex throughout his previous marriage. His ex-wife's accusations had all been true.

Now the devastated Catherine sat in front of me, punishing herself so harshly that she couldn't sleep, was overeating to deal with the pain and was even considering suicide as a way out. Self-blame, the most viciously destructive form of blame, had sunk its talons into her heart and wouldn't let go. She needed relief. She needed to understand and be able to employ the Law of Personal Limitations.

◼ UNDERSTANDING YOUR PERSONAL LIMITATIONS CAN CHANGE YOUR LIFE

Now we come to the most life-changing part of this book: **the Law of Personal Limitations.** I guarantee that once you understand how this "law" works in your life, and begin to apply it, you will be rewarded with greater self-confidence and tranquillity, and far more satisfying relationships.

How can I make such a sweeping statement? Because as you apply the Law of Personal Limitations to your life, you will no longer have any need to use blame in any of its variations. As we've already seen, living Beyond Blame provides countless benefits.

Admittedly, however, the Law of Personal Limitations is complex. Why? Because it's *counterintuitive*, which means it's not in agreement with what we would naturally assume or expect. This psychological "law" (which I'll frequently refer to as the LPL) presents an entirely new way of thinking about why all of us behave the way we do.

Pretty much everything about your usual way of thinking about human behavior will need to change. The LPL *contradicts* the typical way we think about why we do the things we do. We see this in Catherine's objection to discussing her *limitations* rather than the positive aspects of her life.

And at first glance it might indeed seem unproductive to talk about our restrictions and limits rather than our positive qualities.

Actually, though—and paradoxically—it leads us directly to the ultimate solution for blame. It's especially effective in dealing with the most vicious and subtle form of blame afflicting Catherine, self-blame. She has been making herself sick by criticizing, accusing, punishing and humiliating herself for making a mistake.

We'll begin with how the Law of Personal Limitations (LPL) applies to you. And how your own personal limitations affect your life in thousands of ways, big and small.

Then we'll cover how you can use the LPL to deal with the

irritating and frustrating limitations of *others*, especially your closest relationships.

But first, let's return to Catherine's story and how she began to realize that understanding her limitations had led her into a heartbreaking marriage.

■ INTRODUCING THE LAW OF PERSONAL LIMITATIONS

After listening to Catherine's complaints about Bryan's multiple betrayals, I outlined a way for her to *understand* how she came to make such an egregious mistake. This step was essential because her self-blame was so intense that she saw herself as basically defective, incapable of ever having another relationship. Her self-blame was causing her extraordinary amounts of pain. And all that pain was stopping her from healing her emotional wounds.

I asked her to study the Law of Personal Limitations:

THE LAW OF PERSONAL LIMITATIONS

Everyone is always doing as well as they can within their personal limitations, their personal history, what they know and don't know and what they're feeling in that moment. If they could make a healthier decision, they would. This includes YOU.

Catherine's reaction was typical. "So I just tell myself I did as well as I could, and that's that? But I don't believe that for a second. How could I?"

I replied, "Catherine, I'm not offering any shortcuts. You're already suffering from the consequences of your relationship with Bryan. You're going to have to work through the facts of your divorce and the humiliation of making some bad decisions. But right now what you need to do is *stop punishing yourself*."

But, you may ask, if Catherine heaps on the blame and makes herself sick with despair, won't that help pound in the lesson?

The answer is a clear **no**! Excessive self-punishment makes *everything* worse. Criticism is an impediment to clear thinking. *Extreme* criticism can be deadly. This issue is at the heart and soul of this book.

Blame is *not* thoughtful! Recall the definition of Positive Accountability (in Part Two): it requires a ratio of 80 percent thought to 20 percent emotion. To respond thoughtfully to a situation requires lucid thought. Otherwise our negative emotions take over, triggering a Reactive Response.

Excessive self-criticism only infuses an event with negative emotions of anxiety, anger, resentment, pain and fear. These create a thick emotional gunk that fouls up our thoughtful deliberation. **Without thoughtful deliberation, we make more impulsive and reactive decisions that only lead toward greater unhappiness.**

Ironically, some bad decisions are *initially* driven by an excess of what we call positive emotions: joy, excitement, elation, enthusiasm and, in extreme cases, euphoria and delirium. These emotions are often found within romantic love, that euphoric condition that pushed Catherine to rush into an affair with a man she wanted to believe was physically and emotionally available. These euphoric emotions derailed her ability to think clearly.

That's one of the dirty tricks romance can play on us. Romance often involves the least thought of any kind of behavior. How many tragedies could be avoided if romantically delirious couples took some time to think through the consequences of their delirium.

◼ EXPLAINING THE LAW OF PERSONAL LIMITATIONS—ONE PHRASE AT A TIME

Since Catherine was having a hard time understanding how the LPL applied to her, we began by applying the first phrase:

Everyone is always doing AS WELL AS THEY CAN within their personal limitations, their personal history . . .

This beginning phrase, with the emphasis on "as well as they can," typically raises hackles, just as it did for Catherine. Upon hearing it for the first time, people instantly come up with objections and exceptions. "It certainly doesn't apply to my brother-in-law. He's a deliberate loser!" Nor does it apply to someone who's behaved badly in your own world: your ex-husband, ex-wife or ex-anybody. And definitely not your coworker who tried to sabotage your position. Or your boss! Or the neighbor who plays loud music at midnight!

And, you might add, it doesn't even apply to you, or to your own bad decisions!

I'm asking you to bear with me as we work through all of your objections. I promise that I will be able to demonstrate that there are no exceptions to the Law of Personal Limitations.

Returning to Catherine's problem, I asked her about both her personal history growing up, and then her adult relationships.

■ ■ ■ ■ ■

HOW WE GREW UP HELPS
SHAPE OUR LIMITATIONS

Beyond any doubt, our childhood influences who we are as adults. But I try not to place too much emphasis on a patient's *childhood history* because we all need our energy to deal with the present. Once the broad strokes of trauma are understood, and specifically their effects on your life today, it becomes far more effective to focus on your beliefs, attitudes and behaviors as they are now. In the discussion with Catherine, all we need to understand are basic themes from her childhood, and how they influenced her decisions about Bryan.

Catherine said, "My parents divorced when I was twelve and my dad moved away. My mom said my dad was cheating on her. I didn't see him much as a teenager." She recalled those years as difficult and painful.

Then her mother remarried. Her stepfather was a nice guy, but by the time she started college, they had already divorced. Catherine found out later that each accused the other of having an affair. Catherine was busy with college and buried the information in the chaos of student life. But now, in recollection, it came to the surface.

"Catherine," I said, "because you grew up in the midst of sexual infidelity, your *personal history* is filled with deceit that inevitably influenced your ideas. Does that make sense?"

She nodded sadly. "So you think that I absorbed my parents' affairs into my thinking."

I explained that our childhood experiences tend to stick in the subconscious, creating attitudes that we end up acting on much later. We're usually not aware of the connection.

"What about your first marriage?" I asked.

"Jeremy? Hmmm. I've always been attracted to good-looking men. Maybe because my father was handsome. He always dressed really well. That would sure describe Jeremy."

"Was Jeremy unfaithful?" I asked.

"He was too busy spending money. Jeremy was very irresponsible and extremely self-centered. We had to file bankruptcy when I divorced him."

"So, Catherine, would it be fair to say that you choose men who look good on the outside, but may have a loose ethical structure on the inside? Who are self-centered and irresponsible?"

I waited for this question to sink in, and moved on to the next part of the LPL.

■ WHAT YOU DON'T KNOW CAN BE VERY DANGEROUS

The next part of the Law of Personal Limitations is critical, but tricky to discuss and possibly difficult to understand:

What you know and don't know.

This phrase is utterly fundamental to our discussion. It actually refers to two things: First, the obvious external information that you don't know. Second, the unknown information that's buried inside you (or exists outside of you). Together, they make up everything that you *don't know you don't know.*

Next I asked Catherine to focus on what she knew and did not know about Bryan.

Her eyes grew teary at this question. "He's not your typical computer geek. He's very buff, he works out, plays tennis . . ."

"That's what you saw," I said, "the surface impression. What did you know? His character? His ethics, values, goals in life? Specifically, how did his behaviors line up with his words?"

It took her a moment to answer. "Actually, it's really embarrassing. We had sex on our first date, he's a fantastic lover. Frankly, that was about all that I knew. And . . . from then on, it was all about us getting together for sex. Until his wife filed for divorce."

"And what did you know about yourself?" I asked.

Again a long pause. "I knew I wanted a family—" She wiped away tears. "I didn't know he'd already had a vasectomy. He lied about it. So I'd never be able to have a family with him."

"This is very sad," I said. It was obvious that there was so much Catherine hadn't known when she'd begun the relationship with Bryan.

Mostly because of willful impetuosity, she didn't try to find out much about Bryan. There was a great deal that she did not know she didn't know. She wanted what she wanted right away. And she was willing to rush ahead into a relationship without carefully checking out the most basic fact of whether the man she desired was physically and emotionally available for a relationship. Considering that she wanted a family, she was amazingly impetuous about beginning a relationship without knowing if her goals synchronized with his!

Much of the pain Catherine was feeling now was due to her awareness of how big a mistake she had made. But there was a missing piece that she'd needed to know about.

"Catherine, it appears that there's something very important about your personal history that you did not know. Namely, that you grew up in the midst of a lot of deceit and unethical behavior. You did not seem to be aware of that."

She nodded in agreement. "Funny, I kind of thought my childhood was okay. That all the divorce and separation was sort of typical. No big deal."

I said, "I'm pointing this out because you need to put it on your list of personal limitations. Not as something bad, not as something to feel shame or guilt about, just as a fact about your life. Like being born in Illinois rather than Florida. Does that make sense?"

My overall job was helping Catherine to avoid using self-blame, and teach her more effective ways to develop a relationship.

■ THE ROLE OF EMOTIONS IN THE LAW OF PERSONAL LIMITATIONS

Because our emotions typically control our behaviors, it's essential to know which emotions were in charge when a decision was made. In Catherine's case:

What had she been feeling at the time she'd met Bryan?

"Mostly excitement. I don't think anyone has ever affected me as strongly. For months I was almost giddy . . . euphoric." She became serious. "I suppose my excitement at being with Bryan clouded my thinking."

"It definitely did. Your euphoria—what you were feeling at the time—was a definite limitation, as powerful as if you were taking a chemical stimulant."

We typically think of anger as being our most dangerous emotion, but the euphoria of romance can be equally dangerous because decisions are made that have lifelong consequences.

■ THE CONCLUSION OF THE LAW OF PERSONAL LIMITATIONS

Catherine reached the final and most crucial point of the LPL. This conclusion forms the foundation of profound philosophical truths. It also provides the basis for forgiveness, forgiving both oneself and others.

If she could have made a healthier decision, she would have.

"I wish I had!" Catherine replied. "But at the time, it never entered my head. Not once."

"That's true, Catherine. At the time, you simply couldn't. Why? Because your emotions dominated your thinking."

"Yeah, I was in love," she agreed.

"Catherine, here's the main point you need to hear: You had no way to make a healthier decision when you hadn't the slightest thought that one might be available. It hadn't even occurred to you to say no to Bryan. None of us can make another decision if that decision isn't available to us. Therefore, you were doing as well as you could."

This point is the linchpin that holds together the entire structure of the Law of Personal Limitations. Specifically, you can choose a decision (or act on an emotion) only if that decision (or emotion) is available to you. This requires further discussion.

■ YOU CAN CHOOSE *ONLY* FROM WHAT YOU *BELIEVE* IS AVAILABLE TO YOU

There's a crucial intersection between the Law of Personal Limitations and the eternal theme that runs through human history: the question of free will. This question takes many forms. Theologians ask: Are we instruments of God? Are there really no accidents? Philosophers ask: Are we part of a Greater Destiny? Psychologists assert that we are captains of our own ship, but we must deliberately calculate our own course if we're not to end up on the rocks.

Typically, I avoid these Big Questions because the world of psychology is restricted to dealing with emotions, beliefs and behaviors. However, fundamental to our discussion is the question: *Do we actually make choices, or do circumstances and our emotions only make it seem like we do?* Closely connected is the follow-up question: *Why do we make the choices we do?*

Taking the Law of Personal Limitations as our guide, it's clear that **you can choose only from what you *believe* is available to you.** (In this case, belief and knowledge are the same.) If you're standing at a buffet and all you see is fried chicken and tapioca pudding, that's all you can choose. You might argue that you could go around the corner to another cafe. But what if you don't know there is another a cafe? What if you're too hungry or weak to even look? Suppose fried chicken triggers a childhood memory and you're swamped with nostalgia?

Human beings are guided by a complexity of powerful emotions and influenced by strongly held beliefs that restrict our ability to think and feel at the same time. Which is where the Law of Personal Limitations comes in: *We are all limited by what we know and don't know, and especially by what we believe to be true in that moment.*

This is pointedly valid when it comes to making a decision, which gets down to choosing to react one way or another. Which is why I consistently argue for a 4:1 ratio of thinking to feeling. You need to have your wits about you to realize that there's always more than just *one* choice.

Even within the simplest decision there's always a YES or NO, and the third choice, MAYBE. Amazingly, so many people are hardly aware that *maybe* is a viable selection. Catherine didn't know that she could have inserted a "maybe" into her relationship with Bryan. For example, Catherine could have gone out on a date with Bryan and asked him some specific questions. Taking that information, she could have asked around. Very quickly she would have found out the truth about his marriage. But she had to *want* to find out.

◼ OUR ATTITUDES AND BELIEFS DETERMINE OUR REACTIONS AND BEHAVIORS

Psychologists and therapists recognize that people's *attitudes* and *beliefs* (which are both forms of *thinking*) have a powerful influence on their happiness and success in every area of life. There are countless experiments that demonstrate that a person's behaviors can be significantly changed if a person is manipulated to think or believe certain things.

The way we see the world—our expectations in any situation—as well as our hopes, anxiety, fear and levels of trust or suspicion, all exert significant influence over even our physical world.

For example, we generally believe that a medicine's effect is entirely due to its chemical composition, and the stronger the chemical the stronger the effect.

Not so. For instance the effects of morphine, one of our most powerful painkillers, are greatly influenced by the situation in which it's administered. If a doctor (a trustworthy figure) marches in and tells you that he is going to give you a shot of morphine and gives you an injection, you will typically report a much greater easing of pain than if the morphine is administered automatically and secretly through an IV. Your *expectation* of relief, your direct contact with the doctor, influences the relief you feel.

But if a chemical is a chemical, how can this be? In fact *everything* we experience is influenced by our expectation, our attitude and our personal history.

A psychological experiment measured how men's beliefs about masculinity affect their ability to endure pain. In this study one group of men were told that how long they could keep their hands in ice water indicated their levels of testosterone and therefore masculinity. That group was able to tolerate much higher levels of discomfort and pain than another group of men told that the test was about something generic not linked to masculinity. When men believe that their masculinity is being tested, they simply turn off their sensitivity to pain. Because, after all, real men don't complain about pain or feel the cold.

Other experiments have demonstrated how even subtler dynamics, such as generosity or altruism, can be manipulated and changed by how an experiment is set up and what participants are told to expect during the process.

Over and over, experiments and studies have proved beyond a doubt that your attitude in the moment, what you expect and what you believe to be true have a powerful influence on how you feel, think and behave.

This fact is vitally important to our discussion about blame. Because what you *believe* or *think* about a mistake, error, miscalculation, will greatly affect how and even whether you use blame.

Likewise, how you see your personal limitations will affect how and whether you blame yourself. There are two aspects of our attitudes that we need to explore further, both of which greatly influence our use of self-blame. The first is our desire for perfection. The second is our fear of being defective.

◼ HOW OUR MISTAKEN BELIEFS ABOUT PERFECTION CREATE SELF-BLAME

Our highly destructive Mistaken Belief about the possibility of achieving perfection guides much of our behavior. While we human beings are *structurally incapable* of being perfect, we nevertheless *aspire* to perfection. Doing a "good enough" job is not okay. If we make a mistake we believe we're supposed to feel shame, if not consciously, then unconsciously.

The only possible outcome of this thinking is that we come to believe that we *deserve* to be criticized and punished—especially by ourselves. And that is the root of self-blame.

True, we often utter the automatic (and usually meaningless) disclaimers "We all make mistakes" and "I'm not perfect." But there remains deep inside us a very solid Mistaken Belief that seems to have biblical roots that tell us that we're supposed to be perfect at all times. In fact, many religions make extensive lists of ways we fail to reach perfection.

As a boy, I clearly remember the Catholic Church's teachings about sin. The catechism I studied used the image of little milk bottles to illustrate how a mortal sin turned the milk solid black.

Venial sins were little spots. If I were to die with my milk-bottle soul a solid black, I'd go directly to Hell for eternity. Eternity! Venial sins landed you in purgatory, from which you'd ascend to Heaven if enough people on earth prayed for your soul. Paying to have a mass said on your behalf shortened your time in purgatory.

However, the list of mortal sins was vast, and even included "impure" thoughts. I lived in fear of sudden death and instant damnation because my vivid curiosity (especially about sex, which was indisputably a mortal sin) made it quite impossible to maintain a sufficiently pure and milky white soul.

This dogma created a constant struggle to not commit a sin "in thought, word and deed" in order to avoid eternal damnation. Trying to attain that impossible goal guaranteed a constant use of self-blame—not a comfortable way to live.

In ordinary life, if we step out of the unachievable "Circle of Perfection" other people will subject us to judgments that range from subtle disapproval to withering criticism. And we learn to do the same to ourselves. For example:

- When Alexander backs his new car into a steel pole and scrapes his fender, he berates himself all day for being stupid.
- When Joyce misses a meeting at work because she's mis-read the schedule, she becomes nauseous with anxiety and punishes herself by working through lunch without eating.
- When Max drops his cell phone as he's leaving for work, he's so angry with himself that he stays in a bad mood for hours.

Fortunately, the Law of Personal Limitations directly attacks these behaviors, inspired by our dysfunctional attempts to stay within the imaginary Circle of Perfection, by helping us to embrace our human fallibility.

Embracing fallibility, by the way, does not imply supporting self-indulgent incompetence. The difference between them will become more evident as we continue, in the next chapter, to examine the three fundamental supports for the LPL: philosophical, psychological and practical.

■ ■ ■ ■ ■

CHAPTER FIFTEEN

Exploring the Foundations of the Law of Personal Limitations

Now that we've covered the basics of the Law of Personal Limitations, let's look deeper into the underlying concepts that, with practice and over time, will help you make profound changes in your life.

There are three sources of support for the LPL: (1) philosophical, (2) psychological and (3) practical.

At this point I'd like to clarify why I call the LPL a "law." A law applies to all human beings, to all behaviors, at all times, without exception. In physics there's the Law of Gravity, which applies to all objects with substantial mass. So too the Law of Personal Limitations applies to even the most egregious examples of cruel or stupid human behavior; they all fit within its broad definition.

So let's briefly review its philosophical foundations.

■ PHILOSOPHICAL FOUNDATIONS OF THE LAW OF PERSONAL LIMITATIONS

A general difference between Eastern and Western philosophy is that Western thought generally deals with the unsatisfactory present state of things and is always striving to improve our well-being through self-analysis and action. Life can always be richer and happier and there's always a more efficient way of doing things. Traditions have value only as sentimental artifacts pointing out quaint inefficiencies from the past.

The American version of this philosophy says: Don't be satisfied with what you have now; there's always something better coming tomorrow. Strangely, this belief contrasts with American consumerism, which demands going into debt to enjoy life now and not worrying about the future. That's why Americans have one of the world's lowest saving rates: there is no tomorrow!

In contrast, Eastern philosophy is more contemplative and focuses on reflection and meditation as a way to deepen inner knowledge. It tends to be more conducive to accepting life's intrinsic limits, and sees focusing too much on either the past or the future as futile. Eastern disciplines such as yoga emphasize the breath—the most immediate of all biological processes.

Buddhists see life's suffering as caused by excessive attachment to . . . everything. Hanging on to past grudges and resentments only contaminates the present. Nirvana (a state of bliss or paradise) is achieved through "right living" and a rigorous detachment from suffering. Eastern philosophies tend to naturally align themselves with the Law of Personal Limitations.

Meanwhile, American individualism emphasizes the need

to *overcome* limitations, the idea of "pulling yourself up by your bootstraps." We call this the "American Dream." People are encouraged to be dissatisfied with their present condition and work for something better.

For all its laudable aspects, this "dream" is essentially a call for continual striving: whatever we have is not good enough. This striving has infected us all in myriad unconscious ways. From the psychological perspective, most of them are negative.

This pervasive attitude translates psychologically into the idea that whatever we DO is not good enough and whoever we ARE is not good enough. (A popular advertising theme: "You can never be thin enough.") Criticizing and accusing ourselves is an essential part of this constant striving and pushing. This dynamic is not innocuous. In fact it can be deadly.

This leads us to the core theme of *Beyond Blame* as encapsulated in the Law of Personal Limitations: Each one of us is, in fact, inherently flawed, always has been, and always will be. We must develop an active understanding of our fallibility in order to stop projecting our dissatisfaction and negative emotions and not be overwhelmed with self-blame. And we must stop using criticism and accusations in the form of Blame Attacks against others when their behaviors reflect *their* personal limitations.

■ THE PSYCHOLOGICAL BASIS FOR THE LAW OF PERSONAL LIMITATIONS

But is the Law of Personal Limitations true? And if so, how can that be proved?

Psychology offers a solid basis for the LPL. Our search begins with infancy and the theory of "infantile omnipotence." Essentially, this theory states that infants come into the world with the view that they're the center of the world. They need this perspective to help fend off the extreme anxiety of being absolutely dependent on caregivers in order to survive. If an infant really "knew" how vulnerable he was, he might collapse from fear.

For at least the first eight to ten years of life, children imagine themselves to be powerful and virtually omnipotent. Within their imaginations all sorts of wonderful things are possible. A stick becomes an airplane or a gun. Stuffed animals can talk.

As they grow up, however, life teaches children about limits. Skinned knees teach them about force, velocity and gravity. A parent leaving for work teaches a child about absence and the chance of abandonment.

As development continues, an opposing effect takes over. During adolescence, as competition between peers becomes more intense, children often see themselves as agonizingly *insufficient*. They see every little flaw as a catastrophe, and the wrong style of jeans or shoes can result in social ostracism. The child moves from being delusionally omnipotent to being delusionally inadequate.

Approaching adulthood, the adolescent is forced to learn a middle way; to find balance between utter incompetence and delusional omnipotence. Quite a few don't.

Many parents inadvertently contribute to their children's insecurity by aggressively criticizing ordinary mistakes. They believe that if they don't criticize their children's performance, their work ethic will break down and they will become overly confident, arrogantly narcissistic or even wickedly immoral.

All of these dynamics create confusion about the role of criticism in our close relationships.

■ HUMAN FALLIBILITY CONFLICTS WITH OUR NEED TO BE PERFECT

The denial of our human fallibility—our insistence that we should be perfect when we *can't* be—is directly connected to the pervasiveness of criticism in our society. I'm convinced this impulse is woven into our social DNA, and traces its roots back to the inhumanly cruel restrictions of the Middle Ages. In medieval society, for instance, if you were born with a physical defect, the medieval mind assigned the defect to Divine Intention. Either you or someone in your family brought on the curse by sinful behavior. You deserved the defect. The same reasoning explained poverty—the poor deserved to be poor. Many religions explain problems or defects as self-merited: the Will of God. This attitude serves a vital psychological purpose; it protects us from feeling too bad about having a full meal when just down the street someone else is hungry. In other words, it's highly self-protective.

In Europe, this belief system was reinforced for millennia by both the ruling class and the Church because it allowed the privileged to believe that they deserved their privileges: they were blessed by God. The quality of their breeding was a sign of God's favor. "The apple doesn't fall far from the tree" is a cultural reminder of this belief.

American capitalism has transferred pieces of this ideology into our *meritocracy*. This belief system states (or implies) that individual *merit* guides our destiny. Again, people are poor because they deserve to be. Anyone can work their way to the top. Anyone! So if you're not successful, it's because you just haven't tried hard enough. You're lazy, which is a *voluntary* defect of character. There's no shortage of "success" stories to reinforce this belief.

In short, it goes against our ingrained social programming for us to believe that everyone really *wants* to do well and find a successful place in society. The popular myth is that everyone can rise above their familial, economic or personal limitations.

The Law of Personal Limitations counters this popular myth. It asserts that everyone truly wants to successfully fit into society, and build happy relationships. They really are doing as well as they can to fit in and be successful, but are restricted by their personal limitations.

These assertions also apply to you. If you have difficulties fitting in and being successful, it's because of your own personal limitations, your history, and what you know and don't know, and a variety of emotions that constrain or accelerate your behaviors.

Conclusion: Only by understanding and accepting those limitations, and what you don't know, can you begin to effect change. Denying, distorting or minimizing limitations, or (the worse attitude of all) blaming them on others, only keeps you stuck.

But there must be exceptions! In fact, not. Let's explore one of the most obvious.

■ EXCEPTIONS TO THE LPL ARE NOT VALID

Let's briefly look at one of the most visible exceptions to the Law of Personal Limitations: the healthy-looking homeless guy asking for spare change on the corner.

He doesn't seem to be physically disabled and looks healthy enough to work. Obviously he's not doing as well as he can, nor does he have an inherent desire to do well and successfully fit into society. So he must be an exception to the LPL.

Not so fast. Were we to talk with the homeless person, we'd

find out soon enough that he's dealing with either a mental or an emotional illness and/or a traumatic personal history that seriously distorts his ability to think clearly. And he has so completely lost hope that his existence has devolved into a hand-to-mouth struggle.

In fact, he hasn't a clue how to deal with his very real limitations. None of the advice he receives makes sense to him. *If he could act on the advice and make better decisions, he would.*

I recall a patient who was seeking therapy because of stress. He worked for a bank that was having problems because of the subprime mortgage crisis. At one point he chuckled about how stupid people were to take on a half-million-dollar loan when their income was negligible. I was shocked at his cavalier attitude. When I asked him if he had any qualms about the tremendous fees he had earned during that process, he brushed aside my question. "You know, I didn't set up that system. The money was there. I was just making the loans."

His inability to see any ethical problem with giving money to someone who couldn't make the payments was his *glaring personal limitation.* The emotion running his program was desire and greed. He saw himself as ethically correct because he was "just making the loans."

The same argument applies to Catherine as she started her affair with Bryan. Her body was so overwhelmed by the powerful emotions (euphoric romance and lust) *at that time* that she was not capable of making a healthier decision.

Even though an objective observer could see the upcoming tragedy, the person who is enmeshed in the powerful emotions at the time (just as was the mortgage broker) is utterly incapable of seeing it. They are functionally blind!

We can respond to life's challenges only according to our own internal programming, the limitations imposed on us by our family and social status and our ability to think and process information. All of it influenced by our situation and emotions in that moment.

These points are fundamental. Yes, everyone does, in fact, aspire to do well . . . **and** everyone is directly limited by their personal history, what they *know* and *don't know* and *what they're feeling in that moment.*

The phrase about *knowing* is critical because it points us toward a little-known condition whose importance is gathering momentum in psychology: a neurological condition called *anosognosia* (pronounced ano-sog-NO-sia) that has strong psychological effects.

Anosognosia is defined as "a condition in which a person who suffers from a disability seems unaware of or denies the existence of the disability." It's another way of saying that **you don't know that you don't know something about yourself.**

We need to briefly explore this issue before returning to Catherine's situation.

▪ *ANOSOGNOSIA:* NOT KNOWING THAT YOU DON'T KNOW

One of the biggest challenges in therapy is trying to teach a patient what they don't know, both about factual material and the incredibly wide range of emotions.

For example: The father of a four-year-old protests that his son understands perfectly well when he asks him to pick up his toys. "He's just being willfully disobedient. So I swat him on his bottom to get him to obey," just as his father had done to him. While swatting the child will force compliance, the father's parenting would be more effective (and loving) if the father *understood* that his son isn't always able to translate a command into behavior because his brain isn't yet sufficiently developed. The father *doesn't know that he doesn't know about his son's brain development.*

Any situation is made worse when the person is not aware that they don't know something. Thinking is not the only type of not knowing. As already mentioned, there are also many emotional components we might not directly sense.

◼ HOW OUR EMOTIONS BLOCK US FROM BOTH KNOWING AND ACTING

The next issue connected to the Law of Personal Limitations is the emotions we feel but don't know we're feeling. I call this *emotional anosognosia.*

Here's a personal story that involved a quite minor issue that caused me an unnecessary anxiety until I used the LPL to figure it out.

The situation involved a friend I'll call Keith. I'd known Keith casually for a few years, and when I mentioned I needed a website he offered to help. We agreed on a price and he started to work. When we encountered some complications, Keith stepped away from the project.

I still owed Keith some money for his work, but was hanging on to resentment about Keith's performance even though circumstances played a big part. So I didn't send the check. And because he was a casual friend, I was reluctant to tell him I was unhappy. Why did I let months go by without paying him?

Because every time I thought about writing Keith a check, I put it off because the resentment kept popping up. At the time, however, **I did not know that I was feeling resentment.** My personal limitations were both an emotion (resentment) and lack of awareness of the emotion. Both combined to stop me from acting.

The good news is that once I was able to not only identify but also confront the resentment that was limiting my behavior, I realized that hanging on to that minor quantity of negative emotion was unhealthy, and was keeping me from cleaning up an ongoing issue.

After I sent the check, I felt instantly better.

Each of us suffers from literally thousands of these *personal limitations*, both emotional and cognitive, that block our effective functioning in the world.

Here are a few more examples, ranging from basic health to finances to communication:

- Doug, after many delays, reluctantly visits a dentist and finds out he has advanced gum disease. He protests, "But I brush my teeth . . . pretty often." His anxiety about seeing the dentist had kept him from making the appointment, but not knowing about gingivitis gave no protection.

- Miriam receives a letter from the IRS demanding back taxes. "Was I supposed to pay this?" she wonders. Her lack of self-confidence and anxiety about money issues kept her from dealing with the problem, but ignorance about taxes won't help.

- "When I'm pissed off," says Cory, "I yell so my kids know they're in trouble. That's the way I was raised. And it works just fine." Cory's unconscious loyalty to his own father keeps him from wanting to try a different parenting style. That doesn't change that his kids fear him and lead secret lives he knows nothing about.

■ "My mom said some really critical things to me during our last visit, and my husband didn't stand up for me," complains Miriam. "I'm so disappointed in him that I haven't spoken to him in days." She doesn't know that shutting out her husband only deepens the distance between them. She doesn't know there's something she could do about it. Her fear of offending her mother prevents her from confronting her directly.

■ "I almost never have more than, like, maybe, a couple drinks," Heather says with a slight slur. "I'm certainly not an alcoholic." Heather can't admit her alcoholism because once she has a couple of drinks, she slips into denial about how much she's drinking. Her fear of stopping drinking supports her denial.

These are just a few examples of the wide range of *emotional anosognosia*, a state in which both information and underlying emotion you don't know about end up controlling your behavior.

Another enormously important example about *not knowing* is how people use blame. When I try to educate my patients about the destructive effects of blame, one would assume that as soon as they knew something was destructive, they'd stop using it! Wouldn't you?

Not necessarily. It's a bizarre fact of psychology that **people continue behaviors that are either self-destructive or harmful** even when those behaviors are obviously hurting themselves, or the person they love most. Why is this?

■ ANOSOGNOSIA AFFECTS OUR ABILITY TO KNOW OTHERS' LIMITATIONS

If you don't know about your personal limitations, you will act out of ignorance.

Even more potentially tragic is that you will ignore the limitations of others.

If this sounds disturbing, it certainly ought to. Here's a heartbreaking story that illustrates the extremes of this process.

Jim has been dating a woman who has a record of multiple financial and legal problems, some of them quite recent. But she's beautiful and intelligent, and Jim is convinced he's determined to set her life straight. He says she had a terrible childhood and all she needs is what she didn't get—unconditional love—which he's willing to give her.

He tells me this during a therapy session. I'm immediately alarmed. I suggest that his girlfriend likely has Antisocial Personality Disorder, along with other psychiatric complications. I even read Jim the description of the disorder in the *DSM-IV* (the fourth edition of *Diagnostic and Statistical Manual of Mental Disorders*), and she solidly fits the diagnosis.

But Jim is determined to ignore every fact and blames me and the psychiatric cabal for labeling people. He insists, "You haven't seen into her heart. People really can change if they find someone who loves them unconditionally."

I never see Jim again. But I hear through another patient that his girlfriend had stolen money from him and that she's now a fugitive. Apparently, Jim is still trying to find her to offer more help.

In this case, Jim's ignorance about his girlfriend's limitations is pathological and well beyond the ordinary. He utterly refuses to see reality.

While it is absolutely essential to recognize that *everyone is doing as well as they can within their personal limitations*, it's crucial to avoid excusing or minimizing someone's obvious flaws, especially if they're dangerous. Choosing not to know is a dead-end street.

◼ THREE SERIOUS CONCLUSIONS ABOUT OUR LIMITATIONS

From all of the above we can settle upon three very serious psychological facts:

1. Our most damaging limitation is that that we don't accept our own limitations or don't know they exist.
2. Often, even when we do acknowledge our limitations, we blame them on others.
3. When we don't accept that we are all limited, we unrealistically expect more of ourselves and others, thereby ignoring and minimizing everyone's limitations.

These conclusions are serious because they add up to a system-wide state of denial and delusion that can contaminate our decisions, both personal and public.

In the public sphere, we consistently ignore and minimize the disastrous consequences of bad decisions—the inherent limitations of those decisions—and then blame the negative results on others. A popular target is the media. This is a one-size-fits-all response to a problem. In other words, the inherent limitations are not the difficulty, it's the reporting that's the problem.

What to do about this seemingly endless cycle of ignorance and blame and more ignorance and more blame? The answer is found in the third support for the Law of Personal Limitations, the law's practical base.

■ THE PRACTICAL FOUNDATION OF THE LAW OF PERSONAL LIMITATIONS

One definition of the term "practical" is *something that works.*

Something that's practical is functional, realistic and sensible—even though it may not seem that way at first glance. Don't we all want solutions that actually solve a problem? In psychology, however, it sometimes takes a *counterintuitive* leap to discover what's really most effective.

Actively using the LPL stops blame in its tracks, but it doesn't do so by merely shouting "Stop using blame!" Rather, the law's tremendous effectiveness is found within the powerful *paradox* that this law presents.

How can a paradox be powerful? First, we need a definition. *A paradox is something that's counterintuitive, a proposition that seems contradictory, but, in fact, is true.* Science is filled with paradoxes.

Human psychology is also loaded with counterintuitive paradoxes. One of the most common is the idea of vulnerability. A common belief (especially among men) is that *not showing emotion conveys strength.* In fact, the man who's stolid, impassive and unresponsive may not be demonstrating strength. Most likely he's paralyzed with a fear of showing feelings. Expressing an emotion feels frightening, and fear dominates his emotional life.

Someone who can show feelings actually possesses *more* personal power than the unresponsive person. We all respect and admire someone who feels remorse and then admits to making a mistake and apologizes.

The underlying paradox of the LPL is that *by accepting and understanding your own limitations, and becoming comfortable with them, you gain power over them.* This is a psychological paradox.

Two of the most durable psychological paradoxes of proven value are the twin concepts at the heart of Alcoholics Anonymous. The most famous is the first of the Twelve Steps: The admission of being powerless over alcohol. A person new to AA is often confused by the demand that he or she must "admit to being powerless." The Second Step then says the person must "come to believe that a Power greater than ourselves could restore us to sanity."

These two demands contradict our cultural belief in the strength of the individual. AA supplants individuals' attempts at personal strength with fellowship and the belief that people cannot individually control their addictions. Long-term sobriety is found in relying on the strength and hope of others in the AA program.

Recent research about physicians points out another variation on the paradox of vulnerability. When a doctor talks directly to a patient and admits having made a mistake, *the doctor greatly reduces the chances of being sued for malpractice.* This outcome is counterintuitive because physicians often assume a god-like persona. Their Mistaken Belief is that *admitting* a mistake opens him or her for more criticism and punishment. In reality, the great majority of patients really have an inherent desire to recognize vulnerability and not be needlessly vindictive.

Which brings us to another paradox that's *crucial* to our understanding of blame's negative effects on our lives: the Paradox of Criticism.

▪ EXPLORING THE PARADOX OF CRITICISM

We solidly cling to the Mistaken Belief that criticizing makes a person perform better. The Paradox of Criticism refutes this belief. It states: **Criticism, accusation and punishment do not help people change a mistaken behavior; rather, they reinforce the behavior, or create a furor that inhibits change.**

Why? Because, as discussed in Part One, blame (which again consists of actions involving criticism, accusation, punishment and often humiliation) sets up a re-*action* driven by the negative emotions of anxiety, resentment, anger, fear and pain. These powerful emotions *entrench the behaviors we're trying to change*.

Again, why? Because *we all resist change imposed from the outside*. We don't like being told what to do. This universal impulse is called "resistance to change."

The Paradox of Criticism teaches us that NOT criticizing and accusing—but instead using Positive Accountability—encourages the productive change we wish to see. It can "open a space" in the relationship that allows positive emotions to emerge. These emotions promote the desired change from *inside* the person.

Here's a simple example to demonstrate my point.

Imagine you're in the kitchen with your spouse or partner and she says in an irritated, critical tone of voice, "Darn, you left the stove on *again*! Why can't you remember? Do you want to burn the house down?" Three Blame Attacks, one right after another.

How do you feel? Probably not very cooperative or friendly.

Now imagine the same scene, but this time she says, "Oops, looks like the stove was left on." The tone is matter-of-fact and not accusatory. Doesn't that feel better?

Because you're not being criticized, you don't have a bunch of negative emotions to deal with. **You won't feel the need to defend yourself, which can trigger an argument.** So the message about turning off the stove has a chance to sink in.

This is an example of how launching a Blame Attack triggers a power struggle in which each person is forced to use more blame to deflect the criticism. *The power struggle guarantees that the behavior in question does not change.* Or if it does, it's usually only temporary, because the pressure to change is coming from the outside. It's not an internal decision.

Outside pressure only creates resentment toward the person (or entity) pushing for change. That explains why conquering armies may temporarily change a few things about a conquered country, but the "old ways" creep back into practice when the occupier leaves.

A more personal demonstration would be trying to get your spouse to lose weight. It's futile to criticize him for ordering cheesecake for dessert. Trying to control your spouse's intake of calories through criticism and accusation is utterly ineffective, and actually counterproductive.

The one notable exception about criticism is how the military uses it in training new recruits. The military uses harsh criticism and accusation to build instant compliance. The young soldier learns to swallow any individual resentment because he or she is now part of a group that thinks and acts as a team. Individuality is stripped away. But that's a very special environment.

Back in the world of close personal relationships, in which a Blame Attack is a self-defeating tactic, the goal of the Law of Personal Limitations is to entirely eliminate criticism and accusation. No more Blame Attacks!

■ IGNORING THE LAW OF PERSONAL LIMITATIONS CREATES PROBLEMS

There's one more paradox embedded in the LPL, namely, that *not* using the law creates more problems by intensifying resistance to change. In other words we end up achieving the opposite of what we intend to achieve. The following story illustrates this point.

Thomas really dislikes his wife's sister, Patricia, who has strong opinions on every subject from politics to men. Every time Patricia visits, she creates tension.

Thomas's wife says her sister has been difficult to deal with since she was a teenager and there's nothing they can do about it. "She's forty-five, divorced twice and very unhappy. Sure, I can limit her attendance at gatherings with just our nuclear family, but I can't not invite her to gatherings with the whole family. She's my sister."

At the next gathering, Patricia says something provocative, Thomas gets irritated, Patricia escalates, and a terrible argument ensues. Patricia storms out. His wife is angry not with her sister, but with Thomas. "I told you about her, didn't I?" she says.

"There's something really wrong with her," Thomas replies defensively.

"And you're not going to change her. She's completely unaware of how irritating she is. In fact, she believes it's her responsibility to 'set the record straight.' Now you've made things a lot more difficult for me."

Now, here's the psychological paradox: Patricia believes that Thomas is a sexist jerk, and that it's her job to confront him whenever he says the smallest thing she considers offensive, regardless of the consequences! Even if it makes everyone angry at her and doesn't do a darn thing to change anyone's mind.

And have you ever met someone who doesn't believe that their actions are justified? Even someone who's caught stealing has a justification. We all justify our behaviors.

Thomas might be able to express his emotional needs either by asking Patricia to not discuss a certain topic, or, if she bothers him so severely, arranging to not be in her company. Regardless, his campaign to change her will not succeed, and he's going to have to find a different way of handling her visits and his reactions.

Now let's return to Catherine (from the beginning of the previous chapter) and use all this information, including the Law of Lessons Learned from Part Two, to see how to intervene in her situation. Remember, what she needs most right now is relief from the self-punishment that's making her life miserable.

■ HOW CATHERINE USES THE LPL TO FIND RELIEF FROM SELF-BLAME

During Catherine's next therapy session, I asked her to come up with her own assessment of how the Law of Personal Limitations applied to her marriage to Bryan.

"It was really tough to think about this," she said. "I realize now that I was very lonely and sexually frustrated, and that I convinced myself it was worth taking a chance with Bryan. A part of me knew he was risky, but I wanted to do it anyway."

"I understand," I said. "Your loneliness, combined with your sexual desire, overwhelmed your thoughtfulness. Those powerful emotions were part of your limitations. They hindered your ability to think and thoughtfully decide what to do."

"You're right. I always believed you had to follow your feelings, whatever they were. I really believed that. Follow your heart! Isn't that what they say?"

"Yes," I replied, "they do say that. The problem is that your heart can't operate separately from your brain. You need both."

■ ■ ▮ ■ ▪

AN ANTIDOTE TO NOT KNOWING: SHOW ME THE PROOF

In the chapter about blame and dating, I proposed Three Basic Guidelines for Dating. One is "Show me the proof." This admonition can literally be a lifesaver. When we're caught up in the delirium of romance, we all want to be swept along with the powerful flow of romantic energy. The idea of checking out the facts about the person you're dating becomes especially important within that context.

"Catherine," I continued, "it will be very helpful to recognize that you're especially *susceptible* to these emotions. At the time you met Bryan you did not know that you were so susceptible. If you had been *capable* of recognizing what was in fact going on, you could have reacted differently."

"You're saying I should have told the slime bucket to get lost."

"In so many words, yes. But back then you did not know it. Nor *did you know that you didn't know.* Now it's time to stop being excessively punitive. There's enough pain in your situation without you piling on and hurting yourself more."

"I want to make sure I don't repeat this," she said.

"And here's how you can do that. It's called the Law of Lessons Learned. Now you need to extract the lesson to be learned from this experience (see pages 152 and 172 in Part Two). Write it on a three-by-five-inch card and tape it to your bedroom mirror. Review it every few days for a year. The next time you meet a guy, remind yourself of what you learned from the relationship with Bryan. The goal is to never again *allow your emotions to overwhelm your thinking*."

"Can it be that simple? Sounds like not enough."

"Oh, that's not easy. If you really do it correctly, it's a lot of work."

When Catherine arrived at the next session, she looked measurably more relaxed.

"I feel like I've had a breakthrough," she said. "I realize that all my life I've allowed my emotions to push me around, to control my decisions. I've done a lot of soul-searching and I can see how—starting back in high school—I'd just do what felt right, without much thought at all. That's what caused my first divorce. No wonder when it came to Bryan, I didn't want to know things about him. I didn't even ask. I just hoped things would work out. Now I see how shortsighted that was. And I'm going to change it."

I could tell from Catherine's face that she was much more at peace with herself. She had decided to stop using self-blame to punish herself, to "teach herself a lesson," and to instead use that energy to make better choices for her future.

In the next chapter, we'll continue to explore and put to the test how to use the Law of Personal Limitations in your life.

■ ■ ■ ■ ■

CHAPTER SIXTEEN

Testing the Law of Personal Limitations on Yourself

ONE OF THE most common questions about the Law of Personal Limitations, the LPL, I get is "But how does it apply to me, and to my life?"

In fact, the best way to test any conclusion, especially one in the wobbly world of everyday behavior, is to see if it works for you, in your world.

So let's work through two ordinary mistakes. The first will be a simple error: forgetting a friend's birthday, an example of absent-mindedness. The second will be more serious: driving home from a party after drinking too much, getting into an argument with your girlfriend and running into a parked car and causing a lot of damage.

Let's start with forgetting a friend's birthday. We'll call your friend Annie. You've known Annie for years even though she's not your closest friend. Her birthday has come and gone, and a week later you suddenly remember. "Darn! I forgot Annie's birthday!" You also know that Annie makes a big deal about her birthday.

Now answer the following **"Three Questions About Your Personal Intentions."** These questions are designed to penetrate the typical psychological smokescreen we all use to justify our behaviors (almost always using blame) and mask our thinking and attitudes.

IMPORTANT NOTE: As you work through the Three Questions you might notice that you're criticizing and making yourself wrong a lot. Or you might project these behaviors onto the other person or a group. This response is part of our quest to find explanations for everything. Typically we shift responsibility onto others or we criticize ourselves. When you sense that's happening, stop it. Anything that leads to criticizing, accusing or punishing *anyone* moves you away from reaching a solution.

THE THREE QUESTIONS ABOUT YOUR PERSONAL INTENTIONS

1. What is your reason for making the mistake?
2. What was your motive behind making the mistake?
3. At the time, were you functioning as well as you could, considering what was going on in your life?

Question 1 asks about your *reason*, which has to do with thinking. Question 2 asks about your *motive*, which has to do with feelings. Every feeling, from anxiety, resentment, pain, fear and humiliation to desire, greed and lust, influences your behavior. Emotions provide a *motive* for a behavior, even a minor one. Thoughtfully answering these questions will help you get to the core of your fallibility, and thus your limitations.

ANSWERING THE THREE QUESTIONS ABOUT YOUR PERSONAL INTENTIONS

1. **What is your *reason* for making the mistake?** That is, what were you thinking, and how did those thoughts allow you to forget? Were you busy and distracted because you just changed jobs, or were having difficulties in your relationship, or you had a cold . . . and so on? Or maybe you were confused about the time and date? For our purposes, let's say that Annie's birthday slipped your mind because of all the things happening in your life at the time. An ordinary mistake.

2. **What was your *motive* behind making the mistake?** Did you have any emotional problem with Annie? Were you harboring resentment that prompted you to not call her, so you conveniently "forgot"? But as you think about possible resentments, you come up with a "no." You've been on good terms with her. There is no submerged issue. *Conclusion:* You cannot uncover an actual motive for your behavior; you just forgot!

3. **At the time, were you functioning as well as you could, considering what was going on in your life?** That is to say, if you could have *managed* to remember to call her, would you have? This is the trickiest question to answer. In fact, the answer is a solid Yes.

Because . . . unless there were some concealed thoughts or emotions that prompted your behavior, we must accept the idea that you were just *caught up in your own limitations!* You were in the grip of your personal history, and what you knew and didn't know in that moment.

Those limitations—everyone's personal limitations—are part of living. Forgetfulness, confusion and ordinary self-centeredness are intrinsic to all humanity.

And no matter how much you wish that you were less absorbed in your own needs, no matter how much you think you *should* be more generous and giving, less reactive and resentful, less sensitive to perceived slights, and more secure with yourself, *in that moment* when you made the mistake, you were operating only with what you had going for you . . . right then and there.

If you had been more aware, *perhaps* you would have acted differently. *Perhaps* you would have remembered Annie's birthday. Maybe. There's no way of knowing for sure.

Now let's finish working through this issue.

■ BRINGING TOGETHER THE LAW OF PERSONAL LIMITATIONS AND POSITIVE ACCOUNTABILITY

Concluding the Exercise

To conclude this exercise, we need to engage both Positive Accountability and the Law of Personal Limitations. The first process, Positive Accountability, provides a structure to deal with any action that you might need to take.

To refresh your memory, here's the complete description of Positive Accountability:

1. To thoughtfully acknowledge an error, your own or another person's, and consider how to repair it, if necessary.
2. To express an emotion or a need, without using criticism, accusation, punishment or humiliation, with the goal of not triggering negative emotions.

But for any of this to be possible, you need to be significantly in control of your thinking. You need to be operating with at least 80 percent thought and only 20 percent feeling. That's a 4:1 ratio. This ratio also applies to the "positive" emotions that can trigger destructive behavior.

■ ■ ■ ■ ■

POSITIVE EMOTIONS CAN HAVE NEGATIVE CONSEQUENCES

While the positive emotions of joy, elation, excitement, enthusiasm and romantic love are hardly considered as dangerous to our well-being, they certainly can be. As the previous story about Catherine and her affair with Bryan pointed out, she suffered greatly when those emotions overwhelmed her thinking. Consider how the joyful enthusiasm of opening a business of your own can lead you to making disastrous financial decisions. Positive experiences can, like negative ones, overwhelm our ability to make thoughtful, prudent decisions.

In this case, the simple error of forgetting your friend's birthday, all you need to do is thoughtfully acknowledge the error—as part of recognizing your personal limitations—and repair the mistake by offering a heartfelt apology. You don't need to express an emotion other than your regret.

Above all, **there's no need to criticize or punish yourself** because you made a mistake. Nor do you need to self-flagellate as a way of expressing your regret. "Oh, Annie, I'm sooo sorry. I'm such a dunce. There's no excuse . . . I don't know how I can ever apologize . . ." And so on.

Just acknowledge the error, make amends if possible . . . and move on.

In addition, remember that the Law of Lessons Learned teaches that every error contains a lesson, and presents an opportunity to learn about yourself. So the lesson might be to develop the habit of writing important events on your calendar, or inserting dates into your electronic device. These would be simple behavioral changes that would help avoid making similar errors.

Now that we're familiar with the Three Questions let's use them to examine a more dangerous problem—volatility in a relationship—with expensive and potentially dangerous consequences.

■ USING THE LPL TO EXAMINE A SERIOUS RELATIONSHIP PROBLEM

A common problem people face in relationships is volatility, defined as responding angrily to even a slight provocation. Not violently, but with a raised, angry voice. While men tend to be the greatest offenders in using violent language (and actual violence) in relationships, women, too, can be highly volatile. In this case, we're using a male as an example of what *not* to do.

Here's the scene: You and your girlfriend Kristi have been at a friend's party. You've known Kristi for about a year and usually get along well, except for her jealousy—and your very short fuse. The last time you lost your temper over Kristi's jealousy, you threw a glass and broke it, really frightening her.

At this evening's party, you've had three glasses of wine and should not drive. But you're in a jubilant mood when you get to your car.

Kristi suggests she drive, but you tell her that she's had more to drink than you have. "I definitely did not!" she responds. As you start the car and begin maneuvering into the street, Kristi asks you about the woman you were talking to as you were leaving. You say, "Who?"

"You know who! That blonde who put her hand on your shoulder."

You protest that you don't even know her name, that she was just being friendly. Kristi insists that you must know her. Suddenly, you're irritated. Your voice tight, you shoot back, "I'm not lying, for Chrissakes! I don't know her."

"I definitely heard you call her Susan or Suzanne. Why are you denying it? Just admit it!"

You hit the brake hard and turn to face her. "Stop being so friggin' jealous!"

Kristi doesn't back down. Her eyes flaring, she demands, "I'm just trying to get the truth."

A quick thought flashes in your head about your being in a

closed space, having had too much to drink, and Kristi being
upset with you. But that warning of potential danger passes by
and disappears in your anger.

Furious, you step on the gas, but the steering wheel slips from
your hand and you crash into the side of a parked car, crunching
the door and fender. Now you're really furious. You jump out of
the car and stalk off, swearing at Kristi. You've created a real mess,
at least a couple thousand dollars in damage.

Now let's work through this problem using the Three Questions About Your Personal Intentions, the Law of Personal Limitations and Positive Accountability.

The primary issue is this: How are you going to deal *intellectu-
ally*, *emotionally* and *practically* with your major screwup?

Sure, you're responsible for the damage to the other car, and
you'll surely pay for it. But more importantly: What will you
do about your dangerous habit of flying off the handle? You certainly can't live the rest of your life being unpredictably volatile,
can you?

This brief format will not allow us to exhaustively explore
every tangent of this problem, but we certainly can cover the major
issues.

Let's begin with the Three Questions About Your Personal
Intentions. The first question is: **What is your *reason* for making
the mistake?**

What were you *thinking* when you stepped on the gas and lost
control of the car? Thinking? Reasons? Sorry, drawing a blank.
You were not thinking. You were having a temper tantrum, a rage
attack. However, you know that being unjustly accused gets you
really angry, and quickly. And Kristi's jealous insecurities have
provoked a series of fights.

So the best *reason* you come up with for smashing the other car is that you hate being accused. In admitting that, you also have to admit that causing so much damage and raising your insurance rates is a pretty high price to pay for losing your temper just because Kristi had accused you of flirting.

Next, **what was your *motive* behind making the mistake?** You already know that the motive was out-of-control emotions: you were in the grip of a rage attack.

Finally, **at the time, were you functioning as well as you could, considering what was going on in your life?** Definitely not. Your behavior was terribly irresponsible. You could have and should have done better. A lot better.

Then why didn't you?

Why didn't you do better?

Replying with "I don't know" is not an answer. Just like it isn't the answer for why you threw the glass and broke it last time you fought with Kristi. Then, too, you could have and should have done better. So why didn't you?

Because, as always, the Law of Personal Limitations was in force. As it always is.

▪ DEALING WITH YOUR LIMITATIONS THAT CAUSED THE CAR ACCIDENT

In order to avoid more costly episodes like the one that wrecked the car, you need to understand and confront your limitations.

The most important fact about that incident was that you became very quickly irritated when Kristi questioned you about the blonde. Yes, you had a fleeting thought about the danger of getting upset, but it passed by too fast for you to act on it. So I repeat: If you *could have* acted on it, you would have. These tantrums have got to stop. You must learn the lesson from your out-of-control behavior.

In short, it's time you got really serious about the Law of Lessons Learned. An effective way to deal with your potential to rage would be to make a note (ideally written) about the type of situation that puts you at the greatest risk. For instance, drinking too much. You're emotionally more vulnerable when you go beyond one drink. So you need to take steps to control your alcohol intake, especially when you're with Kristi. (Other issues in your relationship, namely her jealousy, need to be addressed, but that would probably require a couples therapist.)

Let's see how using Positive Accountability fits into this scenario. We'll begin by recalling the two parts of the process.

The first is **to thoughtfully acknowledge an error (your own) and repair it.**

So first, you need to apologize to Kristi for frightening her. (Whether that will be sufficient is yet to be seen.)

Next is **to express an emotion or a need without criticism or accusation.**

The first need you must express is to yourself: you need to change your volatile reactions. You must work diligently to control your temper. This is the primary need that comes from this incident.

To that end (and as part of your apology to Kristi), you're likely to need to promise to see a psychotherapist who can help you understand and control your volatility and do whatever the therapist says is necessary to change this reactive behavior.

This is where the Law of Lessons Learned comes in (see page 152). You need to make notes about the *lessons learned* from the incident, and review them often so they remain fixed in your mind.

Above all, you don't allow blame to wipe out the lessons you need to learn, such as accusing Kristi for provoking your rage attack. That approach wouldn't change a thing.

THE BOTTOM LINE: No matter what Kristi says that might irritate you, it's *your* responsibility to overcome your limitations (your tendency to rage) and keep yourself (and others) safe. You must acknowledge that *in that moment* you were in the grip of rage and *not capable* of making a healthier decision.

But now that you're aware of your limitations you must take steps to deal with them. At the very least, whenever you feel your ability to think rationally is at risk, you must take a break and remove yourself from the scene.

Now, it's possible you might believe that raging is just what guys do, that rage is basically okay. It's an inbuilt personal limitation. "What's wrong with blowing off steam?" So let's make something clear: **The Law of Personal Limitations is never an excuse to continue impulsive and destructive behavior.**

THE LPL IS NOT AN EXCUSE FOR SELF-INDULGENT BEHAVIOR

Distorting any maxim or rule to serve an immature, self-indulgent purpose is all too easy. It can be tempting to exploit personal limitations as an excuse to stay stuck or overwhelmed. So far I've made the case that self-indulgent destructive behavior is not and can never be the goal of the LPL or any part of learning to live Beyond Blame.

Remember that living Beyond Blame does not excuse or

exonerate a person who behaves badly or makes a mistake. The LPL does not eliminate anyone's responsibilities. It merely eliminates handling them with blame. Including self-blame and self-punishment.

■ THE LPL IS NOT AN EXCUSE FOR ENGAGING IN SELF-BLAME

The Law of Personal Limitations is not an excuse for staying stuck. It's not okay to take refuge in thoughts like "I have so many limitations, I'm too stupid to learn anything. I might as well give up." Such an attitude is not part of the law's message.

A fundamental strategy behind living Beyond Blame is to figure out what your personal limitations are, to accept them fully and own them—they're yours!—and then to **take action so they don't continue to control your life.**

This is a difficult challenge. But the first time you have the experience of actually accepting and working with your limitations (rather than pretending you don't have them), you will instantly feel more at home in your own life.

It all comes down to diligently studying the Law of Personal Limitations and recognizing that we're all in the same boat, all the time.

The only thing that will save us from repeating damaging mistakes is *awareness* of our own (and others') limitations. It is that awareness itself that leads toward greater thoughtfulness and then increased effectiveness.

The Law of Personal Limitations, properly used, can free us to practice more effective behaviors in all our relationships.

CONCLUSION: Our social, cultural, familial and individual reliance on blame constantly works against our best interests. The Law of Personal Limitations allows us to develop a broader and deeper understanding of how each of us struggles with our inherent restraints to function in a way that advances our best long-term interests.

As we take apart the LPL and digest each of its components, we encounter our natural bias against giving anyone an excuse for self-indulgent behaviors, a "free ride." But we must delve deeper into the counterintuitive and paradoxical aspects of the LPL. We must go beyond our initial objections and our knee-jerk refusals to accept our own limitations and those of others.

Only by accepting without argument our own limitations can we stop criticizing ourselves long enough to take a relaxed breath. To pause. And within that pause to feel some compassion for our lack of perfection . . . and our frequent less-than-brilliant performance, especially with those we care about the most.

In the end, the Law of Personal Limitations contains an intensely hopeful and positive message about our possibilities for interaction, first with ourselves, and then with others.

In the next and final chapter of the book we'll review step-by-step a series of guidelines that bring the entire model together into one practical and functional unit, putting you at the center of the action.

■ ■ ■ ■ ■

CHAPTER SEVENTEEN

Pulling It All Together

Living Beyond Blame

THIS FINAL CHAPTER is all about HOW to eliminate blame in your life using Positive Accountability, the Law of Personal Limitations and the rest of the tools I've presented. It will bring together the book's major concepts into a basic working model you can use in all your relationships. I'll use detailed narratives to illustrate each concept and intervention, and put *you* at the center of the action.

The Blame Syndrome (the initial Blame Attack, the Emotional Impact and the Reactive Response) damages so many areas of life, and it needs to stop. Because blame can appear as everything from an arched eyebrow or a cynical sigh to a shouted accusation, identifying blame is not a simple task. And taking steps to eliminate it takes sustained effort. But it's well worth it.

The payoff of living Beyond Blame is immediate, tangible and permanent.

Time after time when I present the concepts in this book to my patients, I hear, "I grew up with so much blame in my family, if only my parents had been able to . . ." Or, "My first marriage was nothing but a blame-a-thon. If only we could have . . ." Or, "If the managers of my company could understand that criticizing and accusing doesn't help, we'd be so much more efficient!"

Let's start by going back to the earliest concepts in this book, and reviewing the four functions of blame. We use blame:

1. when we want to change another person's behaviors through criticism, accusation, punishment or humiliation;
2. when we want to vent a feeling such as anxiety, anger, resentment, pain or fear;
3. when we want to escape personal responsibility by shifting it onto someone else; or
4. when we try to protect ourselves from being seen as wrong or bad.

Sometimes we'll engage two or three of these functions at the same time. Blame's effects and damage are far-ranging, so logically it will take a wide series of interventions to stop its destructive influence in our lives.

Here's a step-by-step outline of the interventions necessary for living Beyond Blame. They're arranged in a sequence that won't fit every situation; there's just too much variation within human communications. So be ready to adapt them to your own situation, knowing that every major concept will show up somewhere in the process.

■ A STEP-BY-STEP PROCESS FOR
LIVING BEYOND BLAME

What do you do when confronted with blame—when someone criticizes, accuses, punishes or humiliates you? How do you take care of yourself? How do you correct a mistake, or get someone to change a behavior? How do you express an emotion, or communicate your own personal needs, without falling into the trap of using blame?

FIRST STEP: **Use Positive Accountability.** This step always comes first because it's the main structure onto which everything else is attached. To review: When you engage Positive Accountability, you practice two behaviors:

1. To thoughtfully acknowledge an error, your own or another person's, and consider how to repair it, if necessary.
2. To express an emotion, or a need, without using criticism, accusation, punishment or humiliation.

Here's the condensed message of Positive Accountability:

Find a way to express yourself without criticizing or accusing anyone. To do this demands thoughtful consideration, but it's the only way out of the thorny thicket of blame. And it requires careful, rigorous adherence to the second step:

SECOND STEP: **Maintain a 4:1 ratio of thought to emotion.** That's 80 percent thinking to 20 percent feeling. This means that when your sweetheart does something incredibly inconsiderate and you're about to fly into a rage, don't make a move, don't do anything. Stop . . . and *think about the most effective way to respond.* Even during the hormone-drugged phase of romance, keep your wits about you. You cannot allow powerful emotions—negative or positive—to overwhelm your clear thinking.

THIRD STEP: **Ask yourself the Question of Intention:** "What do I want to accomplish right now, in this moment, with this interaction?" Take a few seconds to think about what you really need, what's in your best long-term interests. Clearly, it's to not humiliate the other person, or try to get even. Having a clear intention will help you not be overwhelmed by negative emotions.

Along the way, *always reinforce your intentions* to be sure that any negative emotions are not eroding your plan to solve a problem or bring the other person closer to you. When we're on the receiving end of a Blame Attack, our instinct is to respond in kind. Focusing on your intention helps stifle that reactive instinct. If your particular style leans toward being *passive-aggressive*—which means controlling a situation by withholding action or communication—you will need to be even more overt in clarifying your intention.

FOURTH STEP: **Remember the Law of Personal Limitations,** which states that *everyone's* thinking and behavior is intrinsically limited and fallible. Here's the complete version:

Everyone is always doing as well as they can within their personal limitations, their personal history, what they know and don't know, and what they're feeling in that moment. If they could make a healthier decision, they would. This includes YOU.

Finally, there's:

FIFTH STEP: **Engage the Law of Lessons Learned**—which states:

Every mistake contains a lesson. Make a note of the lesson, process the accompanying emotion, and move on with your life.

This law teaches us the necessity of extracting the lesson from the mistake or experience, writing it down to refer to in the future, then moving on. Taking the lesson to be learned and discarding the incident's details helps to stop brooding over what you could have/should have done. Most important: **it eliminates guilt, the incessant self-criticism for a past mistake.**

This five-step sequence provides a nautical chart to guide you through the jagged rocks that can sink relationships. Using these ethical, psychological, spiritual and practical structures, you have all you need to live completely Beyond Blame. On the philosophical and spiritual level, accepting your personal limitations encourages compassion for yourself and others. Compassion leads to understanding and acceptance, which is an elegant definition of love.

Because the goal of this book is to provide a do-it-at-home method to deal with blame in all its nasty manifestations, we'll integrate each of these concepts into the following stories.

And to help make this process easy to understand and apply and explore how all of this works together in a variety of contexts, I'll analyze each of the following stories in four stages. The goal is for you to have these four stages *as a model* to work out conflict using Positive Accountability. The four parts are:

1. **The Inciting Incident**—The event that triggers the Blame Syndrome.
2. **Personal History and Limitations**—The limitations from your personal history that influence, restrict or control your thinking, feeling and behaviors.

3. **Blame's Damage**—Begins with a Blame Attack or similar behaviors that trigger a host of negative emotions, and create a Blame Cycle.

4. **Resolution and Lessons Learned**—Using Positive Account-ability to repair the mistake or apologize, if necessary, with-out allowing yourself to criticize, accuse, punish or humiliate the other person. Following with extracting the lesson, releas-ing the emotions and moving on with life.

IMPORTANT: **Not every incident will reach a conclusion satisfy-ing for both parties,** because the other person's *intention* may be to *not* solve the problem. This problem brings us back to the most frequently asked question about living Beyond Blame.

"What can I do when the other person insists on using blame, or continues with a destructive behavior?"

Recognizing that the other person's intention, agenda or goal may be entirely different from yours is essential to stepping away from a chronic problem that cannot be fixed. Likewise, it some-times happens that the other person's **personal limitations are too severe to facilitate resolution.** We will discuss these unhappy outcomes in more detail as well.

◼ SIX STORIES ABOUT LIVING LIFE BEYOND BLAME

In the following six accounts, you are the person with the prob-lem. Some of the situations may not resemble your gender, stage in life or exact personal experience, but I'm telling these stories from your perspective to illustrate the possible problems you might incur and the best way to reach a solution.

Sometimes, however, a solution is not possible because the other person's intention is to NOT solve the problem. In that case, you need to know that as soon as possible, and then know what to do about it.

You're Hosting a Big Event and Your Good Friend Abandons You. Your daughter is graduating from high school. Putting on parties and social events is emotionally difficult for you, but you and your extended family really want to celebrate, and over fifty people are scheduled to attend.

Fortunately, your closest friend, whom you've known since college, has promised to help. Sometimes in the past she hasn't been available because her husband is an airline pilot and he's frequently absent. Her youngest son is still in college and she says she's available.

For days you've frantically worked to make the house look antiseptically perfect, pretty much driving your family crazy. Yet it still doesn't feel like enough. A good thing your friend will be there to lend logistical and moral support.

THE INCITING INCIDENT: The morning of the party, your friend sends a text message: "Can't make it 2day; crisis w/ son." *You're stunned!* Instantly you feel close to panic and react angrily. You think: *How could she not know the importance of this event? Her son is always in crisis. Why can't her husband handle it just once? She's so incredibly selfish!* You call her back hoping to change her mind but only get her voice mail.

Despite your friend's absence, the party's a big success. But you remain hurt and angry.

Late the next day your friend calls, but you're not ready

to talk with her. You haven't asked yourself the Question of Intention—what do you want to accomplish? So a flood of negative emotions take over and you *unexpectedly feel very angry*. You are unable to maintain a 4:1 ratio of thought to feeling. You blurt out something harshly critical and hang up.

The next day your friend leaves on vacation and the two of you don't talk for weeks.

PERSONAL HISTORY AND LIMITATIONS: Your family history and personal limitations play a big role in this story. You moved a lot as a child and felt out of place in every new location. This awkwardness made it difficult to develop close friends and you didn't really have a friendship group until college, where you first met your friend. As an adult, you're *aware that you tend to magnify* any slight from your friends because it feels terribly familiar to your school days. Despite your personal accomplishments and your appearance of outward calm, you always feel insecure in large groups. The day of the event, you were exceptionally anxious.

Let's review the Law of Personal Limitations to see how it applies to this crisis:

> *Everyone is always doing as well as they can within their personal limitations, their personal history, what they know and don't know and what they're feeling in that moment. If they could make a healthier decision, they would.*

Which of your personal limitations have affected this situation?
FIRST is your insecurity about hosting an event. You've been exceptionally anxious about making even the smallest mistake.

> SECOND is your ongoing difficulty making friends coupled with a tendency to overreact at the slightest disappointment, which makes it difficult to keep friends.
>
> THIRD is your overreliance on perfectionism to calm your anxiety. You cling to the Mistaken Belief that being utterly perfect at all times will keep you from feeling anxious.

And then there are your friend's personal limitations, which you are well acquainted with and will eventually have to consider because her sudden absence was the Inciting Event.

BLAME'S DAMAGE: When your friend canceled, your mind raged with criticism. You were furious and wanted to *punish* her disloyalty and misplaced priorities. How could she do this to you? When she called to apologize, your surge of strong negative emotions prompted you to speak accusingly.

In addition, your tendency toward perfectionism and **self-criticism** impelled you to obsess about your own faults, which created yet more anxiety—which you blamed on her.

So when she called to apologize, your pent-up negative emotions prompted you to launch into a volley of accusation. You criticized her parenting style, her inability to say no to her son, even her husband's frequent absences. Needless to say, it damaged your relationship.

Over the next few days, as your negative feelings recede, you realized that you had strongly overreacted. But you could realize this only when the ratio of thoughtfulness to emotion returned to at least 80 percent thought to 20 percent emotion. Now you began to think about how to repair the breach using Positive Accountability.

RESOLUTION AND LESSONS LEARNED: You must also ask yourself the Question of Intention. Instantly you know that you must repair the breach in your friendship with her. Your friendship is too important to allow the discord to continue.

So, after a few days, you call her and leave a heartfelt message with a brief apology. She soon calls back and gushes about how extremely happy she is to hear from you and apologizes for allowing her son to once again derail her plans. She admits she needs to toughen up in that regard. The next day you meet in person and share a deep conversation and a meaningful hug. The breach is healed.

The most important lesson is to recognize that you reacted too quickly with criticism, accusation and punishment when under stress. Your first reaction to her cancellation was to see it as a personal rejection. You were allowing no room for anyone to make a mistake, especially yourself. You need to notice how your thinking hardened into criticism, and stop that pattern.

In short, once you apply the LPL to your old friend, you can be more understanding of her limitations.

CONCLUSION: This story points out how our personal history and limitations make us inherently vulnerable to seeing a disappointment as a betrayal. We must be always on guard to not allow our negative emotions to push us toward a potentially damaging interpretation and set of actions.

Now let's look at a couple in their early thirties who have a new baby. The stress is triggering a Blame Cycle that's creating extreme unhappiness.

■ ■ ■

You Are Locked in a Power Struggle with Your Spouse.

You and your husband were overjoyed about having a baby. Or so it seemed. You had worked full-time until the arrival of your son, but now have to stay home during the days and wait tables three nights a week. You feel overwhelmed with the responsibility of child care, shopping, cooking and cleaning.

Your husband, meanwhile, works as a theater director and free-lance writer. You've heard him regaling his theatrical friends with stories of his tremendous involvement in the ultimate drama— child raising. Yet in reality he spends long hours at the theater, including writing a play he believes will bring fame and fortune. When challenged on his schedule he says, "I've had some recognition as a playwright and I can't just give it up! It may seem like a hobby to you, but it's really hard work." To which you reply, "I understand your need to focus on your career, but I feel like a single mother. You need to help out at home more."

THE INCITING INCIDENT: After months of feeling neglected, you're angry, exhausted and, finally, you threaten to leave. You accuse your husband of caring more about his career than you and your son. He denies it, insisting he's only working for his family's benefit.

In desperation you begin couples therapy. Your husband insists he wants you to stay, that he's committed to the marriage, and that he's doing all he can. You're at an impasse.

BLAME'S DAMAGE: As you sit on the couch in my office, it's obvious that the negative emotions of anxiety, anger and pain have taken over your ability and your husband's to think. The ratio of thinking to feeling is instead skewed to the other extreme: maybe 90 percent negative emotion to 10 percent thoughtfulness. You can hardly say a sentence to each other without interrupting and making dismissive gestures or sounds.

He attacks your neediness. "I knew you were insecure when we got together, but I thought it would get better . . . with the baby. But instead it's only gotten worse."

His attack infuriates you, and you shoot back, "That's such typical paternalistic crap. If you didn't want to be a father and a husband, you should have said so. The theater is like your mistress. I'd be better off on my own. At least then I wouldn't have to wait around for you to drop me a crumb of your precious time."

The mutual accusations intensify the negative emotions. In my role as therapist, I try to clarify both spouses' intentions. I say, "Despite high levels of resentment and anxiety, both of you say that you really want to stay together and raise your child. Are you equally committed to staying together?"

Both of you say yes, but I notice much less enthusiasm on your husband's part.

We review together the concepts of Positive Accountability: how to communicate without criticism and accusation. Every single gesture, sentence or even word that implies blame must be eliminated.

Next, we discuss the Law of Personal Limitations. I insist that you see each other as doing as well as he or she can in that moment. As expected, the LPL does not go over well. So I decide to test it on your husband. "Are you aware that you just insulted your wife?"

"When? You mean about her being insecure? But she is!"

"Your comment is demeaning. It's an insult." I turn to you. "Did you hear it that way?"

"Of course I did," you say. "He's always telling me I'm insecure. If I was more secure, I wouldn't mind being left alone at home."

I turn to him again. "Did you intend to insult her, to make her feel bad?"

He looks embarrassed and upset. "Why are you making this all about me? What about her?"

"One at a time," I say. "Allow me to put this in the context of the Law of Personal Limitations. Namely, when you insult your wife, you do so because in that moment, your personal history and your emotions are controlling your thinking. I say this because it seems obvious that insulting the mother of your child, your partner to whom you've sworn lifelong loyalty, is working against your own interests. When your wife feels wounded, she can't be very loving toward you. So my only conclusion can be that, because your thinking is clouded by resentment in that moment, that's as well as you can do."

That was a lot for your husband to absorb, and he's very perplexed and troubled by my statements. But you seem relieved, as though he's finally being taken down a peg.

"I get carried away," he weakly defends himself.

Next, I challenge *you* for constantly criticizing *him*.

"But what am I supposed to do," you ask, "when he says he'll finish rehearsal at six and he comes home at nine, without even a call!"

"What else *can* you do?" I reply. "That's the big question. Obviously, criticizing his behavior hasn't worked. There must be something that's more effective."

I turn to your husband. "You just said your intention is to remain together. But your behaviors don't line up with your intention. From your actions, your behaviors, the conclusion is that you don't *really intend* to be an involved dad. Your profession is more important than your son. But perhaps you'd like to prove that the contrary is true."

The alternative to constantly criticizing your husband for putting his work and career before his family is, first, keep clear records for yourself so you know you're not exaggerating. Second, every week or so *calmly* remind him of his obligations to you and his son. Third, begin to make plans to take care of your needs *without* his cooperation, since **he's determined not to cooperate.** However, you must (as much as humanly possible) maintain the 4:1 ratio of thought to emotion so you are not consumed with anger, anxiety and resentment. If these negative emotions take over your life, you might make a hasty or ill-advised decision.

RESOLUTION AND LESSONS LEARNED: Unfortunately, the story of you and your husband does not wrap up into a neat resolution. Your life continues in conflict for many more months.

However, you learn an important lesson for yourself. You learn that your constant anger at your spouse for his inability (or refusal) to follow through on his promises and commitments has kept you involved in highly nonproductive negative emotions.

This is the most important lesson from this story. Namely:

Being constantly angry about another person's bad behavior keeps you from developing healthy coping skills and making important decisions that are in your own best interests.

Until now you had been unaware of your own personal limitations, the most significant of which is *not knowing what you did not know.* You did not know that your anger kept you stuck in a Blame Cycle which solved nothing. You kept recycling the same negative emotions.

Also, you did not know that staying in a marriage in which

your spouse's *verbal intention* did not ever line up with his actual behaviors created a lose/lose situation.

Your husband's behaviors are both hypocritical and self-centered. His statements to everyone that he's a devoted father and husband is two-faced. In fact, his art and career come first.

As you more completely accept his limitations, you engage the Paradox of the Law of Personal Limitations. That is, as you more openly accept both your own and his limitations, your perceptions shift and you feel less anger. Feeling less anger allows you to think more clearly. Clearer thinking also clarifies what you truly need in your life. What you don't need is a deceptive, hypocritical relationship that causes you nearly constant anxiety.

To that end, you make plans to move in with your sister in a nearby town. You're sad about this decision, but the emotions of sadness and grief are much healthier than anger. Your husband objects, but halfheartedly.

Another paradoxical resolution presents itself now that he has to make a special effort to visit his son. This prompts him to become a better father, because he now has to pick up his son and spend hours with him, without you. Their father-son bond intensifies.

Finally, because you stop criticizing him, you both become more supportive of each other as parents, even though *he still has no intention* of changing his self-centered behaviors.

The value of the **paradoxical resolution** needs to be emphasized. When you are consumed by negative emotions, there's no space for any other opening or resolution to appear. Your personality is like an overheated building in which your brain is sweltering. No one can think clearly in that environment.

But when, as I've witnessed numerous times, an individual backs away from a power struggle, other outcomes never before considered become possible. If one is actually possible. Sometimes it's not.

When it isn't, you need to know that as soon as possible, and stop chasing after the pot of gold at the end of a constantly moving rainbow.

CONCLUSION: Demanding that another person fulfill his duty when he worships at the altar of another god is an exercise in frustration. Declared intentions are important, but it's a person's behaviors that betray how serious those intentions really are.

For our next story, let's explore the challenges of parenting a teen overwhelmed by the intense emotions of her first romance.

Your Daughter's First Boyfriend Has You Really Worried.

A junior in high school, your daughter is a good student but quite shy. She plans to go to art school after graduation. You're her father, and you and your wife get along well. Both of you are regular churchgoers and have relatively progressive ideas.

Everything changes when your daughter gets her first boyfriend, a senior we'll call Jason. As her dad, you want to meet the young man. But your daughter says Jason is afraid because he assumes you'll be critical of him. You notice that Jason drives a big pickup truck, smokes cigarettes and dresses in slacker clothes. Because you work with computers, you find it easy to do some research. You find out that Jason's already nineteen and is attending a continuation high school because he was expelled from the regular school. You and your wife are really worried.

THE INCITING INCIDENT: One evening Jason parks outside and honks his horn for your daughter. You insist that she invite Jason inside. She refuses. "You wouldn't understand him," she says and runs out the door. Later, you try to talk to her but she says angrily, "Jason loves me, he needs me; that's all that matters!" This shocks you! How did this happen so fast? It's also the first big conflict with your daughter. You and your wife feel utterly unprepared and don't know what to do.

PERSONAL HISTORY AND LIMITATIONS: You and your wife have significant personal limitations because of lack of experience with this kind of situation. Your daughter's primary personal limitations are her youth and adolescent inability to see beyond the immediate gratification of having a boyfriend. She's fully in the grip of *anosognosia*, of not knowing what she doesn't know, both about Jason and herself. The attention she's receiving from Jason is overwhelming her ability to think rationally. We won't even start on Jason's limitations.

BLAME'S DAMAGE: Your first reaction is to get angry at your daughter for making an obviously stupid choice in a boyfriend. You even taunt her: "I've always thought you were too smart to pick such a loser!"

Predictably, your criticism and accusation only intensify the drama and increase the separation between yourself and your daughter. For her part, your wife is equally disappointed and hurt by her daughter's sudden angry outbursts.

Meanwhile, your daughter feels completely misunderstood and blames both of you for your strong negative reaction to Jason. She becomes secretive, staying after school, making up excuses and pushing her curfew. When you finally ground her, she climbs out her bedroom window to meet him.

As often happens when parents try to enforce their power over a teenager—especially by using blame—the reaction is defiance. Neither you nor your wife can believe your daughter's reaction. Increasingly desperate, you threaten to send her to live with your brother in another state. Your daughter screams that she'll kill herself if you try. Everyone has reached a toxic dead end.

RESOLUTION AND LESSONS LEARNED: The first lesson you and your wife must learn is the limits of your parental power. In fact, you cannot control who your daughter decides to date. (Remember the tragedy *Romeo and Juliet*.) However, your behaviors are influenced by what you did not know you didn't know. You did not know that using blame would backfire, making your daughter even more determined to see Jason. You believed (mistakenly) that threatening her would be effective.

Fortunately, you and your wife come to your senses and realize that your approach is extremely counterproductive. Despite your fears and extreme frustration, you need to find a way to discuss your Core Values with your daughter, but always within the parameters of Positive Accountability.

But, you wonder, if you stopped criticizing Jason, wouldn't you implicitly be giving your blessing to her relationship?

Sadly, your belief is typical when blame dominates the thinking and behavior of people in a relationship. **If you don't criticize, then you're approving!** *Wrong.* Using Positive Accountability, it's entirely possible to express a need without criticizing.

To that end, you and your wife begin to resolve the crisis by first talking together to reach a consensus, because both of you must act as a team. You realize that forbidding your daughter to see Jason is futile. She is so caught up in her first romance that she is operating at 10 percent thought and 90 percent emotion. The 10 percent thought is still important to note because she hasn't abandoned her other responsibilities. She's signaling to you, her parents, that she has not completely lost touch with reality.

When you and your wife speak with your daughter, you say, "Sweetheart, your mom and I want you to eventually date someone whose goals in life are closer to your own. In the meantime, we will stop saying anything negative about Jason. The only thing we ask is for you to not do anything dangerous. Our first concern is that you never drive with him if he's under the influence of anything. No matter where you are or what time it is, we'll come and get you with no questions asked, at all. Nor will we punish you. And our second big concern is do not get pregnant or pick up a disease."

Later, your wife speaks privately with her daughter. Assuming that she and Jason are having sex, she wants to be sure that your daughter knows about birth control and disease protection. And to make sure she knows Jason's sexual history. She takes your daughter to your family doctor but allows her to go into the appointment alone.

The approach of having *brief* but nonaccusatory conversations with your daughter greatly reduces the tension in the house. When family members stop employing criticism and accusation, they can again begin to relate to each other.

It takes almost two months of behaving this way to effect a change. One day you and your wife realize that your daughter is staying home more often. When your wife mentions it, your daughter casually says she's broken up with Jason. No explanation. Crisis over.

NOTE: This is not an idealized solution. I've assisted many families through similar situations and with similar results. But first, the blame has to stop.

The final lesson you learn about this situation is that reacting without first getting information about what is really going on just pushes everyone further away from one another. The seventeen years of trust and closeness that all three had built quickly vanishes when the powerful negative emotions of fear and anger are triggered . . . by blame.

CONCLUSION: Parents must be constantly aware whether they're pushing against a program that is part of a child's basic development, such as a teenager falling in love. Certain rites of passage must be completed, and romance is one of the most compelling.

In the next story we take a treacherous detour into the minefield known as sibling relations. It's often difficult to come out of such an experience without at least a few scratches.

Your Oldest Brother's Attitude Is Starting a Family Feud.

You have three older brothers and a younger sister, you're all in your late forties and fifties, and you're warmly connected to each of them, except your oldest brother—let's call him Marcus, after Marcus Aurelius, the Roman emperor. Marcus has worked for decades in the family restaurant, eventually expanding the business into a small chain. After your father died, Marcus considered himself the family elder.

You are a schoolteacher and your husband runs his own business. You also have two children in college and recent medical expenses, so you live far less affluently than the free-spending

Marcus. Even though he lives just an hour away, you see Marcus only during the two or three major holidays a year. But you are close to your other siblings, and despite some friction with Marcus, you consider yourself fortunate to have a big and mostly happy family.

THE INCITING INCIDENT: Every few years the entire family organizes a reunion. Typically everyone decides on renting a vacation home at a reasonable cost.

This time, however, Marcus announces a Caribbean cruise. The cost is prohibitive for you and you tell everyone your objection, suggesting a less costly venue. Your siblings express sympathy but they're still going. You are upset because your family is well aware that you can't afford it. Then you learn that Marcus is helping another brother financially with the fare even though Marcus hasn't made you the same offer. So you feel discriminated against, as well.

PERSONAL HISTORY AND LIMITATIONS: Within a family of many adult siblings, personal limitations are intimately connected to your shared history. Almost without exception the siblings carve out (or are assigned) specific roles and these tend to remain relatively unchanged for a lifetime. These roles are not always connected to birth order. In Marcus's case, he's taken over the family business and assumed the role of patriarch, the typical "hero" role. Another typical role is the "scapegoat" or "rebel," the sibling who is seen as a troublemaker. Yet another is the "lost child," the sibling who fades into the background, rarely coming forward with an opinion. In this case, that's you. You see yourself as the "lost child," the sibling whose opinion matters least.

Blame's damage: After stewing about the situation for days, you send a scathing e-mail to every family member—a harsh Blame Attack. You accuse Marcus of selfishness and grandiosity. "He acts like the Godfather, and we're all supposed to go along!" You go on to suggest that your father had favored him in the business and that he owes most of his success to the family and not just to his own efforts.

The e-mail explodes like a bomb. Within hours, everyone has taken sides. Whatever resentments and jealousies were lurking below the surface are now bleeding wounds.

Resolution and lessons learned: You had never considered using Positive Accountability because negative emotions drove your thinking and behavior. How could you express a need without using criticism or accusation when your mind was seething with resentment? After your bombshell e-mail you refuse to talk to your siblings, and the more you talk to your husband, the longer is the list of resentments from your history that have never been entirely resolved.

Finally, in an attempt to make peace, your younger sister and closest sibling comes to visit. You complain, "We have our two kids in college and my husband's barely keeping his business open. Did Marcus think about *us* when he decided on this cruise?"

She listens and commiserates, then presents you with the Law of Personal Limitations. "We all have our issues and problems with the family, starting with Mom and Dad. Marcus sure has his share. But just because he's being his usual bossy egotistical self doesn't mean you should try to outdo him. It's only a cruise."

You counter, "Marcus likes to flaunt his success."

"Yes, that's his personal limitation," she says. "We can't change him."

"So you want me to accept that he's a selfish jerk?"

"Well, being so angry at something you can't change doesn't make sense."

You hesitate. She continues. "Here's something else you need to consider. You're very quick to criticize me if I do something selfish or forgetful, like forgetting one of your children's birthdays, or if I don't call you on Mother's Day. I don't like it when you're so critical, when you let me know I don't measure up."

Over the next few days, you come to an understanding about your own behaviors—based on your own limitations. You realize that growing up, you felt constantly overshadowed by your older brothers. And you realize that, indeed, you had been exaggerating every possible offense since your high school days. Every time Marcus brags about his prosperity, it triggers your insecurity. You feel that Marcus is, in essence, being critical of your restricted family income, and he's dismissive of your dedication to your career as a teacher.

The next step is for you to question your intentions. Do you intend to maintain a grudge against Marcus and ostracize yourself from the family? Will you remain stuck in recycling the negative emotions of anxiety and resentment? Or do you want to find a way to see this issue as part of what sometimes happens between siblings, and move ahead with your life?

To this end, using the Law of Lessons Learned, you extract the lesson. Specifically, you realize that you are powerless to effect any significant change in the family. *And using blame only makes every situation worse!* You accept the idea that it's not Marcus's task to scale down his desires because of your limited resources. That *you* won't expose yourself financially to go on a cruise doesn't mean that Marcus should *never* go on one with the other siblings. You also admit to yourself that sending out an accusatory e-mail to everyone has opened up a lot of old wounds—without any benefit to anyone. What, after all, did you accomplish that was positive?

So you fully engage Positive Accountability. You made an error that you must correct.

IMPORTANT: It is not appropriate or helpful to take the position that because Marcus planned the cruise first, he needs to apologize first. Your error (sending the accusatory e-mail) must be resolved as its own separate episode. *Demanding that the other apologize first is the lifeblood of an everlasting feud.*

So you go to visit Marcus (carefully maintaining your 4:1 ratio of thinking to feeling) and briefly apologize for your harsh e-mail. You don't allow yourself to be drawn into a discussion of irrelevant issues. Nor do you excuse your behavior with the common "I only did it because . . ."

Marcus accepts your apology even as he tries to justify his behaviors. You listen for a few minutes without comment and excuse yourself. He gives you a hug and you leave. You feel greatly relieved . . . and proud of yourself. Then you wish everyone a great time on the cruise.

CONCLUSION: Family dynamics and competition between siblings always stir up everyone's emotional limitations. Even minor events such as not calling on Mother's Day can trigger a reservoir of negative emotions. The lesson is always to learn what you know and don't know about these emotions, and how they influence your life today.

The next situation we'll explore is between a couple who have hit an impasse in their decades-long relationship.

■ ■ ■

Your Relationship Has Settled into Silent Unhappiness. After almost twenty years together, you're considering breaking up with your partner, but you own a home together and are well established in the community. When you come to see me as a couple, you express your exasperation with what you consider your partner's whiny attitude. She responds with a counteraccusation. "You're such a workaholic; you work your regular job, sit on two community boards and volunteer all the time too. You might as well leave. When you're home all you do is watch TV or read and tell me to not bother you."

That doesn't sound like a very satisfying relationship. However, despite your mutual accusations, you both soundly declare your intentions to remain together.

THE INCITING INCIDENT: You call one day in shock and say that your partner has left. "I never thought she'd be the one to leave." A few days later your partner returns and you come into therapy together. Now the stakes are considerably higher because until now it was you who had resented your partner's demands and had threatened to leave.

PERSONAL HISTORY AND LIMITATIONS: Both you and your partner come from families that were emotionally abusive in very different ways. Your partner was the apple of her father's eye, which made her mother jealous. But her father would also rage, especially when drinking, which terrified her. Emotionally, she couldn't depend on either parent. The outside world saw her parents as "wonderful," which made it difficult for her to trust her own feelings and perceptions. In her twenties your partner told her parents she was gay. Her father didn't talk to her for ten years. They eventually reconciled, but the pain of his desertion remains fresh.

In contrast, your family was wealthy but chaotic. Your parents allowed you every privilege, including expensive private schools, and in return demanded loyalty. You dutifully married the man they believed was an ideal match. When he became physically abusive, they refused to believe you. You finally left him and in the process revealed your sexual orientation to your family. An avalanche of blame followed. As with your partner, you eventually reconciled, but the scar remains.

So both of you bring powerful emotional traumas from your respective families of origin into your relationship.

BLAME'S DAMAGE: Neither of you is capable of hearing anything from the other without interrupting and trying to "set the record straight." Neither allows the other to have a separate reality—or even a separate feeling. Each of you feels so much anxiety over the chance of being accused by the other for doing something "wrong" that you launch an immediate accusation—a Blame Attack. Fortunately, your use of blame does not degenerate into a Blame Spiral. After a few minutes of reciprocal Blame Attacks, you retreat into a pained and angry silence.

RESOLUTION AND LESSONS LEARNED: The resolution for this relationship follows the standard treatment for the flagrant use of blame, and must be based on your *sincere intention* to learn more effective communication and repair the relationship.

First, you have to recognize that the LPL is constantly active in your lives and with each other. Acknowledging this fact allows you to feel more compassion toward each other.

The next intervention is to stop all criticism, accusation and punishment. *And also stop making threats to leave the relationship, which is punishment.* Initially you will need considerable guidance to learn this revolutionary set of new behaviors.

When I make this proposal during a therapy session, the reaction is silence. You comment, "But if she's acting like a drippy pouty teenager, what am I supposed to do?"

Your partner responds in kind. "And if you're always working, watching TV or sleeping because you're exhausted, I'm supposed to just tolerate your neglect?"

Since neither of you has a clue about how to correct a mistake, or express a feeling or need without using blame, we'll have to work together to craft phrases that will allow non-critical communication.

I ask your partner to cite a recent situation. She jumps at the chance. "You were away at a conference. We agreed to spend some time together when you came home. But you found something else to do. I ended up calling you a few names." She grimaces at the memory.

You start to defend yourself, but I ask you to wait.

"Try to express that need without blame, please."

She struggles, so I jump in. "How about saying, 'I'm disappointed we haven't spent any time together like we'd agreed.'"

You sigh loudly and smile. "Oh, that sounds sooo adult! That'd be great."

Next I turn to you. "So you're saying you'd respond to her request more readily if she didn't get upset and call you names?"

"You bet I would. If I disappoint her even a tiny bit, she gets so moody. So I just disappear!"

"Okay," I say. "So when you see her getting moody, what

could you say that doesn't use blame? By the way, disappearing can be self-protective, and also a form of punishment."

"I haven't a clue."

"How about saying, 'Please let's sit and talk about what's going on with you.'"

Your partner exclaims, "How I'd love to hear that! That would be wonderful!"

We continue to work out various requests and responses that contain no criticism or accusation. We eliminate behaviors that are punishing. And we also develop a "neutral nonverbal communication" to use when one of you feels criticized or accused. That person is to pull out a white handkerchief and wave it gently.

The most important Lessons Learned for both of you is how tremendously influential your family-of-origin trauma remains in your lives. Once you began the process of expressing your feelings and needs without blame, you quickly became quite skilled. Also, using the flapping white handkerchief helps slow down and control the negative emotions that push toward blame.

CONCLUSION: Bad habits form slowly and are especially difficult to change because they are reinforced by Mistaken Beliefs that track back to childhood. Fortunately, if the positive intention to change is there, learning new and more effective skills is always possible. Just as bad behaviors are learned, they can be unlearned.

This Last Situation Involves an Ongoing Problem with depression complicated by social and personal isolation. It's also unique because there isn't a single incident that triggers the problem. While this situation is common enough, we don't typically ascribe it to the ravages of blame.

You've Blamed Everyone Until You're Completely Isolated.

You retired a year or two ago and have been spending your days playing golf and gardening, but these activities have lost their appeal. A couple months ago, your doctor was concerned that you might be falling into depression and prescribed medications, but they haven't helped. Over the last few weeks, you're feeling even worse. Sometimes you have to struggle to get out of bed in the morning.

THE INCITING INCIDENT: You've made an appointment to see me because your doctor pushed you to do so. At first, you minimize your complaints, but the conversation quickly shifts to accusations about how stupid, selfish and inconsiderate people are. You're quick to criticize people waiting in line at the market, the public's lack of true patriotism, corrupt politicians and even your old school friends who don't return your calls. "I'm sick of calling them, only to not get called back." You're genuinely pissed off at everyone. The crisis has been building inside you for years, but in the last few weeks, your mood has plummeted and you've even had fleeting thoughts of suicide.

PERSONAL HISTORY AND LIMITATIONS: You were the youngest of five children. A ten-year age difference between you and your nearest older brother made you feel like an only child, ignored by everyone. Your father often referred to you as an "accident." He was harshly critical about everything you did. You left home early and put yourself through college. You didn't socialize much because you had to work and study.

You became successful in your profession because you worked harder than everyone else. But you always had to deal with a lot of ungrateful, difficult, dishonest people. You're critical of other people's work ethic. "When I give my word, I keep it. When I have a job to do, I do it. I don't make excuses for myself. Everybody else always finds an excuse."

Your spouse of forty years has an active schedule and mostly ignores you, no longer able to tolerate your negativity. You've raised two successful children together, but when they call, they talk only to your spouse. When they visit, they stay for only one day.

BLAME'S DAMAGE: You are absolutely not aware that the most virulent forms of blame have contaminated your life since childhood. Your father blamed everyone, including you, for all his problems. Blame permeates your life; your thinking is constantly critical and accusatory. Your emotions are negative: anxiety, anger, resentment, pain and fear. You can hardly think of anyone's behavior, no matter how altruistic, without making a cynical comment.

RESOLUTION AND LESSONS LEARNED: You won't be able to learn any lessons until you've changed your corrosively pessimistic ideas and your deep cynicism, which stifles every possible joy or pleasure. To help your depression, you will have to recognize how negative thinking has harmed your life. Any chance of succeeding will require stern and diligent exploration of your attitudes and beliefs.

We start by rigorously applying the Law of Personal Limitations to your own life and the life of everyone else. Initially you react strongly and critically to the LPL because of how tightly you cling to several Mistaken Beliefs about how people function.

I ask, "Are you aware you've set yourself up as the only perfect human being in existence?"

This catches you off guard and you're not sure if you should be offended. But you decide to go along. "Oh, I know I'm not perfect."

"So could you tell me about your limitations, please."

You admit that you're probably too demanding of others, that you're impatient. But, dammit, you just don't suffer fools gladly. You justify your impatience because people are stupid.

"I see. So you have some limitations, but they're justified. That sounds like you really are perfect after all." It's increasingly clear that you're well armored, and only a direct hit will penetrate your protective exterior.

You ask testily, "What do my limitations have to do with anything?"

"Because you're living inside a well-defended hypocrisy, a *fundamental* contradiction. This contradiction absorbs vast amounts of energy to maintain. Psychologically, it's like building a ten-story building on beach sand. It's taken so much energy to keep it from falling over that you end up feeling depressed and hopeless."

"I don't quite . . . get it."

"Then let's go deeper. If you really are human, then you must have human limitations. Just like everyone else. Yet you refuse to accept anyone else's limitations because you believe that you yourself don't have any. Make sense?"

It's quite a struggle to grasp the meaning of my statements. "So my supposed limitations are causing my depression?"

"Look, you're smart and accomplished. But you've utterly ignored your emotional world. In fact, you've pretended it doesn't exist. Now you need to put some energy into psychology, which is the study of emotions and beliefs. I say this because you're suffering, and . . . you don't need to. You are suffering *psychologically*, that is, your emotions are giving you a lot of pain, so you need to solve this problem with psychology."

I give you some homework. Spend an hour a day thinking about this question:

"If everyone is human, and all humans have limitations, what would be the purpose of being critical of what is intrinsically human, namely, everyone's limitations? Including your own? It's like being angry about something that is part of nature, like the weather."

"That's the question. And here's an example of what I mean about the weather. If it rains unexpectedly, you can be upset because it's raining, and you didn't plan on it. But you cannot be *angry* at the rain! Get it?" I ask you to return the following week.

When you come into the session, I notice a change. Soon after we begin, you say, "My spouse and I got into a long discussion— sort of an argument, really—about the Law of Personal Limitations, and your question to me. Well, we talked off and on for most of a day . . . the first real conversation we've had in . . . years!" Your eyes are glistening.

I ask, "Did you come to an understanding?"

You reply, "Well, it's pretty complicated. First, I used to defend my father. Finally I admitted to my wife that he was a terrible bigot. He hated a lot of people. I think I've ended up being a bigot myself. Though I've tried not to, it's been a struggle. But when I applied the complete Law of Personal Limitations to other ethnic groups, it suddenly dawned on me that I was being actually quite stupid. How can I criticize someone for not being white? Or for belonging to another religion? Or for not going to college? Or for not thinking the way I do?"

These realizations represent a big shake-up in your thinking. They can't be absorbed in a few days, although such an important insight can promote a "breakthrough" into a broad new awareness.

So over the next few weeks, you continue to think about these personally revolutionary ideas. You're delving into your fixated way of thinking and taking it apart piece by piece.

This process releases a tremendous amount of pent-up energy. Your depression begins to lighten.

The breakthrough comes one evening when one of your children calls. Typically you say a few words and pass the phone. This time you actually continue chatting and don't make a single *critical* comment about anything. You speak for ten minutes. A record!

From that point on, your mood gets progressively better. You're indeed fortunate to have a spouse who is willing to discuss the ideas behind the LPL. Now that you're not so outwardly cynical, your spouse is also willing to confront you when you slip back into your depression-building habits of negative thinking.

It takes a lot of hard work to break with the past.

CONCLUSION: If your view of the world is pessimistic and cynical, there's no room for interpretations that are life-affirming. Without positive emotions such as hope and gratitude, the only recourse is depression. It's essential to constantly challenge your worldview.

That's It for Stories and Examples. Now it's time to wrap up everything presented in the book in a few paragraphs.

■ ■ ■ ■ ■

The Take-Home Message:
Living Beyond Blame

Writing *Beyond Blame* represents the culmination of a lifetime of experience and twenty-five-plus years of clinical practice.

My intention is for you to have a source to refer to whenever you or someone you know unwittingly uses criticism or accusation.

With these concepts at hand you will know what to do when a seemingly simple sentence or an "ordinary" question turns into a raging conflict.

Until you began reading this book, you likely weren't aware that a "simple sentence" or "ordinary question" could really constitute a sharp criticism, or a pointed accusation, and that someone was going to feel hurt. That someone's negative emotions were going to be triggered. That those actions launched the Blame Syndrome, and that blame was doing its nasty work.

Now you know that there's no such thing as an innocent criticism or a simple accusation. Every single Blame Attack—even the subtlest of them—creates some kind of Emotional Impact. Perhaps not a visible one, perhaps not immediately acted on, perhaps even forgotten in that moment. But the *next* Blame Attack may well unleash the Reactive Response, the counterattack that sets the whole building of your relationship ablaze.

Now, after reading this book with care and thought, you know what to do—how to protect yourself. And how to protect the people you care about. You can no longer fault your personal anosognosia: *not knowing what you don't know.*

Now you know that it really *is* possible to express your emotions, to make a request, to lodge a complaint or correct an error without criticizing, accusing or punishing. It is my sincere hope that somewhere in these pages you found a way to talk to people in any situation far more *effectively* than before you had read this book.

Underlying all your efforts will be the Law of Personal Limitations. Anytime you find yourself pointing blame inward and needlessly criticizing or punishing yourself, go back and study the Law of Personal Limitations, the LPL. This law provides a broad understanding of the thick fog of imperfection within which we all must operate—also known as the Human Condition. The LPL explains exactly why, as I've said many times throughout this book, *there's no one to blame.*

Personal limitations of all sizes, shapes and weights are part of the air we breathe.

Mistakes "Я" Us. Get used to it!

Stop fighting a battle to achieve an impossible perfection, demanding it of others and demanding it of yourself. It's a battle that's impossible to win. At the same time, the LPL is not a license to be vindictive, selfish or heartless. Unless that's your intention. But if it were, I assume you wouldn't be reading this book.

I sincerely hope these pages will guide you toward living a happier and more fulfilled life—a life that is Beyond Blame.

Acknowledgments

The concepts behind *Beyond Blame* inspired several key supporters from the beginning, and each contributed to working through the complex ideas.

The first to lend support was my superb editor, Jake Elwell, with the Harold Ober Literary Agency. Jake helped shape the book's organization through several major revisions. My sister, Elaine Cherkezov, tirelessly read every page and was always ready for a phone consultation. Kedron Bryson, who tragically died before seeing the completed book, brilliantly edited the initial pages. I was truly fortunate to have Paul Wagner take over in mid-stride and lend a sharp eye to the book's completion and refinement.

If you enjoyed this book, visit

www.tarcherbooks.com

and sign up for Tarcher's e-newsletter to receive
special offers, giveaway promotions, and
information on hot upcoming releases.

TARCHER
PENGUIN

Great Lives Begin with Great Ideas

New at **www.tarcherbooks.com**
and **www.penguin.com/tarchertalks**:

TARCHER
TALKS

Tarcher Talks, an online video series featuring
interviews with bestselling authors on everything from creativity and prosperity to 2012
and Freemasonry.